BEHIND THE SCENES

D1482350

The New Historicism: Studies in Cultural Poetics
Stephen Greenblatt, General Editor

BEHIND THE SCENES

YEATS, HORNIMAN,
AND THE STRUGGLE
FOR THE ABBEY THEATRE

ADRIAN FRAZIER

University of California Press

Berkeley · Los Angeles · London

University of California Press
Berkeley and Los Angeles, California

University of California Press, Ltd.
London, England

© 1990 by
The Regents of the University of California

Library of Congress Cataloging-in-Publication Data

Frazier, Adrian.
    Behind the scenes: Yeats, Horniman, and the struggle
for the Abbey Theatre / Adrian Frazier.
        p.   cm.—(The New historicism ; 11)
    Bibliography: p.
    Includes index.
    ISBN 0-520-06549-2 (alk. paper)
    1. Abbey Theatre.   2. Irish Literary Theatre.   3. Yeats,
W. B. (William Butler), 1865–1939.   4. Horniman, Annie
Elizabeth Fredericka, 1860–1937.   5. Theatrical producers
and directors—Ireland—Biography.   I. Title.   II. Series.
PN2602.D82A25   1990
792'.09418'35—dc20   89-5142
                                                                   CIP

Printed in the United States of America
1   2   3   4   5   6   7   8   9

To Russell and Charlotte Durgin

Contents

Illustrations

(following page 148)

A. E. F. Horniman, oil portrait by J. B. Yeats, 1904. Collection: National Theatre Society, Limited; by kind permission of the Abbey Theatre.

William Butler Yeats, pencil sketch by J. B. Yeats, 1899. Collection: Michael B. Yeats.

Isabella Augusta, Lady Gregory, pencil sketch by J. B. Yeats, 1905. Collection: Michael B. Yeats.

J. M. Synge, pencil sketch by J. B. Yeats, 1905. Collection: Michael B. Yeats.

Mary Walker (Maire nic Shiublaigh), pencil sketch by J. B. Yeats, 1906. Collection: Michael B. Yeats.

Sara Allgood, pencil sketch by J. B. Yeats, 1911. Collection: Michael B. Yeats.

Frank Fay, pencil sketch by J. B. Yeats, 1904. Collection: Michael B. Yeats.

Padraic Colum, pencil sketch by J. B. Yeats, 1907. Collection: Michael B. Yeats.

Foyer of the Old Abbey Theatre, sketch by Raymond McGrath. Collection: National Theatre Society, Limited; by kind permission of the Abbey Theatre.

Stage of the Abbey Theatre, photograph. Abbey Theatre Collection: National Library of Ireland.

Abbreviations

The following short titles and acronyms appear in the footnotes:

Alspach   William Butler Yeats. *The Variorum Edition of the Plays of W. B. Yeats.* Edited by Russell K. Alspach and Catherine C. Alspach. New York: Macmillan, 1966.

Finneran, Harper, and Murphy   Richard Finneran, George Mills Harper, and William M. Murphy, eds. *Letters to W. B. Yeats.* 2 vols. New York: Columbia University Press, 1977.

Frayne and Johnson   William Butler Yeats. *Uncollected Prose by W. B. Yeats.* Edited by John P. Frayne and Colton Johnson. 2 vols. New York: Columbia University Press, 1976.

Harper   George Mills Harper. *Yeats's Golden Dawn.* New York: Barnes & Noble, 1974.

Hogan and Kilroy   Hogan, Robert, general editor. *Modern Irish Drama: A Documentary History.* Vols. 1–3. Dublin: Dolmen Press; Atlantic Highlands, N.J.: 1975–78. Vol. 1, *The Irish Literary Theatre 1899–1901,* edited by Robert Hogan and James Kilroy. Vol. 2, *Laying the Foundations 1902–1904,* edited by Robert Hogan and James Kilroy. Vol. 3, *The Abbey Theatre, the Years of Synge 1905–1909,* edited by Robert Hogan and James Kilroy.

Holloway	Joseph Holloway. *Joseph Holloway's Abbey Theatre: A Selection from His Unpublished Journal "Impressions of a Dublin Play-Goer."* Edited by Robert Hogan and Michael J. O'Neill. Carbondale: Southern Illinois University Press; London: Feffer & Simmons, 1967.
JBY	John Butler Yeats
NLI	National Library of Ireland
NYPL	New York Public Library
Saddlemyer	Ann Saddlemyer, ed. *Theatre Business: The Correspondence of the First Abbey Theatre Directors: William Butler Yeats, Lady Gregory, and J. M. Synge.* Gerrards Cross, Bucks.: Colin Smythe; University Park, Pa.: Pennsylvania State University Press, 1982.
Schuchard	Ronald Schuchard. "W. B. Yeats and the London Theatre Societies, 1901–1904." *Review of English Studies* 116 (November 1978): 415–46.
Synge	John Millington Synge. *Collected Works.* Vol. 2, *Prose,* edited by Alan Price. Vols. 3 and 4, *Plays,* edited by Ann Saddlemyer. London: Oxford University Press, 1966–68.
TCD	Library of Trinity College, Dublin
Wade	William Butler Yeats. *Letters.* Edited by Allan Wade. London: R. Hart-Davis, 1954. Reprint. New York: Octagon Books, 1980.
WBY	William Butler Yeats

Preface: Whose Abbey Theatre?

To whom did the Abbey Theatre belong? At various times, many of the Irish people involved in its life thought they had a right to call the Abbey "our Irish theatre": those who started the Irish National Dramatic Society, those who acted in it, those who wrote plays for it, those with a need or use for it, with a wish to make Ireland free, Gaelic, socialist, or feudal. In a legal sense, there can be no question that during its formative years, from 1904 to 1911, the Abbey Theatre belonged to no Irishman at all; it was the property of Annie E. F. Horniman, a middle-aged, middle-class dissenting London spinster. But now it is most often understood to be, as W. B. Yeats tried to make it then, an authors' theatre, even Yeats's very own theatre. To read through the essays of Yeats, one would think that the patron of the Abbey Theatre, Annie Horniman, had little effect on what was written and performed; that the actors were instruments of the will of the authors; and that the audience was unappreciative of the emergence of great literature before them, when not violently opposed to it. This book, in a study of Irish dramatic movements from 1899 to 1911, challenges that view of the theatre; it reevaluates the importance of authors, patrons, actors, and audience in shaping the literature of the stage.

It was Yeats's ambition—both in the Irish Literary Theatre (1899–1901) and in the Irish National Theatre Society that succeeded it—to found a literary theatre in Ireland over which the authors had control. Due largely to his efforts, Yeats, Lady Gregory, and J. M. Synge became the Board of Directors of the fully subsidized Irish National Theatre Society, Ltd., working rent-free out of the Abbey Theatre in Dublin. The First

Principle of the Irish National Theatre Society, as stated by Yeats in the September 1903 issue of its house journal *Samhain*, was to "restore words to their sovereignty" on stage.[1] The second, third, and fourth principles of the INTS follow from this preeminence of the author: the author comes before text, the text before the actor, the actor before the scene, and the audience (if it comes at all) comes last. Nothing must be permitted to rival in importance the author's words as spoken on stage. The sovereignty of the author, Yeats says, is essential because "Literature is always personal, always one man's vision of the world";[2] the rightness of the author's rule is self-evident: "Literature is always justified and needs no justification."

Later in this book, I discuss the social basis of Yeats's individualism and the political determination of his apolitical idea of theatre, but in itself there is nothing uncommon about Yeats's view of literature. Such pronouncements in his essays on dramatic literature are remarkable for their eloquence, not their originality. They take their place in a historical development in which claims for art have become grander with the gradual creation of an elite group of artists, connoisseurs, and critics. In this process, the work of literature has been assigned special status by marking it off from all other types of lettered knowledge, emptying it of utilitarian values, and freeing it at last from its age, place, and even its author.[3] "'Literature' rises to value," as Frank Lentricchia puts it, "by a process of negation," by "a marked disposition to suppress its material conditions."[4] Scholars can suppress such conditions simply by ignoring them, or balkanizing them in prefaces, appendices, and footnotes; in the theatre, Yeats sought to do this by political and economic control.

1. WBY, "The Reform of the Theatre," *Samhain*, September 1903 (Dublin: Sealy Bryers & Walker & T. Fisher Unwin), 9; id., *Explorations* (New York: Macmillan, 1962), 108.
2. WBY, "An Irish National Theatre," in *Explorations*, 115.
3. See Raymond Williams, *Keywords: A Vocabulary of Culture and Society* (New York: Oxford University Press, 1976), 150ff.
4. Frank Lentricchia, *Criticism and Social Change* (Chicago: University of Chicago, 1983), 125.

There is an unquestionable element of truth to the claim that authors and the language in which they embody their individual visions of "beauty and truth" are a necessary condition of literature. However, we have broadened our understanding of literature since the period when the stock conceptions of New Criticism prevailed, in which Literature, in a domain of pure freedom, was secreted from the soul of a great author and distilled in the tropes of a text, which then rose by its own virtue into the orderly formations of the canon, free of the conditions of its production. We are prepared to see that other factors must be considered as necessary to a fully sufficient definition of literature, including the ethics, politics, and rhetorical purposes of the author.[5] Literature, however, arises not just from the author, but from the entire human struggle for power through articulation—more specifically, in the case of literature of the stage, from the actors who raise the text to life, the audiences in whom it takes shape, the patrons who foster it, and all the economic and political stresses in which it is lodged. Indeed, so great is the force of these authorizing conditions that while a definitive feature of a literary context is the text, there are richly significant theatrical events with no authorial text whatsoever.

2

One such event occurred in 1861 on the stage of the theatre that was to become the Abbey forty-three years later. It was

5. As Wayne Booth summarizes the critical situation, now freed of the ideologies of freedom, "We can . . . look at the ethics and politics that were concealed in the professedly anti-ethical and apolitical stances of modern aesthetic movements. We can question the notion, implicit in certain of those movements, that art is more important than people; that artists not only can but should ignore their audiences; that didactic and rhetorical interests are inherently non-aesthetic; that concern with ideologies and with truth or the practical value of art is a sure mark of its enemies; . . . that any true art work must be above politics" ("Freedom of Interpretation," in *The Politics of Interpretation*, ed. W. J. T. Mitchell [Chicago: University of Chicago Press, 1982], 55). Booth is concerned with the politics of those who write, those who first received, and those who now interpret texts. My own interests, while including these concerns, extend as well to the political forces that are actually constitutive of the works themselves.

the most popular and politically effective matinee and evening show ever put on that stage. This was the funeral of Terence Bellew MacManus.[6] After a brief part in a minor uprising, "The Rebellion of 1848," MacManus was tried, convicted, and sentenced to be transported to Van Diemen's Land (now Tasmania). He escaped after three years to San Francisco, where he quietly lived out his final ten years. After he was buried, local Irish-Americans came up with an idea: to dig up the body of Terence MacManus and send him home for a grand republican burial in Glasnevin cemetery, right under the noses of the British authorities. Joseph Mahoney and Michael Doheny of the New York branch of the Fenians promoted the idea and took up the collection of funds; James Stephens, the Irish Fenian chief, eventually seized control of the plan to transport the body of MacManus 6,000 miles on a three-month journey, across the United States by train, by ship to Cobh, again by train to Limerick Junction, and then on to Dublin, where he would lie in state at the Pro-Cathedral, Dublin's largest Catholic church. Both the British authorities and the Catholic Church opposed honoring violent revolutionaries or tolerating Fenian demonstrations disguised as funeral rites, so the body, barred from the Pro-Cathedral, was placed instead on the stage of the Mechanics' Institute in Abbey Street. Thousands entered its doors, witnessed the scene on stage, and departed with fairly precise knowledge of what the performance said. Its speech was eloquent by virtue of the view the audience took of the scene: a reverent gaze at proof that Irishmen suffer under British rule, that they fight against it, that they die for the struggle, that, finally, they are honored for their sacrifice. Collectively, the audience witnessed a generational bond tying together Irish revolutions, renewed through past failures. The muteness of the testimony was its power and clarity.

This scene, clearly, had no text. There were, however, a host of authorizing conditions: Captain John Smith conceived the

6. Oliver MacDonagh, *States of Mind: A Study of Anglo-Irish Conflict, 1790–1980* (London: George Allen & Unwin, 1983), 84–85.

idea, Mahoney and Doheny promoted it, and James Stephens openly defied the clergy, roused the audience, and wrote the graveside address, a sonorous interpretation of the meaning of what had already happened in the theatre on Abbey Street. Without their collaborative authorship, there would have been no theatrical event. However, there were still further authorizing conditions. Four men can at any time decide to disinter a body in one country, transport it to another, leave it lying on a stage, and then reinter it, without any such import at all. To create the significance of "The Last Appearance of Terence Bellew MacManus," it was necessary to have a people who look backward in times of trouble, who have important funeral customs, who for political reasons venerate (and create at need) national martyrs, and who respond quickly to orders from secret and alternative forms of power. These factors were essential to the significance of the event; without them, the Fenian leaders would never have gotten 50,000 people to march in the Dublin funeral cortege. The authorship of "The Last Appearance of Terence Bellew MacManus" consists in the Fenians' conception of how the event would be read and in the conspiracy of the Irish masses to read it as meaningful.

Not only did the event have its authorship (organizational and communal), it also had other elements of dramatic performance, such as an actor. MacManus at the time of his death was an unsuccessful San Francisco businessman; at his height of glory, he was only a minor figure in a civil disturbance requiring the attention of the local constabulary. On stage, however, he was cast in the role of martyred hero. Although there are plays by Beckett with very nearly as little dialogue and action, and hardly so much impact, the 1861 spectacle of the disinterred rebel was not a play. Staged event, enactment of an idea, propaganda ploy, performance with authors, an actor, publicity, audience, and reviews, it may have been all of these, but it was not a play because the body on stage was indeed the corpse of Terence MacManus. Of course, we can posit counterfactual conditions for such an event becoming a play: an author beforehand owns up to an intention to engage the audience's interpretative abilities; he asks them to suppose that a motionless actor is a corpse, or that a corpse is the last remains of Terence MacManus; the audience, consequently, approaches the scene on stage with the special sort of attention one grants to fictive events. Although the same arrangement on stage could serve as a play, there would, in short, have had to be a symbolic substitution for reality, and some rearrangement of intentions and expectations, for the 9 November 1861 spectacle at the Mechanic's Institute to be counted as the first and greatest moment in Irish National Theatre.

The point of this illustration is that while the existence of author and text are by definition essential to dramatic literature, the other factors that figure in making a publicly staged event significant—the promotion, the nature of the fund-raising, the political context, the predisposition of the audience, the character of the actor, the meaning of the scene, the commentary upon the event—are so important that one may discover something very much like an authorless, textless play. These other factors do not cease to be important when there is an author and a text; they continue to be the very stuff of significance. These nutritive, sustaining conditions of literary production can only be suppressed by suppressing the significance of the text as well.

While it is not precisely true to say that this book is about all but the text, its emphasis is obviously not upon textual criticism of the plays of the early Abbey Theatre, either as pieces to be revived for the modern stage or as texts to be appreciated for their formal integrity; it does not aim to show that this play by Yeats is overrated, that one by Lady Gregory underrated, or Synge's *Playboy* justly prized. There are many books offering expert appreciations of this literature, and there will be more such books still, the authors of the Revival having established an enduring claim upon our interest.[7] This

7. Among the critics who have made the strongest claims for the value of Yeats's plays are David R. Clark, who persuasively connects late plays such as *Purgatory* with the dramas of Beckett in *W. B. Yeats and the Theatre of Desolate Reality* (Dublin: Dolmen Press, 1965); James W. Flannery, who argues that

book is less about my appreciation of plays by Yeats, Synge, and others than about the reception of a few of those plays by Dublin audiences from 1899 to 1910. More completely, the aim here is to restore the traditional text to its historical moment, and, in the phrases of Lentricchia's call to contemporary critics, to bring to light "its politically activist, materially textured substance" "in an act of reading that penetrates the idealist myths . . . that have veiled the text's real involvement in the human struggle."[8] No matter what the nature of that involvement, it is not to be passed over, explained away, or excused, as if such matters, being "reductionist," detract from the author and the plays. One need not prove a writer a secular saint in order to preserve for him or her the title of a great writer, although those who of all the millions of speakers of a language have used it to best effect, those whose force of utterance puts them in a league of their own, and to whom we are drawn as crowds to star performers, may seem to merit any honor we grant them. Yeats, certainly, was one such writer: he came early into his force, words obeyed his call, and he mounted up in an ascendancy over his audience; he was indeed, as he bragged to his sister, King of the Cats. But even in his own time, when audiences found a few of his early pieces for the stage less than entertaining, dramatically ineffective, or even thematically repellant, no one questioned

---

Yeats's developing theories of the stage anticipate the ideas of Total Theatre in *W. B. Yeats and the Idea of a Theatre: The Early Abbey Theatre in Theory and Practice* (New Haven: Yale University Press, 1976); Katharine Worth, who relates the plays of Yeats to those of Maeterlinck, and to international modernist drama in general, in *The Irish Drama of Europe from Yeats to Beckett* (Atlantic Highlands, N.J.: Humanities Press, 1978); and, finally, Andrew Carpenter, who aims to make the best possible case for each of Yeats's plays as vehicles for the stage in *The Dramatic Imagination of W. B. Yeats* (Dublin: Gill & Macmillan, 1978). This book differs from theirs in scope (since it does not include the late plays or all of the early ones), in focus (it includes plays by many Abbey authors), and, most important, in purpose. Since they and other scholars have so ably done their work, we may now assume the interest of Yeats's plays to have been established, and need not arrange our remarks as a justification of Yeats the playwright.

8. Lentricchia, *Criticism and Social Change*, 142.

that Yeats's plays were works of a master's hand.[9] In short, Irish audiences awarded him the laurel, but refused him a halo; and while complaining that some plays by Yeats or Synge did not belong in the National Theatre, they did not doubt their honored place in the National Library. So the literary quality of the Abbey authors was not in question then, and, *a fortiori,* it need not be the main issue here. A book that concentrates, not on proving that the plays are works of art, but on showing their considerable political craftiness and social meaning is unlikely to diminish their claims upon our attention. Indeed, one may hope that when these works are fully restored to their context, they cannot be regarded as merely literary, altogether too lofty, or positively hermetic; rather they will appear as freighted with authorial purpose, alive with social suggestion, and dangerous in the intimate violence they harbor against the predispositions of the audience.

In the chapters that follow, instead of writing a chronicle of the Irish Literary Renaissance, or a theoretical analysis of literary production, I have often chosen to take as points of departure (or, in some cases, destination) the first performance of a play by Yeats, Synge, or Lady Gregory. The events of the opening night of *The Countess Cathleen, The King's Threshold, In the Shadow of the Glen, On Baile's Strand, Dervorgilla,* or *The Playboy of the Western World*—what happened with actors, spectators, writers, reviewers, and patrons—are samples of "the materially textured substance" of "the traditional text" that must as a whole be the subject of a reading. The readings in individual chapters, however, are guided toward different theoretical concerns. Chapter 1, on *The Countess Cathleen,* is a general introduction to all those discursive forces around the play that make the meaning of the play. Chapter 2, on Yeats's

9. This characterization of the audiences' judgment of Yeats's early plays is not meant to apply to all those who attended or equally to all plays. *Cathleen ni Houlihan* (co-authored with Lady Gregory), for instance, was universally admired by nationalists; *Deirdre* had a good run with Mrs. Patrick Campbell in the lead; and *On Baile's Strand* was spared adverse reviews. The full complexity of the reception of Abbey plays is addressed below.

early role in the Irish National Theatre Society, is a critique of claims for the autonomy and freedom of the author in the theatre. The third chapter concentrates on the role of the audience; the fourth on the role of the actors; the fifth on the patron, Annie Horniman. The final chapter is given to illustrating that the political perspective is, to borrow Fredric Jameson's phrase, "the absolute horizon of all reading and interpretation."[10]

This type of study would not be possible in the case of some literary periods; the documentary evidence of the "materially textured substance" of history would not be available. The figures involved in the Irish Literary Renaissance lived, however, in an era neither so long past that their communications have been lost nor so recent that they relied on the telephone. Those at the Abbey knew, even as they planned, that they were nation-building, that what they made was history; as a result, they recorded every day in the light of the age and kept nearly every scrip of the multitudinous record. Furthermore, the heroic and scrupulous industry of scholars has made the letters and lives of all the participants, major and minor, available to readers. Few authors have been so well served as these Irish writers were by Richard Finneran, George Mills Harper, Robert Hogan, John Kelly, James Kilroy, William M. Murphy, Ann Saddlemyer, and many others who receive but a poor acknowledgment of their service in the notes and bibliography. Had they not done their work first, and done it so splendidly, I would still be at the National Library of Ireland, the New York Public Library, or another of the many institutions with Irish archives, ruining my eyes over the cursive of Yeats, with no hope of finishing this book for years to come, perhaps without even a glimpse of its picture of the totality of forces around the text.

10. Fredric Jameson, *The Political Unconscious: Narrative as a Socially Symbolic Act* (Ithaca, N.Y.: Cornell University Press, 1981), 17.

Acknowledgments

Russell Durgin was an exceptional teacher and a fine director of plays; his wife Charlotte was, and remains, a designer of ingenious skill and a person of remarkable insight and charity. This book is dedicated to them in memory of the years from 1968 to 1974 in St. Louis, Missouri; during that time, we staged Yeats's *Purgatory* in a ghetto electric with violence and the murder of the Boy by the Old Man caused some on that street-corner square to gasp in recognition; presented the ritualistic murder of his *A Full Moon in March* before the reredos of Christ Church Cathedral to the irritation and wonder of parishioners; and inserted a performance of Synge's *In the Shadow of the Glen* into the uproar of a big, noisy Irish pub, where we played to an accompaniment of lewd jokes. It was in these and the many other performances of those years (presided over by Russell's ironic glee and Charlotte's warmth of understanding) that a leading idea of this book began to germinate—that the meaning of a text is always reshaped by the occasion of the performance, its institutional and political context.

This book is indebted in an unusual way to one person, my colleague William M. Murphy, who suggested the subject, helped me with research materials, answered a hundred queries, and continued to assist in the clarification of my thought even where he did not approve its conclusions. His own *Prodigal Father: The Life of John Butler Yeats (1839–1922)* was my model for style and scholarship. I have also been lucky in my other colleagues at Union College: Felmon Davis of the Philosophy Department improved the reasoning in the second, third, and fourth chapters; Christie Sorum of the Classics Department urged me to a higher degree of formality in the presentation of the first chapter; and Jordan Smith of the English Department, reading the final chapters with the clarity of a poet, found those places where slight changes made for great improvements. Professors Harry Marten and William Thomas scoured the entire manuscript, finding flaws to which I had grown blind. These colleagues—always eager to receive manuscript and quick to return it—were my first readers, and I wrote for their interest and amusement; as they evoked it, the book is partly theirs. Thora Girke, our department secretary, must be mentioned in thanks along with my Union colleagues; without her assistance, we would get little done, and that not competently. Marilyn Schwartz, managing editor of the University of California Press, and Peter Dreyer, the copyeditor, rescued the manuscript from a host of errors; I am grateful that only they know how many.

The Humanities Faculty Development Fund of Union College made research in Ireland possible. The Dana Fund for Summer Research Fellows enabled me to profit from the assistance of my student Joy Runyon, who worked on the bibliography. The staffs of the Huntington Library, the National Library of Ireland, and especially the Union College library lent all necessary assistance. By locating lost titles, purchasing new ones, and borrowing out-of-print volumes from other libraries, David Gerhan, Bruce Connolly, Mary Cahill, Donna Burton, and Maribeth Krupczak made a small college facility serve the functions of a research center.

I am grateful to Colin Smythe for permission to quote from Lady Gregory, to A. P. Watt, Ltd., on behalf of Michael B. Yeats and Macmillan London Limited, for permission to quote from W. B. Yeats, to Macmillan Publishing Company, Inc., New York, for permission to use material from the following published works by W. B. Yeats: *Explorations* (copyright © by Mrs. W. B. Yeats 1962), *Autobiography* (copyright 1916, 1936 by Macmillan Publishing Company, renewed 1944, 1964 by Bertha Georgie Yeats), and *Essays and Introductions* (© by Mrs. W. B. Yeats 1961). I also wish to thank George Core for providing space in the *Sewanee Review* for publication of material that became the first chapter of this book, to Michael B. Yeats for providing the drawings by John Butler Yeats and granting permission to reproduce them, to the Board of Directors of the Abbey Theatre for permission to reproduce photographs of the old Abbey and the painting of Annie Horniman, to the National Library of Ireland for reproducing illustrations from its archives. Stationed in Schenectady, with all the illustrative matter in Dublin, I could not have managed at all without the generous assistance of Mr. Yeats, Mr. Martin Fahy of the Abbey, Mr. D. O Luanaigh of the National Library of Ireland, and Dublin photographers Fergus Bourke and Rex Roberts.

Finally, I would acknowledge publicly my debt to my wife, Alison Frazier, whose historical scholarship is an example to me and whose indulgent affection is my support. My children Rufus and Helen deserve the last word: their amused tolerance of their parents' academic pursuits is remarkable.

The Making of Meaning

Yeats and The Countess Cathleen

The first performance of W. B. Yeats's *The Countess Cathleen*, the 8th of May 1899, was the Irish cultural event of the decade. Seated in the hall of the Antient Concert Rooms in Dublin, on that night or during the following four nights of performance, were representatives of nearly every section of the social and political life of the country. The play had been the subject of a debate in the letter columns of London papers between the producer William Archer and the novelist George Moore on the feasibility of literary drama (Archer said *The Countess Cathleen* would make a boring and expensive production; Yeats and Moore replied that it need not be expensive).[1] Consequently, the *Saturday Review* had sent Max Beerbohm and Arthur Symons from London to cover the play; no doubt, their courtesy tickets placed them toward the front of the hall, where English actors took the stage.[2] Also present, and probably in the first rows, were people of title that Lady Gregory had persuaded to put up their names as guarantors of the

1. Yeats joined the controversy in the *Daily Chronicle* with a letter to the editor on 27 January 1899; see Allan Wade, 308–11. Later in the year, in *Beltaine*, a journal promoting the performances, Yeats made the aggressive concession that Irish literary dramatists appealed to "that limited public which gives understanding," and would "not mind greatly if others are bored" (*Beltaine*, May 1899, 8–9, rpt. in Frayne and Johnson, 2:159–62).

2. Symons came over before the performance for a rehearsal, and then pumped the play in a review of *Poems* (1899) and *The Wind among the Reeds* (1899) in the 6 May 1899 *Saturday Review*, rpt. in *W. B. Yeats: The Critical Heritage*, ed. A. Norman Jeffares (London: Routledge & Kegan Paul, 1977), 109–13. Beerbohm's complimentary review, "In Dublin," appeared in the 13 May 1899 *Saturday Review*.

Irish Literary Theatre, a blessing that seemed to consecrate
Yeats's adventure as more literary than nationalist. But nationalists made the largest part of the crowd, not only officially apolitical nationalists like Douglas Hyde, the Gaelic
League's president, but political ones too, like Arthur Griffith,
editor of the *United Irishman* and future president of Sinn
Fein. He came to show himself in favor of what Cardinal
Michael Logue had said no Catholic should see: a play that
presented the Irish as a people eager to sell their souls for
gold, that said souls came at different prices, and that illustrated as features of Irish life some peasants who stole, some
who committed sacrilege, and one woman hell-bent on for-
nication.[3] Perhaps huddled up in the corner of an aisle was
the intriguer who had raised the alarm about the play—
F. Hugh O'Donnell, author of the pamphlet *Souls for Gold* that
had incited the cardinal to instruct the faithful to shun this
heretical entertainment. A group of Catholic students sat
together close to the back of the theatre just to make sure
that Yeats learned that "the people of the Catholic capital of
Catholic Ireland" could not be "subjected to affront with im-
punity."[4] But not all the students there came to defend the
honor of Ireland or the holiness of the Catholic Church; James
Joyce, for instance, came to bear witness to the independence
of Art. Finally, lined up along the back wall, a deployment of
Dublin policemen stood ready at the request of Yeats to protect the players in case "the mob" got out of hand.

Yeats was often quick to call his opposition a "mob," and
any protest a "riot."[5] How many young men came to pro-

3. WBY, "Dramatis Personae, 1896–1902," in *The Autobiography of William Butler Yeats* (1935; New York: Macmillan, Collier Books, 1965), 278–79, and id., *Memoirs*, ed. Denis Donoghue (New York: Macmillan, 1972), 119–23.
4. *Daily Nation*, 6 May 1899; rpt. in Hogan and Kilroy, vol. 1.
5. In connection with this episode, Elizabeth Cullingford argues that Yeats was "careful to distinguish between 'the mob' and 'the people'" (*Yeats, Ireland and Fascism* [New York: New York University Press, 1981], 49). While it may be doubted that he was always careful to do so, in "The Galway Plains," as Cullingford notes, Yeats did envision the existence of "a people, a commu-nity bound together by imaginative possessions." Great poetry, he believed, "always requires a people to listen to it" (*Essays and Introductions* [New York:

test on different nights during the week is a good question: Joseph Holloway, the diarist of Dublin theatre, says there were twenty, all beardless idiots;[6] T. W. Rolleston, president of the Dublin Irish Literary Society, makes their number only twelve, and says they expressed their hostility without malice or ignorance.[7] Riot, ruckus, protest, civil demonstration of hostility, clerical bans, debate: whatever the appropriate term for the type of controversy aroused, the play was the center of excited discussion for weeks before and after its performance. In the Dublin press, through privately issued pamphlets, through student petitions against the play, at academic debates held by Trinity College's Historical Society, and in speeches after the *Daily Nation*'s celebratory dinner, Ireland discussed the play's theology, plausibility, and symbolic meaning.[8] Without doubt, *The Countess Cathleen* is a fundamentally significant document in the coming to consciousness of the Irish nation.

And yet the play is now as insignificant a piece of drama as a press keeps in print. The modern reader observes the obvious: it is short, but boring; trivial and bad. Critics who write books on the drama of Yeats try to put a little life into the chapter on this, his first play for the Irish Literary Theatre, by explaining it in terms of *A Vision*, the love of Yeats for Maud Gonne, his poetic development, the significance of the five major revisions of the text (1892, 1895, 1900, 1912, 1919), or some law of dramaturgy.[9] In many ways, these critics have

---

Collier, 1961], 213). But it appears that those who make up "the people" should exist silently out on the plains as an ideal audience; when they became visible, strenuous, articulate, and off their leaseholds, they were, in Yeats's usage, a mob.

6. Holloway, 6.

7. T. W. Rolleston, letter, the *Freeman's Journal*, 10 May 1899, 6; Hogan and Kilroy, 1:40.

8. There is a generous sampling of the controversy in Hogan and Kilroy, 1:38–52.

9. See Richard Ellmann, *Yeats: The Man and the Masks* (New York: Macmillan, 1948), 102; Peter Ure, *Yeats the Playwright* (London: Routledge & Kegan Paul, 1963), 9–42; David R. Clark, "Vision and Revision: Yeats's 'Countess Cathleen,'" *The World of W. B. Yeats*, ed. Robin Skelton and Ann

used the play well to give life to their interpretations, but no one has succeeded in finding an interpretation that gives life to the play. We tend to assume that meaning lives in the relation between texts; in signs of literary craft; in the comment of work on life, life on work; or in a vision of humanity; but from whatever source we draw meaning, we have found little of what the original audience found and nothing so exciting. Where did *The Countess Cathleen* get the meanings it once had? If we could find that out in this remarkable case, we might know something about how any work comes to have significance. Certainly, what once seemed an answer both obvious and good—the right words in the right order make great works great—now appears as a truism that is not always true.

2

Of course, not all those in attendance at the Antient Concert Rooms found the same significance, or, for that matter, any significance at all. When George Moore arrived for the second night, he says, he took the noise inside the hall for "the true caoine from Galway," a stage effect to make the death of the countess more authentic, but it turned out to be the audience, howling against the play.[10] Afterwards Yeats explained to him

---

Saddlemyer (Seattle: University of Washington Press, 1967), 140–60; Balachandra Rajan, *W. B. Yeats* (London: Hutchinson, 1965), 24–27; Alex Zwerdling, *Yeats and the Heroic Ideal* (New York: New York University Press, 1965), 75–76, 122–23; Harold Bloom, *Yeats* (New York: Oxford University Press, 1970), 118–19; A. S. Knowland, *W. B. Yeats: Dramatist of Vision* (Gerrards Cross: Colin Smythe, 1983), 10–16; Richard Taylor, *A Reader's Guide to the Plays of W. B. Yeats* (New York: St. Martin's Press, 1984), 24–29. Two critics focus on the historical and political elements of the play and its context, one apologizing for Yeats, the other not: Elizabeth Cullingford interprets the play as an allegory of Maud Gonne's work among the peasantry, which vindicates such political service, but was generally misunderstood by the audience because of unintentional offense given Catholic religious sensibilities (*Yeats, Fascism, and Ireland*, 47–49). My own approach to the play is closest to that of G. J. Watson's *Irish Identity and the Literary Revival* (New York: Barnes and Noble, 1979), which focuses on the matrix of class conflict in which the play developed.

10. George Moore, *Hail and Farewell!* vol. 1, *Ave* (1911; London: William Heinemann, 1937), 76–77.

that having been so long outside of Ireland, Moore might not understand that it was a serious matter to bring over a play that shocked people's feelings. And Moore adds in *Hail and Farewell:* "Of course, the play shocks nobody's feelings, but it gives people the opportunity to think that their feelings are shocked." True, Moore was accustomed to living in a literary beau monde, Paris or London, but he was Irish and Catholic—what does he mean that the play shocks no one's feelings? To us, it may be nothing but dress-ups, pretty poetry, and legendary cartoons, but surely to anyone who was there it had a greater impact?

Not, apparently, to everyone—neither to all Irishmen, nor to all Catholics, nor to all who knew the play well. Lady Gregory says in *Our Irish Theatre* that the actors themselves, being English, could not understand the excitement when there was booing and hooting from the gallery.[11] To them it was a simple morality or mystery play about a time in Ireland's legendary past when famine raged and the peasants were starving. The beautiful Countess Cathleen, attended by a poet and nurse, offers her charity to a peasant family down to her last coin in the first scene. Then two devils appear, disguised as merchants, offering gold to buy food in exchange for the souls of the peasants, many of whom accept the offer. When the Countess Cathleen learns of this horrible commerce across the countryside, she empties her larder, sells her land, and finally barters her own soul in exchange for the return of the peasants' souls. The devils accept and the peasants are freed. After the sudden death swoon of the countess, an angel appears to announce that she too is saved, because God looks on the motive not the deed. With coaching from Yeats himself, the actors had learned the lines, mastered the movements of the characters, and carried this charming play to its conclusion: what, then, did they not know that made them miss the meaning of the play?

They didn't know, according to Lady Gregory, that F. Hugh

---

11. Lady Gregory, *Our Irish Theatre* (1913; rpt., New York: Capricorn Books, 1965), 24–25.

O'Donnell was a master provocateur, a hater of "everything decent in Ireland," such as Yeats and the Anglo-Irish, and probably anyway in the pay of the Crown; or that Cardinal Logue was the supreme authority in Ireland for the majority of its population, and that he, provoked by O'Donnell, had condemned the play. Without this knowledge, no one could find anything objectionable in the play, Lady Gregory concludes, because it is all quite harmless and lovely.

Robert Hogan and James Kilroy allow that the mischief of O'Donnell may have been the first cause of the controversy, but they add that one has to take into account two other necessary conditions, characteristics of the Irish people: first, Ireland, still in the grip of a hyperpuritanical public morality, was quick to sense slights to religion and that morality; second, Ireland, though still a colony, was largely nationalist, and quick to sense slights to its patriotic pride.[12] Once again, there is nothing in the play that makes it significant, but something about the backward Irish. It is possible, however, that where the audience took offense, offense was given.

3

Granted, without the agitation of O'Donnell, the tone of the debate might well have been more gentlemanly: he screamed at what seemed to be small wounds, if wounds at all. His pamphlet *Souls for Gold* is, indeed, as Lady Gregory suggests, hysterical, distorted, and propagandistic. But O'Donnell makes some just observations, though in unjustly inflated language.[13] It is true that WBY shows peasants "crouched in degraded awe" before sowlths, sheogues, and demons; true that in a small cast he introduces one Irish thief, one Irish adulteress, and one Irish iconoclast.[14] Neither O'Donnell nor

12. Hogan and Kilroy, 1:30–31.
13. F. Hugh O'Donnell, *Souls for Gold* (London: Nassau Press, 1899); selections rpt. in Hogan and Kilroy, 1:31–33.
14. *The Countess Cathleen*, in Alspach, lines 178, 182e, 535z, 543r, 543cc, 732, 777. The acting text is a revised version of the one appearing in *Poems*, (London: T. Fisher Unwin, 1899). These revisions, and others, were incorporated in *Poems* (London: T. Fisher Unwin, 1901).

Cardinal Logue were far from the mark when they asked, "Is this Irish?"[15]

But one might well ask, how much does it matter if the play is Irish? To an extent plays are meant to be read on their own terms, not by comparing them with some phantom called "reality." It mattered a great deal to that audience in 1899, however, because WBY had told them beforehand that for the first time on stage, he was going to show the Irish people who they really were. In the formal statement of purpose for the Irish Literary Theatre, Yeats and Lady Gregory concluded: "We will show that Ireland is not the home of buffoonery and of easy sentiment, as it has been represented, but the home of ancient idealism. We are confident of the support of all Irish people, who are weary of misrepresentation, in carrying out a work that is outside all the political questions that divide us."[16] The howls in the gallery when *The Countess Cathleen* was staged showed just how little representation was outside the political questions that divided loyalist and nationalist, Protestant and Catholic, aristocrat and democrat. The advertisement by the founders was, in fact, likely to divide them more, because it makes contradictory promises: the authors will show the real Ireland and the ideal Ireland. *The Countess Cathleen* certainly disappoints one of these expectations: an ideal Ireland would not be so richly populated with sinners.

The real Ireland may or may not have the particular vices—and virtues—the play attributes to it; that depends on what we call "vice" and on how the Irish people behaved in the nineteenth century. Then (as later in controversies over the works of Synge and Joyce) Irish nationalists claimed that their

15. It is difficult to accept Elizabeth Cullingford's characterization that opposition to the play, while expressive of "genuine religious feeling" can be laid to "artificially manufactured bigotry," or even to agree with her opinion—drawn from Yeats's own account—that "those who attacked 'The Countess Cathleen' were motivated more by religious than political fervour" (*Yeats, Ireland and Fascism*, 48). In the Irish context of theological politics and political theology, of class conflict determined by religious affiliation, the drawing of this distinction has the effect of dismissing the force of both the play and the opposition to it.

16. Lady Gregory, *Our Irish Theatre*, 20.

men were brave, their women pure, and their people pious. Scholars have usually followed the writers in mocking these claims, saying that the nationalists were puritans, chauvinists, and philistines. Whatever their stock responses to drama, in order to judge *The Countess Cathleen* as a representation of reality, we need to know something about the general moral conduct of the Irish: whether the women were characteristically chaste or adulterous, the men courageous or cowardly and thieving, the people strong or weak in their faith.

First of all, it is a fact everywhere in evidence and by all acknowledged that the Irish of the last half of the nineteenth century and first half of the twentieth were remarkably reserved in their sexual behavior. Up to the Famine, apparently, they played more, married younger, and scamped about a bit; after the Famine, the average age of marriage rose to about thirty-nine for men, thirty for women.[17] The Famine came in a fashion that seemed to many a punishment for having too many children, and, with the help of Jansenist theology and Victorian morality, brought about a blessedly virginal nation. By the end of the nineteenth century, the purity of Ireland's women had become a plank in the nationalist program: every crown colony is bound to be thought of as a slut, used at the pleasure of the Empire—Ireland alone, though poor, is pure. Critics may mock the status of chastity as a virtue, but one cannot deny its importance both to Irish nationalist thought and in Irish behavior.

As for the second and third sins representing the faults of the Irish in the play—robbery and sacrilege—they are even less characteristic than adultery. No doubt, some Irishmen at some time stole property, but for cultural reasons the Irish of

17. In the 1830s, 28 percent of Irish women who married did so before their twenty-first year; only 11 percent of English women in that decade did so. After the Famine, the rate of marriages declined severely, and the age at which people married increased, until in 1951, the average age at which farmers married was thirty-nine for men and thirty for women, while a quarter of the men remained unmarried. See K. H. Connell, *The Population of Ireland, 1750–1845* (1950; rpt., Westport, Conn.: Greenwood Press, 1975), 39; and F. S. L. Lyons, *Ireland since the Famine* (1971; rpt., London: Fontana, 1973), 45–46.

the nineteenth century did not make much use of the small opportunities for larceny a poor country provides. To steal a sheep in Ireland was not just to make yourself one sheep richer; it would quite possibly have been to starve your neighbor. For this reason, the Irish queerly regarded assault and even murder (of certain persons) as less heinous crimes than theft. (This peculiarity is, of course, one basis of Synge's ironies in *The Playboy of the Western World*: because he is believed to have killed his father, Christy Mahon is a good man to guard the shop of Michael James from thieves; in fact, he is an all-around hero.) As for sacrilege, Yeats included a spectacular scene in which a peasant kicks a shrine of the Virgin Mary to pieces just after struggling with his wife.[18] The audience did not object to his browbeating his wife, but they did not at all like seeing the man crush a statue of the Virgin under his boot. It was not that the Irish did not commit sins, but that they typically did not commit *those* sins singled out in the play—lechery, robbery, and iconoclasm.

The plot of *The Countess Cathleen* called for sins of some sort in act 3, during which the demon-merchants price the souls of the peasants by adding up their sins. The playwright might have provoked less reaction from his audience if he had made one sinner a miser, another an incendiary, and a third a believer in faeries—typical vices of the people in nineteenth-century Irish novels and in the eyes of the Church. But for Yeats, superstition was not a sin but a strength of the peasant; incendiarism suggested the possibility of peasant anguish and revolt, which he tended to ignore; and miserliness contradicted his thesis that the Irish, unlike the English, were a spiritual people, caring little for material gain.

4

The Catholic "mob" that objected so much to the sort of vices Yeats gave the Irish masses did not much mention the virtues he assigned to the play's representative of the Irish classes,

18. Alspach, 31; line 182e.

but it could have. The picture of the countess was so flattering, and that of the peasants so amusing, that the ladies of the
Chief Secretary's Lodge—Lady Balfour, the countess of
Fingall, and others—begged Yeats to let them perform the
work as nine *tableaux vivants* six months before the performance scheduled for the Antient Concert Rooms. Yeats wrote
his sister that of course, as a nationalist, he could not go any-
where near the residence of Britain's representative in
Ireland, much less take part in the performance, but as a
gentleman he did not refuse to meet the ladies in Betty Balfour's house to advise them about costumes.[19] Their performance was a complete success: it was such fun for the gentry
to act the peasants, who must have seemed like fabulous talking beasts out of Grimm. The chief secretary, Arthur Balfour,
also found a pleasant satisfaction in the graceful way the
countess of Fingall, as Countless Cathleen, died to save the
peasants who could not save themselves.[20] Certainly, the
chief virtue in the ethical scheme of the play is *generosity,* a
quality most accessible to the rich.[21] The main virtue to which
the poor may aspire is gratitude—as in the one blameless
peasant character, Maire, who shows exaggerated respect
and thankfulness to the countess, then dies of starvation.[22]

These differences between the "quality" (Anglo-Irish word
for the upper classes) and the peasants did, however, attract
the attention of theological critics. A rather sensible Catholic
reviewer for the *Daily Express* concluded that Yeats, though "a
king in Fairyland," was completely ignorant of the way an
Irishman thought: "the central conception of the excessive
value of the beautiful Countess's soul" was "foreign to any-

19. WBY to Lily Yeats, 25 December 1898; Wade, 306.
20. Elizabeth, countess of Fingall, and Pamela Hinkson, *Seventy Years
Young* (London: Collins, 1937), 234–35.
21. Malcolm Brown correctly judges that Yeats's "attention to Irish grievances"—such as the Famine—"was always slight and sustained only with
difficulty"; his real aim in the play was "a more congenial theme . . . the exaltation of the supernatural benevolence of the Irish aristocracy toward the
deserving poor" (*The Politics of Irish Literature: From Thomas Davis to W. B.
Yeats* [Seattle: University of Washington Press, 1972], 144).
22. Alspach, 15–25; lines 69–138; 728b.

thing" that could be called Irish "in spiritual outlook."[23] In
the play, the highest price brought by the soul of a peasant—
that of an ugly old woman—is a thousand crowns; but for the
soul of the countess, the demons are glad to give five hundred thousand.[24] When Yeats was attacked on this score, he
claimed the opinion belonged to the devil, not to him. But actually, as the *Daily Express* reviewer notes, the entire play is
constructed on this conception. Not only do the demons as-
say certain values, they pay the gold pieces. And the peasants
show no surprise that one soul is worth more than another, or
that the soul of the countess is worth many times more than
all others. Indeed, at the end of the play, God himself, decid-
ing that the countess is too valuable a property to go down to
the house of hell, repossesses her soul.

   Yeats's kinder critics, such as T. P. Gill and the reviewer for
the *Daily Nation*, charitably assumed that he had a poor grip
on the theological principles of Catholicism, but the real problem lay in his powerful hold on certain beliefs about society,
not about God, beliefs the majority of his audience could not
accept. The weakest claim for the countess, necessary to the
working of the plot, is that this particular individual is simply
good, in a selfless and absolute way. But the contingencies of
social casting permit, and indeed invite, a stronger claim: that
those of the countess's rank and station in life are naturally
more noble than others. To cite a later poem, there are "loftier
thought, / Sweeter emotion working in their veins, / Like
gentle blood."[25] The fact is, Yeats believed some people to be
more valuable than others—more beautiful, thus more noble,
thus more virtuous; or, in the idiom of the peasant Maire,

   23. *Daily Express*, 9 May 1899; Hogan and Kilroy, 1:42.
   24. Alspach, 117, line 586; 145, line 774. G. J. Watson also notes that
"these going rates seem entirely appropriate to Yeats's peasants." Concerning the play as a whole, Watson makes the valuable point that *"The Countess
Cathleen* expresses a consciousness in many ways alien to that of its audience" and "the gap between 'Ascendancy' and 'native' ensured its hostile reception" (*Irish Identity and the Literary Revival*, 66–67).
   25. "To A Shade" (29 September 1913), in *The Collected Poems of W. B.
Yeats* (New York: Macmillan, 1956; 1968), 108.

more wealthy, therefore more wise.[26] Catholic members of the audience could no doubt see for themselves that beauty, wealth, and status were important facts of life, but they did not take them as facts of the afterlife as well. For them, the values of this world stood opposed to those of the other world; for Yeats, they seemed sometimes to be the same. This belief in a natural social hierarchy was the very reason he hated democracy.

In the debate over the play, Yeats denied that it had any proper historical setting or said anything about the social character of the Irish people: "His play, of course, was purely symbolic, and as such it must be regarded"—the countess just a symbol of subjective life, the bad peasants and demons of material life.[27] But Yeats's revisions of the folktale actually made the countess and the peasants more identifiable as historical Irish types, if not accurately representative of them.

For example, one oddity often noticed in the play's action is the entrance of the countess into a peasant's cottage.[28] First, she comes in for the queer reason that she is lost, though she is in her own demesne, not far from the immense castle the peasants mention in awe. Many take this as clumsy dramaturgy, but there were plenty of Irish lords and ladies, either largely absent from Ireland or garrisoned in great houses, who could not have found their way around their own property, had they ventured into it.

Second, when the countess comes into the cottage, she arrives accompanied by a lutanist and other musicians, which causes the "bad peasant" Shemus to rumble, "They are off again: some lady or gentleman . . . in the woods with tympan

26. To be precise, Maire's words are as follows: "When wealthy and wise folk wander from their peace / And fear wood things, poor folk may draw the bolt / And pray before the fire" (Alspach, 27, line 146).

27. "Irish Literary Theatre: Dinner at the Shelbourne Hotel," *Daily Express*, 12 May 1899, 5–6; Hogan and Kilroy, 1:50.

28. Alspach, 15, lines 69d–121. Peter Ure notes that the scene is "a trifle grotesque" and says it can be "justified" by the "economies" of Yeats's revision and by the effective "pictorial stage-contrast between real rags and gorgeous livery" (*Yeats the Playwright*, 21).

and with harp." [29] After all, his family is starving, and all he has in the kitchen is a dead wolf. Thematically, this seems a heavy-handed way for the playwright to establish that the countess suffers a spiritual sorrow only music can soften, while the best the peasants can do is suffer a physical hunger. But once again, there is a kind of historical accuracy: the immense social distance between the Protestant Ascendancy of Ireland and its Catholic peasantry appears in the highly cultured loneliness of the rich and the brutal, ignorant suffering of the poor.

Third, here, for the first but not last time in the play, we notice how little there is for the heroine to do. She wanders in, empties a few last coins from her purse, and wanders out, sorrowful she cannot do more. She does not struggle for anything, against anyone. In the end, of course, she offers herself for sale, and in her highest act signs her last will and testament (with a quill from the cock that crowed when St. Peter—the first pope—betrayed Christ!). Here too the play idealizes the life of a class of landlords that had little to do but leave smaller fortunes behind at their deaths. Yeats's subsequent defense that the characters were "purely symbolic," because "literature is the expression of universal truths," seems in this instance to have been offered to obstruct an inquiry into the more particular truths—and untruths—embodied in the play. The aesthetic argument, in other words, was offered for a political purpose.

5

In fact, there was a political purpose to *The Countess Cathleen*, over and above the eulogy on the landlord and libel on the peasants that appear in the characterization. The purpose is found in the setting and plot of the play: in a famine, peasants sell their souls until they are saved by their landlord. George Moore reports a conversation with T. P. Gill, editor of the *Daily Express*, in which the latter said that the setting and plot

29. Alspach, 15, lines 58–58a.

of *The Countess Cathleen* were "calculated to wound the religious susceptibilities of the Irish people." Gill, Moore says, "while stroking his beard, . . . continued to speak of the famine times and of proselytizing by Protestants: memories like these were too deep to be washed away by mere poetry."[30]

Memory indeed is too weak a word to express how the Irish psyche was convulsed by the Famine that began in 1845—by its end, the population was cut in half, millions dying, millions emigrating. Meanwhile, Protestant landlords offered to give them soup if they changed their religion. Not many changed it, however, and those who did are remembered and ridiculed today—"soupers," they are called.

Though Yeats denied the association between the setting of his play and the Irish Famine, his adaptation of the source, "The Countess Kathleen O'Shea" (collected in WBY's *Fairy and Folk Tales of the Irish Peasantry*), actually enforces it.[31] In the original, a "dearth" is mentioned, but only a few times, and then not until almost half the tale is done. In the play, Famine is the premise from start to finish. What Yeats had done was to transvalue the greatest national experience of the Irish, turning a Protestant moral catastrophe into a miracle of benevolence, and one of the world's remarkable cases of a people's devotion to a faith into wholesale infidelity.[32]

This transvaluation of the historical roles of the classes is

30. Moore, *Hail and Farewell*, 1:95. A leading article in the 9 May 1899 *Irish Times* also complained that the play "offends against the tenor of Irish history in regard to the Theological connection and against the position of the Irish peasant in the face of physical pain" (*Critical Heritage*, ed. Jeffares, 114).

31. W. B. Yeats, ed., *Fairy and Folk Tales of Ireland*, rpt. of *Fairy and Folk Tales of the Irish Peasantry* (London, 1888) and *Irish Fairy Tales* (London, 1892) (Gerrards Cross, Bucks.: Colin Smythe, 1977). Yeats later discovered that the tale was translated from the French *Les Matinées de Timothe Trimm;* the actual source was named in the 1895 and following editions of *Poems* (Alspach, 170–77).

32. The transvaluation by Protestants began even in the midst of the deaths and forced emigration of the famine years. Malcolm Brown sharply observes that Sir Robert Peel's ineffective relief measures during the 1846 Famine—in which finances were left to the voluntary impulses of local landlords—incited "in the donors a maudlin self-congratulation by which they read their niggardliness as heroic benevolence, in the manner of Yeats's 'Countess Cathleen'" (*Politics of Irish Literature*, 89).

cunningly worked into the plot. Fredric Jameson's explanation of Vladimir Propp's morphology of the folktale elucidates
the changes Yeats made in his source.[33] Propp, the first to
break folktales down into their signifying elements and to define the rules of combination for those elements, found that
most tales begin with a situation of lack in the home. The hero
is then driven out by this initial problem either to do battle
with a malignant enemy or to carry out a series of perplexing
tasks. Jameson observes here that the main reality of a world
of scarcity is not just that one cannot meet one's needs without work, but that one's very existence—as one who eats and
strives to gather food—is a threat to the existence of others.
One is therefore given the bleak choice of either competing
with others (doing battle with the villain) or working (carrying out the perplexing tasks). Both ultimately have the same
meaning: the war of man upon man. The fairy tale reflects
this world of scarcity by making the Other, the figure outside
the family circle, appear as a primal enemy or supernatural
friend, there being no such thing as a natural friend. The
great value for societies of this popular form is in the sturdy
hope of the standard denouement. As Bruno Bettelheim em-
phasizes, folktales teach self-reliance: the hero who sets out
at the start always in the end brings home the boon that fills
the initial lack, even if he has a bit of heavenly help along
the way.[34]

   In *The Countess Cathleen* the initial situation is typical: there
is no food in the home, and the father is out foraging. When
he returns, he tells his wife of his failure to find anything to
eat, except for the wolf he killed before their door. At this
time, half a scene into the play, the countess enters with her
"fantastically dressed musicians." Now, in this situation of
famine, and a war of man upon man, the starving peasants,
having made depredations upon one another's flocks, then

33. Jameson, *The Prison-House of Language* (Princeton: Princeton University Press, 1972), 68; Propp, *The Morphology of the Folktale,* trans. Laurence
Scott (Austin: University of Texas Press, 1968).
   34. Bettelheim, *The Uses of Enchantment: The Meaning and Importance of
Fairy Tales* (New York: Knopf, 1976).

having turned to violence against one another, at last recognize that the estate of the countess offers a way through to the next harvest. In act 2, Cathleen learns from the gardener that peasants are stealing her apples, and from the herdsman that they have rustled her sheep.[35] This recognition that her wealth can save them is only a short step from another perception for the peasants: the countess creates the Famine—her immense wealth causes their poverty. But before this perception can break upon the mind, Yeats turns the tale so that the countess is not the villain, but the supernatural donor, and, then, more than the donor, the tale's one true hero. The shape of the play's plot makes a compelling depiction of the masses as helplessly dependent.

In Yeats's source, "The Countess Kathleen O'Shea," this message of peasant helplessness does not come through, because in that version there is no peasant family at the start, just a generalized Irish town populated with unspecified townspeople; the first named and individualized character is the countess, who is thus seen from the start as the heroine.[36] But in *The Countess Cathleen*, Yeats puts Shemus, the father of the family, in the position of hero—the first character developed, the first to journey forth, and the first to struggle with the demons—and then makes him fail, allowing the countess to take over the role of hero. In this way, rather than being the natural enemy of the peasants, the landlord becomes their supernatural savior. Furthermore, the demons are suggestively transformed from being the supernatural villians to appearing like the natural enemy of the Irish, the British—strangers with good manners who operate on principles of Free Trade even in times of Famine.[37] A social contradiction

35. Alspach, 61, lines 365–66d; 65, lines 378rr–78ss.
36. Yeats, *Fairy and Folk Tales of Ireland*, 213.
37. Andrew Parkin believes that in the early version of the play the devils "display a bitter, brutal streak" "giving the impression that they are melodramatic caricatures of ruthless landlords," not just of specifically English commercialism (*The Dramatic Imagination of W. B. Yeats* [Dublin: Gill & Macmillan, 1978], 71). I follow Malcolm Brown (*Politics of Irish Literature*, 89) in associating them more strictly with English Free Trade policies during the Famine, and in general with the English mercantile character; thus I see the play as using xenophobia as a distraction from class hatred.

(harmony of aristocracy and peasantry in time of scarcity) is turned into an imaginary unity by means of gathering the potentially opposed classes together against an external enemy: under the leadership of the Protestants, Ireland will be saved from England. Yeats can thus be seen to have colonized a typical narrative expression of the poorer classes, altering its plot and thus its social meaning, with the apparent goal of uniting Ireland against England and subordinating the peasantry to the landlords. One must remember that Yeats was a nationalist but not a democrat.

6

We now know something of what the play meant to different parts of the audience (nationalist, Catholic, and Ascendancy), what it means in relation to Irish history and its folklore basis; we must next consider if the political statements implied in the play are what Yeats himself meant to say. In addition, we need to decide whether such statements are the main blow the poet wished to deal, a passing side-swipe, or just an unintentional, if bruising, collision with the sensitivities of a part of his audience. In either of the first two cases—as a main, or a subordinate intention—such statements would be intentional propaganda—writing that aims to shape opinions and attitudes, and in the last, it could nonetheless be propaganda, though unintentionally so. Yeats himself declared many times that his work was not propaganda, but art, and that he was not interested in forming the opinions of people.

This distinction between art and propaganda may be a useful rhetorical trope in certain kinds of political argument, but logically it is false. Any work of art can become propaganda if it is used in a certain way; any work of propaganda can become art if viewed in the right light.[38] Pope's "The Rape of the Lock," for instance, becomes propaganda if a minister of propaganda sends it to British troops on the Somme to

38. This availability of one work of art to many conflicting political uses is a major theme of A. P. Foulkes in *Literature and Propaganda* (New York: Methuen, 1983), esp. 105.

show them the light grace and cultural refinement they are fighting for. And works can take on quite contradictory functions as propaganda in different settings: *The Playboy of the Western World* in its first production was antinationalist propaganda about the Protestant virtues of wildness and extravagance, about the falsity of prim Gaelic League views of the peasant, and even about the freedom of the Protestant artists from political interference. Many years later, produced at a state-owned Abbey Theatre, the same play becomes nationalist propaganda about the tolerant union of hearts in the new nation and about its modern, sophisticated view of its own past. In its 1899 production, Yeats's play is certainly propaganda as well as art; the questions are what sort of propaganda and for what purpose.

Jacques Ellul has made the best classification of propaganda.[39] In his terms, Yeats's play would be "sociological" rather than "political propaganda." In political propaganda, an organization uses techniques of influence to achieve a specific change in society; in sociological propaganda, an individual who has assimilated a dominant ideology uses it to form what he takes to be spontaneous, natural, and right judgments of value, with the expectation that his work will, among other things, confirm the audience in a set of values it already honors. In particular, Yeats picked up certain attitudes from a group of upper-class nationalists—figures like Standish O'Grady, Lady Gregory, and the younger Edward Martyn—about the value of tradition, noble manners, and the whole feudal way of life. He gave expression to such values as if they were universal truths rather than the beliefs of a class.

Yeats offered his dramatization of these values as what Ellul calls "integration propaganda" rather than "agitation propaganda." Agitation is subversive work opposed to the status quo; integration tries to conserve the status quo and create contentment with it. One way to describe the clamor over *The Countess Cathleen* is to observe that what Yeats of-

---

39. Ellul, *Propaganda: The Formation of Men's Attitudes*, trans. Konrad Kellen and Jean Lerner (1966; rpt., New York: Vintage Books, 1973). Foulkes develops the ideas of Ellul in *Literature and Propaganda*, 12–13, passim.

fered as integration and sociological propaganda was taken
by the nationalist part of the audience as political and subversive propaganda. They had become accustomed to a nationalist view of the Irish people as valiant, pious rebels winning a
war against an unjust land settlement (in which a few thousand largely Unionist and Protestant landlords lived off the
rents of millions of predominantly Catholic and nationalist
tenants), and Yeats's idealization of the status quo ante bellum
struck them as a move by a powerful minority to recapture
control of the political momentum in the country. They refused to assimilate the values of the aristocracy as their own.
Furthermore, because the setting of the Famine became the
key by which they interpreted the play, they did not give
Yeats credit for the progressive side of his nationalism: his
suggestion that the landlords could increase their glory by
serving their tenants and even selling off a part of their estates
to enlarge peasant smallholdings.

The political meaning Yeats gave the play appears in a comparison of the picture of Irish society Yeats painted and
the picture most of his countrymen saw before them. They
looked upon an Ireland with an irresponsible aristocracy and
a rebellious tenantry struggling for equality and independence; he exhibited for their admiration an Ireland with a
conscientious aristocracy and a suffering, misguided tenantry
at last happy to settle back down into their position in the hierarchy. But the audience did not admire his utopia: the
world of *The Countess Cathleen* was neither what Ireland really
was nor what they wanted it to be. Yeats certainly produced
propaganda, but the first production did not succeed completely because it was recognized to be propaganda.

Not a complete success at first, in the end it became one.
During the controversy after the first production, and even
before it, Yeats argued (a) that every civilized country should
permit free artistic expression, (b) that every work of art deserved a fair hearing from a tolerant audience, and (c) that his
play was a work of art and should be appreciated, or at least
tolerated, as one. If Yeats could get the public to come to his
play, sit quietly through it, and comment principally upon its
dramatic verse, scenery, and acting, then he could achieve a

situation in which sociological and integrationist propaganda could work. The political values of the play might then be assimilated by part of the audience simply through the habit of aesthetic suspension of disbelief. When the case was argued on grounds of artistic freedom, Yeats found his supporters and made his brief. Lady Gregory proudly declares that they won that battle because the play was produced several times later at the Abbey and no one made any protest at all.[40] Of course, it has to be added that when the significance the audience first found in the work is excluded from discussion, there is little left in the play to resent, and less to admire; it has become a thing to tolerate.

In 1899, those who saw *The Countess Cathleen* as the object of an argument between artists asking for freedom and clerics requiring censorship came to the defense of Yeats. Joyce, seated in the gallery on the first night, for instance, liked the lyric "Who Goes with Fergus," didn't mind the depiction of peasants as ignorant and superstitious (he thought they were too), and clapped vigorously at the end of the play.[41] James Cousins—another young Catholic intellectual—also came to root for writers: "In the duel of hiss and cheer, cheer won. I give my word for the victory, for I was one of the victors, and possessed as spoils of conquest a hat with a broken rim through which I had clenched my fingers when waving it in wild applause at nothing in the play but something in the rising spirit of the Arts in Ireland as against the spirit of obscurantism and dishonest censorship," he says.[42] With such foot soldiers, Yeats and Lady Gregory indeed had their victory, but at a price: people cheered at nothing in the play; their "wild applause" was for "Art" in the abstract.[43] In fact,

40. Lady Gregory, *Our Irish Theatre*, 25.
41. Richard Ellmann, *James Joyce* (Oxford: Oxford University Press, 1959), 68–69.
42. James H. and Margaret E. Cousins, *We Two Together* (Madras: Ganesh, 1950), 57.
43. In declaring his victory over Cardinal Logue and the Catholic Celtophiles, Yeats also pointed to the applause as proof: "The applause in the theatre has shown what party has the victory" (WBY to the editor, *Morning Leader*, 13 May 1899; Wade, 320).

from this report, it is a wonder that anyone made anything of the play itself, the room being filled with hisses, cheers, boos, verse-speaking, and musical interludes. But ultimately what mattered, and perhaps what always matters, is the argument over the work of art, not simply the argument in it.

7

One who saw him in action in the *Playboy* row, Mary Colum, said that she never saw a man fight so hard as Yeats fought, nor one who had so many weapons in his armory.[44] But by fighting for his work as art and only art, and winning that fight, Yeats began the unmaking of the meanings made out of *The Countess Cathleen*. The critical tradition that finds in this work only verses, gestures, eternal emotions, and allegories of the spirit begins right here with Yeats's own argument against the nationalists. A play or a poem is not essentially an artifice, and what it stands for is not eternity. In the case of this play, the result of splitting the aesthetic from the political, and the philosophical from the historical, is a general erasure of significance. The meanings Yeats put into the play and provoked around it he himself dispelled.

Yeats was a great genius, and remains one, because of his magisterial ability to create and control the interest of his readers. Some of that management of interest occurs through figures of speech and the hosts of other literary effects within the work, but more of it occurs in the activities of the poet around the work—in manifestoes, charters for committees, newspaper editorials, press releases, prefaces, lists of guarantors, costume designs, actresses, musical interludes, symbolic treatises, folklore collections, and so on. And once he has directed our attention to certain things he says are in the work, and away from others, the ways in which the work is discussed are changed forever. This is the perpetual conundrum of the inside and the outside, one every magician and

44. Colum, *The Life and the Dream* (1958; rev. ed., Dublin: Dolmen Press, 1966), 121.

symbolist must master: to make a thing that is nothing in itself signify many things, to make the swan "a concentration of the sky."

An encomium on Yeats in a 1912 work on theatre by Edward Martyn illustrates how much Yeats's work as public figure adds to his stature as phrase-maker. Martyn is trying to understand why his own literary career aborted after *The Heather Field* was produced on that opening night with *The Countess Cathleen*, whereas Yeats's dramatic career became so prominent. The decline in his own fortunes must have been especially puzzling to Martyn because his own play received much kinder, if shorter, notices than Yeats's did. Looking at the success of the Abbey from 1904 to 1912 before considering how to take up a new theatrical plan for himself, Martyn apologizes: "I am humbly conscious of my inferiority as an impresario to the two experts [Yeats and Lady Gregory] whose feats I have the temerity to imitate."[45] *Impresario* is the correct word for the type of artistic genius Yeats so grandly is. And not only Yeats: if Martyn could not excite interest in his work—through being fashionable, controversial, or somehow relevant—he could not be a good writer. For a work to make an impression, the impresario has to create the ways in which the work is perceived, not simply the work itself, which may well remain invisible until one is taught how to see it.

Indeed, the very materials of the work—the words of the language—always already belong to a polity of discourse about many topics that seem external to the work, and using those words, the writer is performing an act of power over others, defining how they are seen, and how they see themselves, just as in receiving those words from others, the writer is an effect of the way others have constituted a world and him out of words.[46] From the first word that is written, then,

45. Denis Gwynn, *Edward Martyn and the Irish Revival* (London: Jonathan Cape, 1930), 156.
46. For an excellent discussion of the "polity of discourse," see J. G. A. Pocock, "Verbalizing a Political Act: Toward a Politics of Speech," in *Language and Politics*, ed. Michael J. Shapiro (New York: New York University Press, 1984), 27–43.

the author enters upon a long conversation that continues until the last word is said, a conversation that is continuous with
other acts of language and acts of power in the society. The
immense volume, scope, and ambition of Yeats's activities in
every aspect of this polity of discourse is one main reason his
plays and poems have such great meaning for us.[47] Discussion
of the work of art, in a simple sense, makes the meaning of
the work, if not its capacity for meaning.

This conclusion may seem debunking, but that is not my
purpose. The public relations work of Yeats had a greater result than raising an audience or increasing sales figures for his
books. It made his writing an enduring object of our attention. We may refuse to discuss the work in the terms he pro-
poses, but we shall continue to discuss it. Looking back over
the poetry of Yeats some years ago, Denis Donoghue decided
with coy judiciousness that there were five or six excellent
poems out of the lot; the rest were period pieces, inchoate
symbolic ruminations, or exercises in personal mannerism.
The reason Yeats had been taken for a great poet on such
small achievement, Donoghue said, is that he had mixed his
poetry up with a legendary biography (especially the unrequited love for Maud Gonne) and with the history of his nation.[48] I think Donoghue is right at least in this—Yeats did en-
hance his poetry by giving it a backdrop of Irish history and a
cast of noble-looking figures. But that does not make him less
a poet; that makes him a great poet. A jar in Tennessee, a mirror in the roadway, or a swan in the sky: what is in the work
comes from what we make of it with what lies around it.

47. Hilton Edwards, formerly co-director of the Gate Theatre, Dublin, made a similar observation about the Abbey's plays in general: "When you come to think of it the Abbey's reputation . . . has been built up upon, I would say, five plays, and I would have great difficulty finding the fifth. . . . The reputation of the Irish theatre . . . depends more on . . . the brilliance of the various people that have been writing about her than on what the Irish theatre has done" (*Journal of Irish Literature*, 2, no. 3 [May 1973]: 87).

48. Donoghue, "The Hard Case of Yeats," *New York Review of Books* 24, no. 9 (26 May 1977): 3–4. In regard to Yeats's dramatic efforts, Donoghue says, "I cannot see any good reason for staging . . . most of the early plays, which are interesting only to students of Yeats."

2

Freedom and Individuality

The Politics of Yeats's Theatre,
1900–1903

Nearly a year after the first production of *The Countess Cathleen*, W. B. Yeats wrote a letter to Lady Gregory in which he explained the aims of his recent political moves and made a forecast for the theatrical movement.[1] A startling epigram from this letter of 10 April 1900—"One must accept the baptism of the gutter"—is sometimes cited by literary historians to show that Yeats had attitudes native to his class toward those who were poor and lived in cities; such people called up in him associations with dirt, ditchwater, and the sweepings of the street. He had, according to G. J. Watson, "an almost eastern sense of caste pollution," and Conor Cruise O'Brien, on the basis of this letter, speculates that Yeats was relieved when he found himself free to fight the Catholic "mob" rather than to work within it.[2] However, this important letter shows more than the way in which Yeats re-

1. Wade, 338–39.
2. Watson, *Irish Identity and the Literary Revival* (New York: Barnes & Noble, 1979), 38; Conor Cruise O'Brien, "Passion and Cunning: An Essay on the Politics of W. B. Yeats," in *In Excited Reverie*, ed. A. Norman Jeffares and K. G. W. Cross (New York: St. Martin's Press, 1965), esp. 225–26. Watson elaborates O'Brien's argument that class conflict was a crucial element in the life and work of Yeats, and he extends the argument to Synge, whose work, he says, shows a "residue of quasi-aristocratic contempt for the 'natives' he was never able to expunge totally" (Watson, 38). For two of the many critics attacking O'Brien's article, see Patrick Cosgrave, "Yeats, Fascism, and Conor O'Brien," *London Magazine*, July 1971, and esp. Elizabeth Cullingford, *Yeats, Ireland and Fascism* (New York: New York University Press, 1981), discussed at length below.

sponded to the force of class feeling; other passages enable one also to measure the forces of politics and patronage as they determine the shape taken by Yeats's intellectual ambitions. An inquiry into this particular letter sets the stage for an analysis of the political identity of the poet in the years between the beginning of the Irish Literary Theatre (1899) and the establishment of the Irish National Theatre Society in the Abbey (1904).

The entire paragraph moves through a chain of subjects—theatre, money, politics, and popularity—to the final remark on "the baptism of the gutter":

> I don't think we need be anxious about next year's theatre. Moore talks confidently of finding the money, and I feel sure that our present politics will have done more good than harm. Clever Unionists will take us on our merits and the rest would never like us at any time. I have found a greatly increased friendliness on the part of some of the young men here. In a battle, like Ireland's, which is one of poverty against wealth, one must prove one's sincerity, by making oneself unpopular to wealth. One must accept the baptism of the gutter. Have not all teachers done the like?[3]

The "present politics" that Yeats expected would do him and his theatre "more good than harm" were the extreme anti-British politics into which he had thrown himself in the previous months. In the columns of the *Freeman's Journal* (20 March 1900) and the *Daily Express* (3 April 1900),[4] WBY had called Queen Victoria's April tour of Ireland a junket to recruit soldiers for the suppression of liberty in South Africa in the Boer War. Anyone who stood by the road and cheered the queen, he said, dishonored Ireland and condoned a crime. Furthermore, he set forth a plan for a committee to organize protest so that public demonstrations of national spirit did not lead to riot. There is a piquant mix of the provocateur and the politician here, the old O'Connell monster-meeting style, the Parnell Land League style, of appearing to hold back the blood-

3. Wade, 338–39.
4. Frayne and Johnson, 2:207–8.

thirsty masses that one has first roused to high passion. Yeats's "present politics," in short, were disloyal, provocative, and spectacularly nationalistic.

"Present politics," however, suggest that there are "future politics" and "past politics"; that the tactics of the moment shift about in the play of the battles, perhaps in light of long-term strategy. The past politics were those of a more gentle-manly, "cultural" nationalism that aimed to set forth Irish scenes and Irish characters in a fashion that was artistic, "outside the questions that divide" Irishmen,[5] and did not necessarily involve disloyalty to England. With those politics, Yeats and Lady Gregory had managed to assemble a list of notable Irishmen as guarantors of the Irish Literary Theatre, many of them Protestants, and some Unionists, such as Horace Plunkett, a Unionist leader of rural cooperatives, and the Trinity College historian W. H. Lecky.

The theatre ultimately did not have to call upon its patrons for the full cost of production, because Edward Martyn had agreed to pay for the first and then the second season of performances, each of which featured his work along with plays by Yeats or Moore. But after Martyn's third play, *A Tale of a Town*, was rejected, and then reconstructed by Yeats and Moore as *The Bending of the Bough*, Martyn began to let it be known that he was not going to pay for other men's work.[6]

5. "Prospectus," Irish Literary Theatre, January 1899, rpt. in Lady Gregory, *Our Irish Theatre* (1913; rpt. New York: Capricorn Books, 1965), 9.

6. Martyn's commitment to a joint theatre project with Yeats wavered from the beginning with the clerical opposition to *The Countess Cathleen* in April 1899, but it did not entirely fail for several years. On 31 January 1900, WBY wrote to Lady Gregory that "Moore promises to raise a certain amount of money if Martyn goes out . . . but at any rate I shall do all I can to keep Martyn, but make plain that what is indispensable is the good work we may yet do and not the money which another may give as well as he" (Wade, 334). Martyn ultimately paid for the third season of the Irish Literary Theatre, and did not completely lose interest in working with Yeats and funding his theatre until the time of his gift of £50,000 to the Pro-Cathedral for founding a Palestrina choir, in the late spring of 1902, after the first performance of the Irish National Dramatic Society in April, by which time it was clear to Martyn that Yeats had no room in his plans for Martyn's work or his type of realistic drama about middle-class Irishmen. As late as 25 July 1902, Frank Fay held out hope that Martyn would lend the Irish National Dramatic Society "sufficient money to build a hall" (Finneran, Harper, and Murphy, 2:101).

Moore subsequently looked elsewhere for funding, and by
the time WBY wrote to Lady Gregory on 10 April 1900, Moore
"talk[ed] confidently of finding" it. But even as early as 31
January 1900, Yeats had thought he could pick up additional
money from a source of his own, a "Miss ——."[7] "One must
of course not mention her name in the matter," he quickly
added in this letter, and Lady Gregory obediently blotted it
on the page, but one would be very surprised if the unmarried woman in question were not the English spinster Annie
Horniman. She had not wished it to be known that she had
financed the production of Yeats's first play, *The Land of Heart's
Desire*, at the Avenue Theatre in 1894; and in 1900 Yeats would
not have liked it to be known that an Englishwoman might
become a financial backer of what he wished to be seen as a
more directly nationalist theatre. The new possibilities of patronage from Moore's friend and Yeats's passionate lover of
art, it appears, allowed the directors of the Literary Theatre
some freedom of movement in the local political scene.

When Yeats, Lady Gregory, and Martyn first began discussions of an Irish Literary Theatre, they sought guarantors for
the sake of publicity, capital, and even legitimacy; indeed,
one of them, Lecky, an Irish M.P., had a government regula-
tion amended to permit nonprofit performances of plays by
literary societies. The sponsorship of the class Yeats called
"the class of wealth" when he disapproved of them, and "the
educated class" when he approved had, then, been important
at the start, but it had soon turned into a liability. During the
arguments over *The Countess Cathleen*, Yeats had reason to
worry that his work would be received with suspicion as long
as it was put before the world by Unionist sponsors.

Even before the May 1899 performance of *The Countess
Cathleen*, Yeats published an essay in the *Daily Nation* that distinguished his own social and political position from that of
many other educated Protestants.[8] This defends Irish folklore
against the Trinity don Robert Atkinson's charge that it was

7. Wade, 334.
8. WBY, "The Academic Class and the Agrarian Revolution," *Daily Nation*, 11 March 1899, in Frayne and Johnson, 2:148–52.

all "silly or indecent."[9] Clearly, WBY could not take the charge that folklore was "at bottom, abominable" lying down. He had based much of his work on the premise that folklore was the source of universal wisdom and a treasury of racial dignity. Yeats, however, does more in this essay than defend folklore: he offers an explanation of the character of Protestant intellectuals as an effect of the land wars, during which the Protestants, if they did not lose their Ascendancy, lost the basis of it in property. "The true explanation" of Atkinson's fury over Gaelic classes, he says, is that he "like most people on both sides in politics of the last generation which had to endure the bitterness of the agrarian revolution, is still in a fume of political excitement, and cannot consider any Irish matter without this excitement."[10] In Yeats's view at this time, neither the Anglo-Irish establishment nor the revolutionary Catholic masses were capable of leading the nation. Once, he says, Thomas Davis and the Young Ireland movement of the 1840s had released a pure stream of ideal nationality, but the "inevitably imperfect ideals" of the revolutionary masses had muddied the stream, and the Ascendancy class had dried it up altogether. Who was to lead the nation and again open clear streams of national life?

During this period, 1899–1901, WBY sometimes imagined himself as a kind of Moses, one who could strike water from the rock, threaten an empire, bring ideal laws from the mountaintop, and lead the people to a promised land. The ascendancy class, he ominously says, would "wander forty years in the wilderness that all who have sinned a particular sin might die there." But the leadership of the tribe would then pass into the hands of a few men "who are seeking to create a criticism of life which will weigh all Irish interests, and bind the rich and the poor in one brotherhood."[11] The chief ambition of the poet during this period was to found and lead that small band of Levites. It is worth remembering that Moses

9. *Daily Express*, 23 February 1899; Frayne and Johnson, 2:148.
10. Frayne and Johnson, 2:150.
11. Ibid., 151.

originally lived among the Egyptians. Yeats surely believed that the leadership of the Irish should come from disaffiliated Protestants like Davis, Parnell, and himself. As Yeats remarked in the 1901 *Samhain*, "Moses was little good to his people until he had killed an Egyptian."[12]
Thus the present politics. And they had an effect that, if not intended, was still welcomed: the "Egyptian" Lecky publicly resigned from the board of the Irish Literary Theatre because of Yeats's disloyal and rabble-rousing letters to the press. Early in that letter of 10 April 1900, WBY says he may write again to the press to needle Lecky a little more by saying he could not resign; he had already been dropped from membership for not paying dues. This charge, Yeats hoped, would so annoy Lecky that it would spread into a long public controversy concerning the queen, which "would make Moore and myself quite happy."[13] Surely everyone would then see that there were not only Unionist Protestants but nationalist ones too, and Yeats could look to "greatly increased friendliness" from the young Catholic nationalists, many of whom had fought him on *The Countess Cathleen.*[14]
I am not saying that in making a public attack on the queen's Irish tour, Yeats was not a nationalist, that he felt neither sympathy for Irish recruits, nor solidarity with the Boers, nor indignation against Irishmen loyal to the British Empire. But why did he make these sentiments public in language that could cause a break with men who had before been his friends?[15] In the letter before us, it is quite clear that after his

12. WBY, *Explorations* (New York: Macmillan, 1962), 83.
13. Wade, 338.
14. As early as 18 February 1900, Yeats had planned this strategy, for on that day Lady Gregory recorded a conversation between Yeats and T. W. Rolleston at an art exhibit in which WBY said "he must do something to violently annoy the upper classes to redeem his character" (*Seventy Years: Being the Autobiography of Lady Gregory*, ed. Colin Smythe [Gerrards Cross, Bucks.: Colin Smythe, 1973], 358).
15. To be precise, Lecky was more the friend of Lady Gregory than of Yeats. To Lecky, Yeats was just one of "those Celtic people," as expressed in a dinner-table conversation entered into Lady Gregory's diary: "Dined Lecky's; he rather cross. Took me down to dinner and said first thing, 'What silly

first "Queen letters," he continued the controversy because these "present politics" would do the theatre "more good than harm." Had they done more harm than good, it seems probable that Yeats would have expressed his sense of the political situation differently, perhaps privately among friends, not in the pages of Dublin daily papers. When the Irish Literary Theatre needed to raise money and gain legitimacy, Lecky was welcome. Now what it most needed (at least if Moore and Yeats were right in their hopes of money) was political credibility with the nationalist audience, and for that the class among which Lecky lived and from which he took his values had to be made at least temporarily unwelcome.

This letter tells us a number of things about the role of Yeats in the politics of theatre and in the theatre of politics. First, he was never unmindful of the way in which his role in the practical politics of events like the Jubilee Riots (1897), the Wolfe Tone Commemoration (1898), the queen's visit to Dublin during the Boer War (1900), or Edward VII's call on his Western colony (1903) affected his popularity with nationalists, Catholic and Protestant, and with Unionists, giving him more or less freedom of maneuver as a maker of plays and popular opinion in Ireland. Second, the welcome given his theatrical initiatives dictated to some extent the particular costume he assumed in his political roles. For example, in 1899, when he seeks a broad coalition to back the Irish Literary Theatre, he is a gentleman asking the support of other gentlemen; when that theatre is under way, he is a member of "the aristocracy of art,"[16] claiming to stand above all parties and to

---

speeches your Celtic people have been making!' 'Moore?' I said, 'Yes, and Yeats, oh very silly'" (1 March [1900]; *Seventy Years*, 362). As a consequence, it was Lady Gregory and not Yeats who suffered the personal loss when Lecky resigned, even though WBY explained to her that it would help the theatre: "4 April 1900: I looked at *The Times* and saw Mr. Lecky has withdrawn his support from the Irish Literary Theatre in consequence of 'the discreditable conduct of Mr. W. B. Yeats, Mr. George Moore and other prominent supporters of the movement.' It will do the theatre no harm, rather good I think . . . but that little want of courtesy in his decision being sent to the papers with no private notice to me hurts me" (*Seventy Years*, 368).
    16. Frayne and Johnson, 2:324.

weigh the opposed interests of rich and poor; finally, in 1900, after the uproar among Catholic nationalists over *The Countess Cathleen*, he is a rebel trying to embarrass an old queen. Amid these past and present politics, the real question is, What is the ultimate future political aim, the vision of the strategist behind the tactical masks?

2

Elizabeth Cullingford sees only one Yeats, who means what he says, and is just as he appears to be.[17] Yeats, in her opinion, always stuck to the same principles, those of the school of John O'Leary: a belief in Irish nationality and a belief in the liberty of the individual. When forced to choose between independence for all or liberty for one, he would choose liberty.[18] "There are things a man must not do to save a nation," O'Leary said and Yeats forever repeated. Asked for an example, O'Leary offered, "Cry in public."[19] It is not hard to figure out, although Cullingford does not press the point, that the list of things that one should not do even to save a nation is long. Indeed, from other things O'Leary said or Yeats did, one can add that a good nationalist does not insult a lady, kill a civilian, participate in an election, or bend to the will of the majority. "Yeats's overriding passion," Cullingford rightly says, "is the passion for liberty," his own liberty in particular. The freedom of the Irish nation as a whole could wait a long time, even forever, if its attainment required the sacrifice of

17. Cullingford, *Yeats, Ireland and Fascism* (New York: New York University Press, 1981); on the first page of her book, for example, she takes Yeats's aphorism "Our intellects at twenty contain all the truths we shall ever find" as her text.
18. Ibid., 13.
19. *The Autobiography of William Butler Yeats* (1938; rpt., New York: Collier, 1965), 64, 143. From WBY's account of O'Leary's character and thought, it is clear that O'Leary "hated democracy" (141), thought "No gentleman can be a socialist" (141), did "not approve of bombs" (67), and "derided . . . sentimentality," "philanthropy," and "humanitarianism" (141). Yeats thinks O'Leary if pressed "would have added [to the list of those things a man must not do even to save a nation] . . . 'To write oratorical or insincere verse'" (143).

the individual freedoms enjoyed by Yeats and granted him by a colony of the English empire. Cullingford's book aims to change the picture Conor Cruise O'Brien drew of Yeats in his essay "Passion and Cunning"—a complex portrait of the poet as calculating, snobbish, authoritarian, patriarchal, and sometimes delighting in violence— very nearly the type of the authoritarian personality that emerged in right-wing movements of the 1930s. O'Brien's Yeats looks for the main chance to impose his will; Cullingford's Yeats sees a distant vision of a free Ireland, but keeps an eye out to stay clear of any group that would impose upon his privileges. While these formulations can be reconciled—one emphasizing Yeats's power over others, and the other his insistence that none should have power over him—the general characterizations of the poet by the two critics are absolutely contradictory: O'Brien depicts Yeats as an aristocratic colonist and possible fascist; Cullingford rehabilitates Yeats as a liberal nationalist.

While Cullingford's book, written under the guidance of Richard Ellmann, is well documented and scrupulously dated, her conviction that Yeats is morally and politically consistent causes her to overlook the importance of occasion to the content of Yeats's remarks. For example, much of her evidence that Yeats was a liberal thoroughly in sympathy with the mass movement toward nationality, even after Maud Gonne's marriage in February 1903 and Horniman's offer of a theatre in October 1903, comes from a speech Yeats made to the Clan na Gael in New York in January 1904. It is possible that Yeats gave the Irish-Americans what they wanted: an individualist, democratic, and heatedly nationalist Ireland, not unlike America. After his return to Ireland, Arthur Griffith brought up Yeats's remark to a New York reporter that the Irish dramatists "now study what the people want, and they give it to them in such form that thirty or forty police must often be stationed inside the theatre to prevent riots."[20] Of course, whatever public demonstrations there had been—protests over

20. *United Irishman*, 11 February 1905, from the *New York Daily News;* rpt. in Hogan and Kilroy, 3:3.

The Countess Cathleen—were directed against the Irish Literary Theatre, not the government, and the police were called in to protect Yeats's theatre against its audience. Yeats answered Griffith by saying he had never said such things, or even mentioned "politics of any kind" while in America. One must be cautious in dealing with a writer who sometimes turns out not to say what he said and often to have meant something different from what he intended to be understood. Even if Yeats can be found to have cast into noble language certain thoughts about freedom and the individual, he was certainly not a liberal, and not simply because he might better be conceived as a conservative. It is not clear that individuality can be stated in terms of principle, or that the social and historical conditions were present in nineteenth- and twentieth-century Ireland for persons to achieve individuality, if individuality is understood in Mill's sense as the full and free expression of the unique powers of a person. If such conditions were not in place, one could not choose between a morally repugnant, opportunist Yeats and a morally attractive, principled Yeats;[21] all men of the time would have been faced with diminished opportunities for self-expression in keeping with a constant principle. Before we can summarize Yeats's political identity, we must examine individuality and freedom in light of their historical rise and decline.

3

Max Horkheimer and Theodor Adorno, leaders of the school of Critical Theory, argue in their genealogy of the authoritarian personality that the economic basis of individuality disintegrated from the nineteenth to the twentieth century, leav-

21. In "Passion and Cunning," O'Brien offers a political description of Yeats, not a moral judgment of him, though his account is laced with irony. It is clear that O'Brien admires Yeats's political skills—his dexterity, patience, timing, and organizational power—although he has no sympathy with Yeats's more right-wing views. Neither Yeats's political skills nor his views diminish O'Brien's sense of the great value of his poetry. In *Yeats, Ireland and Fascism*, Cullingford, however, is representative of many Yeats critics in taking O'Brien's essay as character assassination, and responding with testimonials to the poet's moral acceptability.

ing individualist values as a superstructure without a real social basis.[22] Individuality, they explain, is not the birthright of all persons; it depends on a variety of social conditions—gender, education, property, religious beliefs, and so on. The first qualifying condition of individuality is a degree of separation from society: one is an individual because one is not a part of a group, so only in cultures in which there is a realm of experience that is not communal can there be individuality. A second condition is that the life of the individual must be distinguished from the existence of the species and other lifeforms, so that only in cultures in which the fact of individual death has taken on absolute importance can there be individuality.[23] These are elementary requirements, and certain parts of the populations of all Western cultures since the Middle Ages have met them. But there are further conditions for individuality necessary before the phenomenon can become a widespread social value. To be an individual in the full sense of the term, one needs to be a man of property. Only a man who has to his name a home, a wife, children, a retinue of servants, and a large balance at the bank, preferably in gold, possesses the power to plan his life, the leisure to manifest private interests in hobbies or forms of art, and the authority to give shape to his own little society.[24] Within his

22. See especially Max Horkheimer, "The Rise and Decline of the Individual," in *The Eclipse of Reason* (New York: Continuum, 1974), 129–57. I have also drawn upon Theodor W. Adorno and Max Horkheimer, *Dialectic of Enlightenment*, trans. John Cumming (1944; rpt., New York: Herder & Herder, 1972), and Max Horkheimer, *Critical Theory: Selected Essays* (New York: Herder & Herder, 1972). The Critical Theorists are pertinent because they concentrated their work upon the connection between bourgeois individualism and the authoritarian personality that emerged in fascism; they are reliable to the extent that they succeed in maintaining a critical distance from both Marxist and liberal ideologies, while making arguments whose rigor and scope—including psychology, economics, sociology, and history—appeal to reason.

23. Horkheimer, *Eclipse of Reason*, 137.

24. Ibid., 140–57; esp. 140–41. Nietzsche argues in a similar way in *The Genealogy of Morals*, ii, where he defines the autonomous individual as one with "an independent long-range will, which dares to make promises"; this raises him above the mass of people "who are unable to stand security for themselves."

house the man of property can arrange the education of his young, medical care for sick dependents, provision for parents in their old age, and labor relations with servants; he can see to it, in short, that by the authority of his will, his life is stamped on the world in his own time and, through his children, for generations to come. It is apparent that in its origins, individuality is inseparable from aristocratic features democratized among the middle classes during the great movement of nineteenth-century British capitalism: private property, privilege, male dominance, and authoritarianism.

This definition will seem too narrow and historically specific to some, who would like to think that anyone, rich or poor, can be an individual, indeed, that nothing can eradicate the unique qualities of each person. Horkheimer and Adorno are arguing that this completely open definition of individuality obscures the way in which individuality is dependent on society and prevents us from seeing that the realization of an enduring and integrated self is the end of a long and deliberate labor for emancipation from animal desires, material needs, and social compulsion. A person who must agree to take a factory job in order to eat may achieve little expression through his work; and if he must work all the time when he is not asleep or exhausted, he may find little expression outside his work. If he cannot afford a home and moves from shelter to shelter, he may acquire none of the symbols of identity. If he never acquires the capital to educate his children or leave them a family estate, he may find no self-expression through procreation. If his access to thought is limited to the productions of a mass-culture entertainment industry, even his mental life may become subject to supervision.[25]

How many are there in this class of people whose chances for individuality are so severely limited? Certainly, one must be able to speak of degrees of individuality, and neither Horkheimer nor Adorno is perfectly clear about what degree

---

25. See Horkheimer, "Art and Mass Culture," in *Critical Theory*, 277–88; and Horkheimer and Adorno, "The Culture Industry: Enlightenment as Mass Deception," in *Dialectic of Enlightenment*, 121–67; esp. 144.

counts for full individuality in the nineteenth-century British sense of the ideal that they outline. What about independent artisans with their own implements of labor and their own style of manufacture, but very little fixed property? Or—more to the point—artists not completely deterred by their straitened circumstances?[26] Horkheimer and Adorno do not take up such cases; they offer a theoretical model, not an adequate social history. In this model, those who miss the chance for full bourgeois individuality include most of those, to begin with, who are not adult males, and of the males, many whose work gives them no more than a subsistence. Individuality, then, widely existed only among the bourgeoisie, and by the end of the nineteenth century, Horkheimer argues, the growth of capitalism into a world market, ruled by laws of supply and demand, international conflicts, natural disasters, and the collision of vast industrial interests, severely limited the freedom and economic security of most private entrepreneurs. Many people were left in the end with just that degree of individuality with which they were born: a biological difference, specially determined by the psychology of the nuclear family and then forcibly adapted to the social forms of a new economic order. In these circumstances, to continue to speak without qualification of "freedom" and "individuality" is to indulge in ideology.[27]

4

A generation earlier, Yeats's family had consisted of merchants and rectors, owners of a small country estate, and members of a privileged class in a colonial society. But the poet's father,

26. I am grateful to my colleague Felmon Davis for alerting me to several questions about the Critical Theorists' account of individuality.

27. *Ideology* is here used pejoratively to refer to the class character of the ideas, in the sense developed by Marx and Engels in *The German Ideology* (New York: International Publishers, 1972)—"the illusion of a class about itself" that represents the interests of a group as the interest of mankind. For a discussion of the meanings of "ideology," see Raymond Williams, *Keywords: A Vocabulary of Culture and Society* (New York: Oxford University Press, 1976), 126–30.

J. B. Yeats, had sold the country estate at Thomastown,[28] dropped his study of law, and sought to make a life for himself as a portrait painter, moving from residence to residence in Dublin and London, always in and out of debt. In his early years, then, WBY experienced the dissolution of the economic basis of his membership in an elite. But this did not occur simply through the prodigality of his father. The 1848 Encumbered Estates Act and the 1885 Ashbourne Act under which his father's estate was sold brought about a massive redistribution of property in Ireland—what WBY called "the Agrarian Revolution"—the encumbered estates of Protestants passing into the hands of their former Catholic renters, now peasant proprietors and future tradespeople. The whole solid structure of Irish feudalism began to melt into the air. To a vast new class of private farmers were added a mass of industrial workers, mainly in Belfast and the Lagan Valley; a middle class of men engaged in trade in Dublin and provincial towns; and a new intellectual class, many of them artisans, clerks, and journalists, demanding political expression for these new elements in Irish society.[29] In a few generations, Ireland changed from a society in which a small, basically Protestant, class possessed the means to attain individuality, while a huge inarticulate Catholic peasantry did not, to one in

28. The Yeats estate was 560 English or American acres, with seventeen farm tenancies, mostly engaged in the dairy business. However, it was so heavily mortgaged that income from rents did not suffice to support WBY's grandfather's family, much less his father's. It was sold in 1889 for £7,032, all but £1,004 of which went to pay off loans against the property, the remainder being used immediately to meet other debts. Even had the estate been kept in the family, and passed entirely to WBY, the eldest son, it would not have freed him from work. For the details, see William M. Murphy, *Prodigal Father: The Life of John Butler Yeats (1839–1922)* (Ithaca, N.Y.: Cornell University Press, 1978), 151, 574.

29. W. J. McCormack argues along similar lines that "Too much has been made of [Ireland's] 'generally remarked upon lack of a capitalist bourgeoisie,'" and notes the importance of the industrial sector around Belfast, the commercial districts in Dublin, and the "petit bourgeois" character of the Land League—all ignored, even repressed, in the writings of Yeats, Synge, and Lady Gregory. See *Ascendancy and Tradition* (Oxford: Clarendon Press, 1985), 249–51.

which the economic basis of the Protestant identity was shattered and new classes of farmers, tradesmen, and artisans vociferously sought some sort of collective identity as citizens of a de-Anglicized republic. For them the goal was not to refine the isolated individual, but to realize the national being as a whole, with its own language, manners, dress, industry, and government.

In the early summer, Yeats would return from his London residence to a grandfather's or uncle's home in Sligo, and after 1896 to Lady Gregory's estate at Coole, where he could enjoy the leisure of a gentleman, fly-fishing for trout, writing poems, or conducting spiritual investigations, but come autumn he went back to London to write what he could sell, a review for five pounds, an edition of folk stories for ten guineas.[30] To a remarkable degree, Yeats did the work he wanted to do rather than simply what he was told to do, or what readers would in the greatest number buy, but if he had been born forty years earlier, he could imagine, he might have written entirely at his leisure.[31] It is no surprise, therefore, to hear the poet sing of his dream of the noble and the beggarman, to hear him lament the destruction of a great house and wonder whether it was worth it to make many small houses a little stronger, or, finally, to hear him trumpet the absolute necessity of individuality and freedom. As Kenneth Burke suggests, when we analyze the element of *comfort* in beauty, in order to be dia-

30. An impression of Yeats's money difficulties can be gained from the eloquent index of John Kelly and Eric Domville's edition of *The Collected Letters of W. B. Yeats*, vol. 1 (Oxford: Clarendon Press, 1986), 546: "FINANCES: 95, 'cleared out,' 102, 103, 148, 158; 'low these times,' 159, 160, 183, 218; 'a trifle short,' 220; 'a financial crisis,' 223, 224, 228, 233, 260; 'in a fix for a pound,' 261, 262, 272," etc.

31. Born forty years earlier, Yeats would have reached maturity during the Famine years, when peasants paid few rents, if any. For three generations, the family property was insufficient to provide a complete living to the Yeatses. These facts, however, do not prevent WBY from looking back to better days. W. J. McCormack has a stimulating discussion of the perpetual "backdating" of the good life that is characteristic of Ascendancy thinking (and not unknown to other classes in other lands!) (*Ascendancy and Tradition*, 308–9, and passim).

lectical, we should include "the element of *discomfort* (actual or threatened) for which poetry is the medicine."[32] By this dialectical reasoning, Yeats's assertions of individual freedoms are an elegy for what was lost: the feudal privileges of a great man in a big house.

In his prose notes to "Upon a House Shaken by the Land Agitation" (1910), Yeats himself describes the deeply felt difference between the struggle for identity under the old regime and in the new Ireland. He wrote this poem, he says, when he heard that the courts had reduced the rents allowed to landlords, a structural change in Irish society that he thought had large costs: "I am always feeling a lack of life's own values behind my thought—work had to create its own values. Here [in Lady Gregory's house] there has been no compelled labor, no poverty-thwarted impulse. One feels that when all must make their living, they will not live for life's sake but the work's and be poorer."[33] This is Yeats's hard task: to make real in literature certain values of his class—personal power, energy, precision, family memories, and the eccentric cultivation of intellect—that have been cut loose from their social setting. They must be created by writing; they exist only in that writing.

How, then, can we define the political identity of Yeats? First, that identity cannot simply be reduced to its private property: there is little equivalence between Yeats in 1900 and his rented room at 18 Woburn Place, London, with its books, pictures, and the services of a cleaning woman named Mrs. Olds. Second, Yeats cannot be accurately accounted for by reflection upon receipts for work done or money borrowed—so much for commissions, so much for royalties, unpaid loans

---

32. Burke, *The Philosophy of Literary Form* (3d ed.; Berkeley and Los Angeles: University of California Press, 1973), 61. I am indebted to Frank Lentricchia's *Criticism and Social Change* (Chicago: University of Chicago Press, 1983) for calling attention to this passage, and in general for his spirited rereading of Burke.

33. WBY, *Memoirs: Autobiography—First Draft, Journal*, transcribed and edited by Denis Donoghue (New York: Macmillan, 1972), 226.

from Lady Gregory. Third, he cannot be completely understood by being reinstated in the class of educated Protestant
Irishmen from whom he took some of his values. Yeats is a
petit bourgeois Irish Protestant of large ambition and little
property; but, of course, not every petit bourgeois Irish Protestant of similar ambition is a Yeats.[34] His individuality, of
course, is his writing. But the first, second, and third factors
(property, labor, and class) all determine to some extent the
form of that individuality, in the Burkean light of prescribing
specific medicines for those otherwise untreatable discom-
forts. In each case, Yeats turns a material deprivation into an
aesthetic ideal and a world imprisoned in the past into a free
utopia of poetry.[35] The London flat is the scene in which a poetry is made laying claim to all the islands, mountains, and
streams of Sligo. The real material impoverishment of his
early years becomes a literature that is a monument to the victory of the soul. And, finally, a broken Ascendancy—"the

34. This adapts Sartre's *mot:* "Valéry was a petit-bourgeois intellectual. Of
that there is no doubt. But not every petit-bourgeois intellectual is Valéry"
(quoted in the *Times Literary Supplement,* 11 July 1986, 753).

35. In *The Space Between: Literature and Politics* (Baltimore: Johns Hopkins
University Press, 1981), Jay Cantor shows the relevance of another Critical
Theorist's thought—that of Herbert Marcuse—to this effort in Yeats's poetry
to recapture a lost world. Marcuse sees the main function of art as being to
conceive a world other than the one we live in, and to embody utopia, not
reality. But Cantor argues that "Yeats's technique for recapturing the lost
world insures that the past remains lost" because the life of the self for Yeats
is dependent on the absence of reality (Cantor, 42). For Cantor, this consti-
tutes a defect in Yeats's art, because a symbolic world that was, is, and will
always be absent "cannot nourish" (Cantor, 43). If Yeats's combination of elegy and utopia is a defect at all, however, it is one only in terms of Cantor's
political morality, not in terms of aesthetics, even, I think, Marcuse's aesthetics. Cantor would have Yeats submit his self to the transformations of a revolutionary moment; it is enough for Marcuse that the artist transform the
world through the aesthetic illusion, giving "the things of the world a new
meaning and function" (Marcuse, *Counterrevolution and Revolt,* 81; quoted in
Cantor, 127). So majestic are Yeats's transformations of the world that the escape from fact is at one with the triumph over fact. The bad conscience that
haunts his poetry is that its world is one in which only some may fulfill their
wishes. Made through the dominion of self, it would require for its realization continuing domination. The appeal of that world to us is also a criticism
of the structure of our wishes.

dying mind of a dying class," he called it—is transfigured into an "aristocracy of art."[36] But the material deprivation upon which the utopia is raised limits the reality, the possibility of actual achievement, of the values expressed. The freedom found in his poetry is that of a world of everything that is not the case.[37]

5

In moving from belles lettres into the theatre as a field of individual expression, Yeats encountered, of course, greater obstacles to the transformation of facts to wishes, a world into a self. For the poet individuality may be in part conditioned by the external factors of property, labor, and class. These simply define his status; they do not deny him the chance to write in rebellion against that status, and make a world in the world's despite, as Yeats does in his poetry. For the man of the theatre, however, individuality depends on still further conditions, because theatre is a large cooperative enterprise. It takes not just an author but also a company of actors, set and costume designers, a business manager, an auditorium, patrons, and, of course, a paying audience. Each of these elements of the society may look upon the theatre as its field of self-expression, the scene in which its own social wishes can be represented as fulfilled.

When a part of the audience of *The Countess Cathleen* repudiated the play as a picture of Ireland, Yeats was left with the defense that his play was art, and like all works of art represented one man's vision of spiritual truths, not a conten-

36. WBY, letter to the *All Ireland Review,* 22 September, 1900, rpt. in Frayne and Johnson, 242–43. A characteristic passage on the "aristocracy of artists, the only aristocracy which has never oppressed the people," occurs in WBY's New York address to the Clan na Gael on "Emmet the Apostle of Irish Liberty," 28 February 1904, rpt. in Frayne and Johnson, 324.

37. I lately discovered that this sentence must have been a recollection of Frank Tuohy's dry remark "Yeats's world, it might be said, comprised everything that is not the case" in his biography, *Yeats* (New York: Macmillan, 1976), 60.

tious account of the social history of its audience. It is clear that in the aftermath of the performance, Yeats was troubled. He was taken off guard by being attacked in Ireland by nationalists; he had thought of himself with good reason as having acted as a nationalist politician himself during, for instance, the recent Wolfe Tone Commemoration (1898). Furthermore, his defense of art did not enable him to make a claim upon the attention of the broad public essential to a theatre. Why should citizens pay to see a play made up out of heterodox spiritual beliefs, showing little sympathy to their national ideals, written by a poet who lived in London? If he wanted to be a playwright in Ireland, he had to repair the damage to his public stature done by *The Countess Cathleen*.

Between the letter of 10 April 1900, in which he expressed confidence about the future of the theatre and laid out plans to rehabilitate his nationalist standing by an attack on the queen, and October 1901, Yeats certainly lost hope in the Irish Literary Theatre as a vehicle for the expression of his individuality. The amazing system invented for the composition of *Diarmuid and Grania* (scheduled for the third season), with George Moore on one end of the production line, Yeats on the other, and a pack of translators in between to move the text between French, English, Gaelic, and Kiltartan dialect, could have been patented as a technique for the elimination of personality from literature. It ended in a predictable quarrel over just whose property the play was, and who could make the final judgments on its form.[38] By this stage, Yeats had sacrificed many personal preferences to the idol of theatrical success: he relinquished for a time his right to do verse drama, to choose whatever subject he liked, to supply no propaganda, to make his friends among educated Protestant Unionists,

38. See WBY's letter to Moore of January 1901, complaining that he has "continually given up motives and ideas that I preferred to yours. . . . Remember that our original compact was that the final words were to be mine" (Wade, 347), and Moore's answer: "If it was your intention all along to be supreme in command I wish you had taken the scenario and written the play. . . . For me to hand over a play the greater part of which is written by me, for *final* correction is an impossible proposal" (Finneran, Harper, and Murphy, 1:78).

and, finally, even to write the plays he signed.[39] With all this lost, there was little left in the Irish Literary Theatre that could be called the free expression of the poet's individuality. During the same period, Yeats began to look beyond Ireland for the fulfillment of his hopes for individual expression in drama. In his theatre journal *Samhain* for the final season of the Irish Literary Theatre, October 1901, Yeats went over the plans others had made for continuing the movement in Ireland: Moore and Martyn wanted a touring English company, endowed by the Dublin Corporation, to do foreign and Irish plays, and train new Irish actors; W. G. Fay and Frank Fay wanted a resident amateur company of Irish actors, free to "touch on politics, the most vital passion and vital interest of the country."[40] Outside the circle of the Irish Literary Theatre, there was much activity—both practical and theoretical—in Irish theatre. Amateur societies, many of them organized by the Gaelic League, performed nationalist plays, and intellectual leaders discussed the shortcomings of the Irish Literary Theatre in light of what a national theatre ought to be. Douglas Hyde thought it might be a Gaelic theatre; Standish O'Grady thought it should not deal with heroic myths, because they were too lofty and aristocratic a subject for common people; Æ thought it should be spiritual and beautiful; John Eglington thought it should deal with the modern, mostly economic, facts of urban Ireland.[41] But as for

39. According to Lady Gregory (*Our Irish Theatre*, 27), WBY said: "The financial question touched on in 'The Bending of the Bough' was chosen, because on it all parties are united," chosen, therefore, for the sake of the audience, although WBY added that it was "the cause nearest each of our hearts." Yeats called the play, upon its completion, an "intricate gospel of nationality" that might prove "almost epoch-making in Ireland," words that well describe agitation propaganda (Wade, 332). Lecky, of course, was the Unionist friend forsaken; *Diarmuid and Grania* was the play Yeats signed but over which he had difficulty asserting authorship (Wade, 347).

40. WBY, *Explorations*, 76.

41. See the exchange of articles from the Dublin *Daily Express* republished as *Literary Ideals in Ireland*, John Eglinton, W. B. Yeats, AE, and W. Larminie (London: Fisher Unwin, 1899; rpt., New York: Lemma Press, 1973), and *Letters from AE*, ed. Alan Denson (London: Abelard-Schuman, 1961), 40–41, for a discussion of O'Grady's objections to saga material in Irish drama.

Yeats himself, he said he did not care what happened. He was going off alone to write his plays in poetry about old stories, and he did not care who acted them as long as they acted them well (meaning, just as he liked) or how many saw them (as long as they were his friends). Frustrated in his search for fame or beauty in national drama, Yeats turned back to an austere hope for a "Theatre of Beauty" suitable for the few.[42]

The *Samhain* of 1901 could have been Yeats's farewell as a leader of the Irish theatre. In May 1901 he was disturbed by how little welcome his publisher A. H. Bullen received in Ireland: no one wanted Yeats's books, not his mystical *Secret Rose* or even his lyrical drama *The Shadowy Waters*. He wrote to Lady Gregory that the Catholic priests and the nationalist D. P. Moran did not like him because of his "heterodox" mysticism, and the Trinity College bookseller and the men of the Ascendancy Constitutional Club did not like him because they suspected him of revolutionary designs: too Protestant for one group, too Irish for the other.[43] All this news, Yeats went on, "only confirms the idea I had at the time that 'The Countess Cathleen' would make a very serious difference in my position." His plunge into radical politics had separated him from his own class without winning over the Catholic nationalists. Finally, he planned to "withdraw from politics"; indeed, he undertook to withdraw from Ireland altogether.

42. William M. Murphy reads this "strange farewell" as "in fact a maneuver by WBY to set Moore ashore and continue his voyage with new companions"—W. G. and Frank Fay (*Prodigal Father*, 229). This reading has much in favor of it, aside from WBY's capacity for mutinous conspiracies and his ambition always to be captain of his soul, not to mention the souls of others. He had seen the Fays act in the summer of 1901, and he had dreamed of the play Lady Gregory wrote, *Cathleen ni Houlihan*, more suitable to the Fays than to either the Irish Literary Theatre or the London literary societies. However, I think at the time, Yeats was keeping all options open—the Fays' group, the London societies, and even the Irish Literary Theatre. As late as January 1902 he was still trying to raise money for the Irish Literary Theatre, getting ready to send a play to Martyn for his approval, and hoping that Martyn would not pull out of the project (see WBY to Lady Gregory, 14 and 20 January 1902; Wade, 363–64).

43. Wade, 349–51.

6

Information from unpublished papers of Sturge Moore, Gilbert Murray, and Charles Ricketts, brought to light in an article by Ronald Schuchard, shows to what degree Yeats turned his theatrical ambitions from Ireland to London in 1901.[44] After all, his first play, *The Land of Heart's Desire*, had been produced in London in 1894, his sole residence was there, and even when the plans for the Irish Literary Theatre were under way in 1898, Schuchard points out, Yeats and Florence Farr were also looking for "a little theatre somewhere in the suburbs" of London.[45] A month after the quarrelsome committee of authors brought *Diarmuid and Grania* to a close in December 1900, Yeats set in motion plans for a London "Theatre of Beauty" by gathering a group consisting of Florence Farr, Sturge Moore, and Lawrence Binyon, to be called "The Literary Theatre Club." When Yeats said farewell to Irish theatre in the *Samhain* of October 1901, he went off to London to join efforts with this group.

The great importance of Schuchard's article is that it shows that things might well have been otherwise: the Irish Literary Theatre did not lead inevitably to the Irish National Theatre Society of 1902 or the Abbey Theatre of 1904; furthermore, one can infer from the information Schuchard gives that Yeats was committed, not to nationalist drama centered in Dublin, but to literary drama laid in Irish scenes, and that his identity as a writer defined by the full Irish context was not determined by an unflagging individual principle. Wilde found his fortune on the London stage in the 1890s; Shaw followed the same path as Yeats through alternative London theatre societies and ended in the limelight with the 1903 Court Theatre production of *John Bull's Other Island*; Yeats might well have done as they did and ended as a London author from Dublin (although specializing in Irish scenes and colors).

Yeats's path, however, followed a detour back to Dublin.

44. Schuchard, 415–46.
45. Lady Gregory, *Our Irish Theatre*, 2–3; Schuchard, 416.

The way to theatrical success in London that appeared to open in 1901 and 1902 closed in 1903 for a variety of reasons. Yeats did well in recruiting and drilling a battalion of verse-speakers, writers of literary drama, fund-raisers, and set-designers, but once in the field they marched off in all directions. The campaign, however, failed for reasons of money, organization, and the labyrinth of human fortuities; not from any diminishment of Yeats's ambition for a London literary triumph.

7

Two other major developments during this period determined the direction of Yeats's ambitions. The first was his relationship with Annie Horniman, to whom he looked to fund his future; and the second was his developing relation to Frank Fay and to his brother W. G. Fay's group of Irish actors, out of which grew the Irish National Theatre Society. There was no similarity, no basis for sympathy, and no connection between Horniman and the Fays—not in personal ability, aesthetic taste, social class, national identity, or political conviction—except that both knew Yeats. It shows the remarkable versatility of Yeats's identity that he played a part (half foil, half hero) in the lives of both. It is as if one character were placed in both a West End closet drama of intrigue and a rebel peasant play, a casual, but successful, improvisateur along the general *hodos chameleontos*, with a view to some distant denouement, unknown but impending in the future, for which these were subplots. For when Yeats brought Horniman and Fay together, the Irish National Theatre Society had a troupe, a theatre, money, and a host of unaddressed misunderstandings.

Horniman was best described by Lady Gregory: "Miss Horniman is like a shilling in a tub of electrified water; everybody tries to get the shilling out." [46] Of all those who tried and were burned, none showed more perseverance or had greater

---

46. Repeated by WBY in a July 1907 letter to Florence Farr (Wade, 490).

success than Yeats. He became acquainted with Horniman in that peculiar London demimonde of nineties magical societies, particularly the Order of the Golden Dawn. Macgregor Mathers, chief wizard of the Golden Dawn, managed to get £420 a year out of Horniman between 1892 and 1896, but when his subsidy was stopped, he exiled Horniman to the outer darkness, saying that if she was not insane, she was so arrogant, self-conceited, and narrow-minded that she was about to go insane. Mathers in turn was expelled from his own order for saying that its original mystical manuscript in cipher was a forgery by his fellow leader, Dr. William Wynn Westcott. (As George Harper puts it, this was like Moses saying Aaron wrote the Ten Commandments.)[47] Yeats immediately invited Horniman back into the Second Temple with all her seniority restored and an important new position as "Scribe" added. That was in April 1900, the same month of the same year he told Lady Gregory he thought he could get money for the theatre from a "Miss ———."

It did not take long for the reinstated Miss Horniman to quarrel with everyone. She was "appalled" at the informality of the society under the leadership of Florence Farr; older members like herself did not receive their due respect. Minutes had not been well kept. Secret groups for the study of Egyptology had sprung up around Farr in Horniman's four-year absence.[48] Horniman immediately set about to put a stop to all these irregularities. She did not wish to accuse the new members of Evil, she said, but she could only judge their works by their fruits, which were "ignorance, selfishness and discourtesy." She expected that the members would show "gratitude for [her] forbearance" in merely "hushing up the scandal" of the recent departures from the regulations of the order. It is no surprise that the other members were ungrateful; they thought her just what Mathers had thought her—arrogant,

47. For information on Horniman, Yeats, and the Golden Dawn, I rely upon George Mills Harper's *Yeats's Golden Dawn*. The figures for Horniman's subsidy to Mathers are from a personal communication from Ellic Howe to Harper (Harper, 163).
48. Harper, 32ff.

narrow-minded, and dangerously domineering. At her first official meeting with the executive council, the members opposed every suggestion she made—all the members save one, W. B. Yeats.[49]

It is difficult to understand why Yeats stood by Horniman in the Golden Dawn quarrels, why he kept up a friendship with her, or how he got through hours, days, and years sitting in a parlor with this wealthy, but unbeautiful and unwitty, woman. He worked with her on internal reports on the future of the "Order of R.R. and A.C."; he read her his plays; accepted little gifts; permitted her to shake the dustballs from his clothes' drawers and comment on the state of his undershorts; he dictated letters, and as a last resort, picked up a book.[50] One can see she loved him; one cannot easily see what he saw in her if it were not that bright shilling at the bottom of the electrified tub.[51]

49. Harper, 42–44, for the "Record of Executive Difficulty."

50. See Annie Horniman to WBY, 10 December 1906: "When you get back I must have a number of questions answered, I'll remove all reading matter within reach & you will have to give me your full attention whether you are bored or no"; and Annie Horniman to WBY, 7 July 1907, for a record of Horniman's house-cleaning attentions at 18 Woburn Buildings (ms. 13068, NLI).

51. While the simplest explanation of their relationship is pure exploitation, George Harper, the best scholar on the Golden Dawn, has a more interesting and complex explanation of his defense of Horniman in the quarrel over discipline. Harper claims that Yeats's countercharge to those members who opposed and insulted Horniman reflects his basic beliefs about the world. The document in which the countercharge appeared—"Is the Order of R.R. and A.C. to remain a Magical Order?"—argues that if the sacred text is a sham, all that makes the order a possibly valid entity, even "an Actual Being," is the hierarchy of members, which is established by seniority, intellectual mastery of ritual doctrine (certified by formal examinations), and the authority of regulations made in the past. This hierarchy, Yeats supposes, may form "a link with invisible Degrees," and make possible future intuitions of "higher knowledge." The elitist society of the magical order rests on beliefs remarkably similar to those that underpin Yeats's conception of an "aristocracy of art," made up in part out of members of the former, now discredited, aristocracy, but based on values that have lost their social and economic basis. Yeats showed in his countercharge to the members of the Golden Dawn a rich belief in the power of pure self-assertion, in the claim of something being the same as the possession of the thing, reflecting a characteristic mystical habit of thought, a belief that to prophesy meant one had had a vision, and that to look down on others meant that one was elevated.

Out of the Horniman-Yeats alliance in the Golden Dawn came the offer of Horniman money for a Yeats theatre venture. Horniman had previously shown signs of a desire to patronize the theatre: she had for years been an ardent Wagnerite, undertaking the annual pilgrimage to Bayreuth; she had funded the first performances of Yeats and Shaw at the Avenue Theatre in 1894; and lately she had taken an interest in the Florence Farr/W. B. Yeats verse-speaking classes. Whatever the basis for a common interest in theatre, in the letter cited at the beginning of this chapter, WBY writes that he thought he could get money from a woman, who could only have been Miss Horniman; by January 1901, after the completion of *Diarmuid and Grania* and Yeats's turn to London, he knew he could get the money. Although the letter is not dated, Harper thinks that it was in January that Yeats wrote to Florence Farr,[52] leader of the rebel group of Egyptologists, and verse-speaker, and told her that if she behaved herself in the Golden Dawn, he would give her a big part in a new theatrical project he planned. The letter is marked in Horniman's hand, "Demon's letter about the compromise to Sapientia," DEMON EST DEUS INVERSUS being WBY's secret motto in the Order, and SAPIENTIA Farr's. Harper thinks this big new theatre project was the performance of *Diarmuid and Grania;* Schuchard thinks it was Yeats's London literary theatre societies.[53] It turned out, at last, to be the Abbey Theatre.

Not until April 1902 did Horniman pen the letter in which

The difference between Horniman and Yeats may be no more than the difference between one who was nakedly arrogant and another who said it was important for the masses to believe in clothes, between, that is, visceral and theoretical pride. While Yeats may not have sold out on any principle in a bid for the "freedom" Horniman could grant him, his treatise on the magical order shows the extraordinary lengths to which he went to reconcile his beliefs and Horniman's deeds. See Harper, 259–68, for the text of Yeats's essay, and 69–91 for Harper's interpretation that it embodied "his profoundest religious and philosophical convictions about man's place in the universe" (69). Harper stresses WBY's "faith in order, authority, and degree" (74); I stress his skepticism about everything but order, authority, and degree.

52. Harper, 34–35.
53. Schuchard, 415–16.

Yeats made a veiled offer of an endowment for Fay's company if he promised to work hard for a year "along the lines" of Yeats's "rigorous" "theories of the stage."[54] And only in October 1903 did she say she was going to buy a Dublin theatre for them.[55] But after January 1901, the shilling was out of the tub, ready to spend.

8

In his history of the Abbey Theatre, W. G. Fay claims with some cause that the National Theatre Society was "first and foremost a theatrical, not a literary movement."[56] When Yeats was turning his attention to London, Fay and his brother Frank were chief players in the vastly popular amateur theatre activity that grew out the ruins of the Literary Theatre. For if the Yeats-Martyn-Moore venture failed to create plays of lasting interest, to stage successful performances, or to grant the authors the satisfactions of self-expression, it succeeded in stirring others to create a National Theatre. This movement was not led by authors and did not aim to create great literature.

The last year of the Irish Literary Theatre, 1901, saw two main results of the enterprise: Yeats gave up on theatre in Ireland, and Ireland took up the theatre on its own in a large

54. Horniman was the amanuensis for WBY's letter of 21 April 1902 to Frank Fay, which mentions a wealthy friend with an interest in Yeats's plays. The letter says that after a year's work by the company, this wealthy friend would consider an appeal "for capital to carry out [Yeats's] idea" (Wade, 371–72). Horniman's identity is concealed under a masculine pronoun, but it is clear that she was the "wealthy friend."

55. James Flannery reproduces the letter of 8 October 1903 from Horniman to Yeats in which she decided on the cast of Tarot cards to subsidize the Irish National Theatre Company in *Miss Annie F. Horniman and the Abbey Theatre* (Dublin: Dolmen Press, 1970), 9. Flannery also discusses three other letters in which Horniman interpreted the Tarot to predict Yeats's theatrical success. The earliest of these letters is dated 1 March 1903; it concludes that "work for love [would] bring Divine Wisdom."

56. W. G. Fay and Catherine Carswell, *The Fays of the Abbey Theatre* (New York: Harcourt, Brace, 1935), 106. Fay drives his point home by saying, "We of the Abbey made our theatre first and then got plays to suit it."

way. Padraic Pearse, future leader of the Easter Rebellion, reported that more than a dozen Irish dramas in Gaelic were presented in 1901 and 1902.[57] There were plays in Gaelic at the Pan-Celtic Conference in Dublin and at the Feis in Galway during August 1901. The plays were, in some sense, authorless: at the request of amateur acting companies, and to meet the demand of massive and enthusiastic audiences, they were put together by priests, teachers, and patriotic women. Literary quality was irrelevant to their success. They formed the occasion for practicing Gaelic speech, singing Gaelic songs, wearing traditional clothes, and in general manifesting national enthusiasm. In scale, this dramatic activity amounted to a mass movement. Not only did the audiences run to 3,000 at the Dublin Rotunda, but the theatre movement had become part of an immense political network, the Gaelic League. With chapters in every village, town, and city, with a large bureaucratic organization, with the power to produce regular newsletters and booklets, the Gaelic League incited demand for plays, disseminated them throughout the population, organized their consumption, and spelled out their purpose: to educate Irishmen in the lost art of being Irish. Drama now was under way in Ireland, under the control not of a few Anglo-Irish authors but of a vast national apparatus.

Irish history during this period provides an instance of a literary movement leading to a social and industrial movement for self-reliance, which contradicts the vulgar Marxist assumption that the cultural superstructure will always echo the base. Not only did Yeats and Hyde's National Literary Society give utterance to the shift to cultural nationalism in 1892,[58] but for another ten years literary and cultural societies continued the de-Anglicization of Ireland. For instance, in

57. Hogan and Kilroy, 2:21.
58. John S. Kelly in *The Fall of Parnell and the Rise of Irish Literature: An Investigation*, Anglo-Irish Studies, 2 (1976), 3, shows that Yeats in prophesying "that a political lull would mean a literary revival . . . was doing no more than voicing generally received opinion," but nonetheless the literary movement led to a political and economic movement of self-reliance; in effect, to the policy of Sinn Fein.

1903, the "Cork Celtic Literary Society" formed the "Cork Industrial Development Association" to regain the Irish market for Irish goods.[59] And various nationalist clubs and newspapers aggressively carried forward the social revolution to make Ireland Irish. There were Irish cycling clubs, Irish singing groups, Irish hurling associations. The journalists worked to embarrass "shoneen" Irishmen into buying the caps, wearing the boots, eating the jam, spreading the mustard, speaking the language, playing the games, and naming their children according to the customs of their country. For instance, the peckish D. P. Moran, editor of the *Leader*, posted himself outside Catholic churches in Dublin nationalist districts in order to report on "the truly National congregation" emerging with "their recreant skins" clothed in a foreign covering.[60] The message, more than implied, was that any Irishman not in Donegal tweeds and Ulster linens should walk in shame. In the *United Irishman* Arthur Griffith exposed those Dublin businesses that advertised abroad for work that could be done by Irishmen, as when he indignantly reported that Browne & Nolan, "which has gained more from the Irish revival than any other printing firm in Ireland," had advertised in the Glasgow Herald for a printer's case room foreman when scores of Irish compositors were out of work.[61] Finally, both Moran and Griffith printed lists of Irish names, so that parents could at least "put an Irish name on every boy and girl born to the country." The great number of theatrical societies, carried forward by the momentum of this many-sided social revolution, themselves served the valuable propaganda service of representing on stage an ideal, spiritual, and militant version of that revolution as already achieved. Its slogan was *Today, on the stage; tomorrow, on the streets*.

These nationalist theatrical groups, even the most artistic ones such as "W. G. Fay's National Dramatic Society," were not only independent of Yeats; they were also profoundly op-

---

59. *United Irishman* 11, no. 273 (21 May 1904): 4.
60. Moran, "The Clothes We Wear," *Leader*, 20 October 1900, 117.
61. *United Irishman* 10, no. 242 (20 November 1903): 5.

posed to him in their conception of drama. It is often noted that Yeats and the Fays had much in common. The Fays were actors in search of an author and capital; he was an author with capital in search of actors. Frank Fay and Yeats shared an interest in elocution, in grave and simple acting, and in "sincere" dramatic writing, by which both Fay and Yeats meant writing that was not commercial.[62] It is also true that in his series of theatre reviews and essays for the *United Irishman*, Frank Fay made an obvious public appeal that Yeats should write plays for Ireland to be performed by amateur Irish actors, actors like those his brother directed. Yeats was, after all, Ireland's greatest poet and a famous man; they wanted his talent. But the Fays had their own conception of drama and nationalism, and they wanted Yeats only if he would take up the trade of playwright on their terms.[63]

Frank Fay makes clear in his *United Irishman* articles just what those terms were. In the issue dated 4 May 1901, Fay wrote a criticism of Yeats's dramatic ideals as Yeats defined them in an essay on "The Theatre of Beauty" published in *Poems* (1901). A national theatre, for Fay, was first not a theatre of English plays about Ireland; second, not a theatre for the few; third, not a theatre acted by English professionals. It should ideally be an Irish language theatre with Irish actors, serving the "marvellously sympathetic, intelligent, and refined audience" who attended recent commemorations of Thomas Davis and Robert Emmet, the Gaelic League Oireachtas, and the Leinster Feis Concert—in short,

---

62. See Fay's 23 November 1901 *United Irishman* article on "The Irish Literary Theatre" for a statement of Fay's belief that interesting writing was writing that was "sincere" and "uncommercial" (Frank J. Fay, *Towards a National Theatre: The Dramatic Criticism of Frank J. Fay*, ed. Robert Hogan [London: Oxford University Press; Dublin: Dolmen Press, 1970], 83–86). Yeats most often opposes "sincerity" to "morality" rather than commercialism, as in "The Freedom of the Theatre" (Frayne and Johnson, 297–99).

63. James W. Flannery does an excellent job of treating Frank Fay as a dramatic thinker in his own right, rather than simply as an elocutionist in Yeats's plays (*W. B. Yeats and the Idea of a Theatre: The Early Abbey Theatre in Theory and Practice* [New Haven: Yale University Press, 1976]). I depart from his account in emphasizing the populist-socialist grounds for Fay's antipathy to commercial theatre.

nationalists from the Gaelic League, the Gaelic Athletic Association, and the United Irish League. These people, Fay tells Yeats, want more "vigorous themes" than those the poet finds in the land of faery. His plays may be charming, but "they do not send men away with a desire for deeds." If Yeats wanted to be an Irish playwright, he had to write what the Irish people needed, not what he might desire to write. If they were to be his audience, he had to be their voice.

Fay frankly stated his reservations about the literary products of the Yeats-Martyn-Moore combination. Their works, he says, show little "familiarity with the footlights"; written "in the study," they "won't act" on the stage. Ultimately, Fay allowed, Ireland might have a need for the more subtle effects of a theatre dedicated to art; but first it must begin as all national dramas had begun, with simple folk plays—miracle, morality, and mystery plays—that would feed the new popular appetite for native drama.

More important even than Fay's beliefs about the subjects and style of national drama was his belief about its economic basis. Both Fay and Yeats hated commercial theatre, but for different reasons. Yeats complained it had little use for fine writing, being a theatre of big stage effects, coarse oratory, and grandiose scenery. Fay disliked these features as well, but he had another reason for hating commercialism. When John Whitbread's popular theatre company took up a powerful political issue, like the land agitation in *The Irishman*, it turned the subject into a sideshow, with the conventions of melodrama and the circus tricks of the stage spectacular in the center ring.[64] Fay said he wanted to jump the orchestra pit and murder the virtuous persons of such melodramas, and he lamented the popularity of the sensationalist trick of introducing the dreaded battering ram on stage during the climactic scene of eviction when bailiffs knocked down the doors of peasant cottages. This type of theatricality, in Fay's view, was just a way for English money to enable "Saxon swine" to fatten on the Irish by turning a colony into a cartoon.[65] For Yeats,

64. Fay, *Towards a National Theatre*, 27–29.
65. Ibid., 53.

commercialism spoils the subtle aspirations to beauty of the individual artist; for Fay, it diverts the entire people from a recognition of their real oppression. Fay discovered a dangerous affinity between business and amusement: the purpose of both is to defend the status quo. For an audience to be amused at the land question, to enjoy its conversion to a commodity, is to say yes to its settlement, while making a flight not just from reality, but from any thought of resistance to that reality. When letters to the press suggested that a national theatre could be formed by subscription from patrons or by floating a company for stockholders, Fay was furious: "We don't want any of the financial gang, who would run the Universe, Limited, if they could, in connection with an Irish National Theatre." [66] The capitalist syndicates, he said, were "the real authors" of the plays seen in Dublin: the measure of a commercial play's merit was the amount of conspicuous expenditure on its production; its meaning was just business turned into an ideology.

The Irish culture industry, run by foreign investors, had been the subject of a public investigation by the indefatigable D. P. Moran in the pages of the *Leader*,[67] to which Fay and Yeats were regular subscribers. To its three theatres and two music halls, Dublin paid out £200 a working night, or roughly £60,000 a year. In addition, Dublin doubled the expense by importing "jingo panoramas, travelling circuses, merry-go-rounds," "Bray coons," and "dancing Grenadiers." The total for Dublin was again doubled for the country as a whole, so that Ireland, Moran calculated, paid out £250,000 a year for entertainment. What it got in return was "a regular night-school of Anglicization," and "powerful propaganda of the lowest . . . moral standards." Moran, a puritanical Catholic nationalist, was especially worried about the moral effect of a theatre in which "religion is besmeared; idling is glorified; cadging and thieving are presented as 'smart' arts; the heroes are cads and the heroines are—well, the modern theatre has a name for them—'women with a past.'" He described part of

66. *United Irishman*, 11 May 1901; Fay, *Toward a National Theatre*, 56–58.
67. *Leader*, 15 September 1900, 40.

the program on a typical evening at a Burgh Quay music hall: "One of [the comedian's] songs, which excited great applause, described . . . how he got seasick, another how he collected in church and went off with the proceeds, and a further 'lyric' was partly about a girl who falls off a bicycle, with the usual low jokes . . . which are invariably the point of such incidents."[68] To Fay, such stuff was not only vulgar and ethically undignified, as it was to Yeats; and not only demoralizing and sinful, as it was to Moran; it was also an opiate of oppression administered by foreign capitalists, both exploitative and profoundly alienating. If there were to be an Irish National Theatre, Fay argued, it must be created outside the capitalist culture industry, without the help of "financial bounders or aristocratic patrons." Basically, the difference between attitudes of Yeats and Fay on commercialism is that Fay, a naive socialist, sought freedom from money;[69] Yeats, a naive aristocrat, sought freedom through money; Fay sought freedom by giving himself up to a political movement; Yeats sought freedom from political movements by achieving control over them.

9

Early in his series of articles, Fay shows that he suspected Yeats of being too popular with wealth. But after Yeats had "killed an Egyptian" (W. H. Lecky), attacked the queen, and finally, in the *Samhain* of October 1901, restated Fay's own view that a theatre to be free to speak of politics must be amateur, Fay (mistaking Yeats's restatement of his views as agreement with them) wrote with relief "that Mr. Yeats has at last

68. *Leader*, 1 September 1900, 2–3.
69. It is certain that Frank Fay came in contact with socialist thinkers. James Connolly was in Dublin running the Irish Workers' party and publishing a Marxist propaganda paper. Connolly was a friend through Maud Gonne of Arthur Griffith, Fay's editor at the *United Irishman*. If Fay did not know Connolly (who did not have a large following), he certainly knew Fred Ryan, the secretary of the Irish National Dramatic Society, and author of the radically socialist *Laying of the Foundations*, first performed 29 October 1902.

cut himself adrift from the so-called 'upper' classes and . . . he recognizes that an Irish theatre would be worthless if it were in the hands of people who could in any way prevent it from acting outspoken plays."[70] As badly as both Fays wanted a theatre and the work of well-known playwrights, Frank Fay insists again and again that the work must be popular and political, and the theatre cannot be compromised by the form of its support—no money "made out of the misery of millions."[71] And Yeats, even as he turned toward London and toward Horniman, allowed Fay to receive the impression that he agreed with his aims. The extraordinary mobility of Yeats's political identity—something Cullingford calls his "freedom" and Conor Cruise O'Brien his "cunning"—is really, I think, his uncertainty. He sought individual success, but the achievement of individuality depended on a host of factors outside his control. Paradoxically, he had to keep his political identity in a state of flux in order to keep alive any possibility of realizing some individual identity. Fenian agitator, defender of the poor, initiate of the Golden Dawn, régisseur of the London "Theatre of Beauty," guru of the amateur arts of London ladies in "cantillation": one can see the Masks, but one must infer the existence of the Man.

From the start of his direct correspondence with Frank Fay, Yeats cultivated the character of a like-minded nationalist seeking to stir up a popular political movement. His first direct communication with Fay followed from a letter Lady Gregory urged him to write Arthur Griffith, editor of the *United Irishman*, asking for some help in increasing his popularity in his native land.[72] *The Land of Heart's Desire* had been given a successful American performance, and Yeats wanted

70. *United Irishman*, 26 October 1901; Fay, *Towards a National Theatre*, 25–26.
71. Fay, *Towards a National Theatre*, 85.
72. Wade, 352–53. It is in this letter that WBY says, "I always write for my own people though I am content perforce to let my work come to them slowly." He also gossips to Griffith about an attack on the Ascendancy professor J. P. Mahaffy, "which is certain to be amusing." Altogether, an astutely nationalist performance.

to know if Griffith would have the press notices Lady Gregory copied out turned into a little article. The job was given to Frank Fay, theatre critic for the *United Irishman*. Fay offered a small paragraph of praise for the "beautiful little play," but asked why the author could not write plays for his own people to act.[73]

Yeats tried to do just that: he set out to meet all the terms Fay set down. He laid aside a treatment of the Cuchulain legend in Shakespearian blank verse on which he had been working and turned to a simpler and more directly nationalist theme. On 21 April 1900, after his attacks on the forthcoming visit of Queen Victoria to Ireland, he had published "Noble and Ignoble Loyalties," an essay comparing the loyalty of people to Queen Victoria, based on egotism and greed, to loyalty to Cathleen ni Houlihan, based on self-sacrifice and love of country.[74] Now he dreamed of writing a play on the popular nationalist theme of the Rising of '98 and the poor old woman who is Ireland, and while he could not manage to write realistic dialogue for the peasants, or to work out action among the characters, Lady Gregory was equal to the task. *Cathleen ni Houlihan*—the result of Yeats's dream and Lady Gregory's first writing for the stage—perfectly answers to the demands Frank Fay had been making of Yeats and Irish playwrights: it is a miracle play, in realistic dialogue, about a major political issue, that drives men to deeds.[75]

73. Fay, *Towards a National Theatre*, 69–70. WBY wrote to Frank Fay shortly after publication of the notice, claiming to be "altogether pleased" with it. He went on to disengage himself from the antinationalist Anglo-Irish: "The ordinary theatre-going person in Dublin, of the wealthier classes, dislikes our movement so much" the director of the Gaiety Theatre wants to hide from the public the fact that Yeats and Moore are the authors of a play set for performance at the Gaiety. Yeats concludes the letter with a remarkable statement that he wishes his work were in the Irish language (Wade, 355).

74. Frayne and Johnson, 2:211–13.

75. The fact of Lady Gregory's authorship of *Cathleen ni Houlihan* casts light on the question of why Yeats never repeated the popular success of that play. He could not repeat what he had never done once. Lady Gregory, however, could, and she did with *The Rising of the Moon*, *The Gaol Gate*, and other works of broadly nationalist propaganda.

Yeats's next play, under way a week after the production of *Cathleen ni Houlihan* on 6 April 1902, was just as deliberate an attempt to show himself an obliging servant of the needs of the Irish theatre. In a letter of 10 April 1902, Yeats describes what was to become *The Hour-Glass* as "a little religious play in one act with quite as striking a plot as Kathleen—it cannot offend anybody and may propitiate Holy Church" (presumably for the heterodoxical sins of *The Countess Cathleen*). With *Cathleen ni Houlihan,* he provided nationalist credentials; with *The Hour-Glass,* he wished to prove his religious ones. Even Frank Fay was taken aback by the piety of the play's morality. Whatever the quality of the writing (really "very fine," Fay allowed), Fay was "not in favor of holding an unbeliever up to the scorn . . . of this pretentiously pious country."[76] Yeats had hoped if he ridiculed an atheist, he would seem to the audience an orthodox believer. In fact, the audience appears to have regarded the play as a very suspicious offering. "Chanel," reviewer for the *Leader,* thought Yeats had "composed a satire on himself," but considered that he must have done so unconsciously, while working at some "inner-guard significance" outside the audience's reckoning.[77] Yeats tried to explain to Fay why, after he had done his best to please the people, they still withheld their enthusiasm: "Some of them felt that because I had written it, it must contain some hidden heresy, while others, finding it impossible to believe I really thought those things, supposed . . . it was a mere literary experiment."[78]

Yeats's later doubts about *The Hour-Glass,* and his subsequent revisions, reveal the distaste he felt while writing to Fay's instructions, working for the movement, and having a daily bath in what he called "the gutter." In the original play, a wise man who can persuade anyone to believe anything convinces an entire land that there are no gods, angels, or

76. Hogan and Kilroy, 2:30–31.
77. "Broken Soil," *Leader,* 12 December 1903, 266–67.
78. WBY letter to Frank Fay, 30 December 1903; rpt. in Gerard Fay, *The Abbey Theatre: Cradle of Genius* (New York: Macmillan, 1958), 69.

spiritual worlds. An angel then appears and promises him eternal pain in death unless in his last remaining hour he can find one believer. The only remaining believer turns out to be a fool, before whom the wise man must kneel and do penance in order to obtain salvation. When he watched the play, Yeats said, he "was always ashamed" to see the wise man abase himself by kneeling before the fool.[79] He had put in the play his own meanings—that the invisible world is true, the visible an illusion—but others just saw the meaning of the action: educated people are cowards, and the Church is a true guide. Surely, Yeats watched himself on stage, his own "propitiations" of the priests and nationalists, and he found the sight intolerable. Consequently in 1914, he revised the play in such a way that the wise man never receives salvation, and finally declares that men never see the truth, but God sees the truth in men; and when the mind is broken, that truth comes through like "peas from a broken peascod."[80] With this close, the wise man becomes a truly tragic, Lear-like figure. Through disbelief, he finds understanding; through suffering, an extreme joy. The main character of the play is thus transformed from a butt of satire to a hero of tragedy, and Yeats from one who is told the truth to one who declares it.

10

Altogether, Yeats gave the Fays three plays designed to meet their requirements: *Cathleen ni Houlihan*, *The Pot of Broth* (both largely written by Lady Gregory), and *The Hour-Glass*. With these works, Yeats won the trust of the company, saw it gain some skill, and obtained its presidency. Now was the time, after a successful London tour in April 1903, to introduce the money to the company and Horniman to the Fays.

For the fall 1903 season of the Irish National Theatre Society, when Horniman was to come to Dublin as costume designer, Yeats was faced with a real difficulty. He had no power

79. Alspach, 645–46.
80. Alspach, 634.

to carry out his desire to write romantic, mystical verse drama in England, because the London theatre societies had by then disintegrated. He had no power to do so in Ireland, because the Irish theatre society was still dictating to Yeats the terms of the playwright's trade. Horniman, he hoped, would free him from such work through her capital. But Horniman liked plays only without politics; and the Fays liked only plays free to do politics; moreover, they did not want money from "aristocratic patrons or financial bounders."

In the play that Yeats wrote for this occasion, *The King's Threshold*, the several parties could see, not their contradictory demands fulfilled, but some personal preferences gratified.[81] It has a part for Frank Fay with fine elocutionary opportunities,[82] elaborate antique costumes for Horniman to design, and a romantic legendary Irish setting for the audience. The profound demands made by Yeats himself are those in the plot of the play. Seanchan, the chief bard of Ireland, denied his privilege to sit with the makers of law at the King Guaire's table, has gone on hunger-strike at the palace doors. On the third day, the king calls together the bard's students, town mayor, old family retainers, and beloved, as well as the king's own chamberlain, soldier, and princesses, each of whom tempts Seanchan to break his fast and submit to the king. The bard, however, spurns every offer tendered, ready to die rather than give up a right "established when the

---

81. A few months after the performance of *The King's Threshold*, during a tour of the United States, Yeats penciled in the margins of Thomas Common's selections from Nietzsche his agreement that one has obligations only to one's equals, that "the lower . . . cannot make obligations to the higher." Nonetheless, "in the last analysis the 'noble' man will serve the weak as much as the 'good' man, but in the first case the 'noble' man creates the *form* of the gift, and in the second the weaker." In *The King's Threshold* (a play in many ways showing the first flush of WBY's Nietzscheanism), Yeats gives not what is asked but what he is disposed to give. See Cullingford, *Yeats, Ireland and Fascism*, 74, and Frances Nesbitt Oppel, *Mask and Tragedy: Yeats and Nietzsche, 1902-10* (University Press of Virginia: Charlottesville, 1987), 94-101, for discussions of Yeats's annotations to Common's *Nietzsche as Critic, Philosopher, Poet, and Prophet.*

82. The play is dedicated "IN MEMORY OF FRANK FAY AND HIS BEAUTIFUL SPEAKING IN THE CHARACTER OF SEANCHAN" (Alspach, 256).

world / Was first established."[83] At the play's end, Guaire is brought to kneel before Seanchan, putting his crown in the hands of the bard, who in turn places it again on the head of the king. In this play, one message at least is clear: ancient Irish tradition declares that the poet rules; patriots, take note.

The King's Threshold spread a banquet of ghostly food, a special course for each guest. Horniman thought she got what she wanted, a deep-laid promise that art would be free from politics; as a result, she unloosed her purse-strings. The Fays thought they got what they wanted, an offer of the free use of a theatre for Irish audiences, on national subjects. Finally, Yeats thought he got what he aimed for, freedom from control and freedom to control.

All would soon find out that their separate understandings were a collective misunderstanding and that none was free from the others. However, what is important to this chapter is that in the moment in which Yeats might well be thought to have at last found his freedom of expression in a romantic verse-drama—with his patron, by his players, and in his country—the form of that play was determined down to points of characterization, costume, setting, and theme by a network of relations outside the poet. Yeats sought freedom and power, and he did not much care if the only way to get them was to take them from others. But he did not consider that freedom and power may not be commodities, things that can be appropriated for individual consumption. Power may perhaps be better conceived after the metaphor of Foucault: "Power exists as a network,"[84] or rather as groups of interwoven networks. In this case, the network included Horniman, her money, and her investments in British ventures in Hudson Bay (income from which paid for the Abbey Theatre); it also included the Fays, their players, nationalist organizations, the radical press, and the Gaelic League, which spon-

83. Alspach, 259. The 1904 text of *The King's Threshold* is used throughout.

84. Michel Foucault, *Power/Knowledge: Selected Interviews and Other Writings, 1972–77*, ed. Colin Gordon (New York: Pantheon Books, 1972; rev. ed., 1980), 130, passim.

sored massive participation in national theatre. An individual or group could colonize a political organization for aesthetic purposes, or a cultural organization for political ones, but when an "individual" such as Yeats grants expression to this network, in doing so he is constituted as one of its effects, one singing string at the center of a web of tensions. Once Yeats was funded by Horniman, aided by Lady Gregory, committed to folk plots and Irish traditions, acted by the Fays, and performed for Irish nationalists, we know him, not as an autonomous being, but as a vivid cloud of potentialities, his individuality indeterminate outside its appearances in a letter, poem, or play, when it is made actual as the point of intersection of oblique forces always outside him and beyond his compass.[85]

85. Years later, when writing *Discoveries*, the poet began to conceive the self much in this fashion, though expressed in the language of alchemical pursuits. Once, he says, he thought of himself as "something unmoving and silent living in the middle of my own mind and body," then one day he suddenly understood that he was seeking something "always outside myself, a Stone or Elixir that was always out of reach, and that *I myself was the fleeting thing that held out its hand*" (WBY, *Essays and Introductions* [New York: Macmillan, 1961], 172; emphasis added).

3

Author and Audience

Stealing the Symbols

If the plot of *The King's Threshold* implied that privilege and authority belonged to the Irish poet by ancient right, then its style, costume, and setting could be understood to show that a poet thus enfranchised would be disposed, out of the abundance of his Nietzschean heroic will, to shower gifts upon others.[1] When Yeats's play was staged on 8 October 1903 at Molesworth Hall, Dublin, along with John Millington Synge's *In the Shadow of the Glen*, the nationalist press was by no means beguiled by the evening's performances. Arthur Griffith, editor of the *United Irishman*, was irritated by the hunger-striking bard's pretensions in Yeats's play: it is not freedom Seanchan demands, but place, power, and wealth, all without accountability. The sympathy of the audience, according to Griffith, "went out to the honest soldier who wished to put his sword into the selfish old man who lay on the King's steps . . . contending for a soft life in a King's bosom instead of an eternal one in a people's heart. We hold it a pity that King Guaire did not hang Seanchan."[2] While Griffith had grown embittered

1. Yeats had been sent Nietzsche's works by John Quinn in September 1902 (Finneran, Harper, and Murphy, 2:106); according to John Kelly's chronology, Yeats had fallen under the spell of this "strong enchanter" by December 1902 (*The Collected Letters of W. B. Yeats,* vol. 1, ed. John Kelly and Eric Domville [Oxford: Clarendon Press, 1986] xx). One of Yeats's most enthusiastically annotated passages in Nietzsche is the section on "Gift-giving" as the sole responsibility of great individuals. Gifts are the fruits of strong natures that may not be otherwise taxed by the masses of weak natures. Nietzsche's influence is further discussed below.

2. "All Ireland," *United Irishman* 10, no. 242 (17 October 1903): 1.

with the Irish National Theatre Society over censorship of Padraic Colum's anti-recruiting *The Saxon Shillin'*,[3] it is still a shock that he should, even on a symbolic level, be suggesting the national poet be lynched. But other papers went just as far in their condemnation of the evening's performances. To Yeats's appeal for an "audience so tolerant that the half-dozen minds who are likely to be the dramatic imagination of Ireland for this generation may put their own thoughts and their own characters into their works,"[4] the *Irish Daily Independent and Nation* responded with the "sincere hope and belief that no such tolerance will be extended," a statement that could be construed as public incitement to riot. So much for Yeats's attempt to reconcile factions under the authority of the poet: one paper insinuates that he be lynched; the other that the people riot. *The King's Threshold* soon became part of the second great public controversy in Irish theatre, resounding with the aftershocks of the *Countess Cathleen* uproar and deepening the discussion of fundamental literary issues.

In his statements in *Samhain* on the character of a national theatre, the difference between propaganda and literature, the rights of artists, and the proper means of financial support for a national theatre, Yeats began a rhetorical conflict with the nationalist part of the audience that continued throughout the performances of *In the Shadow of the Glen* and *The King's Threshold*, and long after they had left the stage. This conflict

3. Colum's play had won Griffith's *United Irishman* annual contest for the best propaganda play in English. In a 30 January 1903 letter to WBY, W. G. Fay claimed that he had asked Colum to change the ending of *The Saxon Shillin'* only for the sake of "stage business," not out of a fear of Unionist backlash. Nonetheless, in the ensuing dispute with Griffith and Maud Gonne, Fay insisted that "a Theatre is no more a political party than its [*sic*] a Temperance platform" (Finneran, Harper, and Murphy, 1:117–19). Yeats drew the conclusion that "Fay wants to get out of acting political plays," and, while Yeats told Lady Gregory that he "certainly differ[ed] from him on the point," Yeats supported Fay against Griffith, and *The Saxon Shillin'* was not produced by the Irish National Theatre Society (WBY, letter to Lady Gregory, 18 November 1903, quoted in Cullingford, *Yeats, Ireland and Fascism* [New York: New York University Press, 1981], 54).

4. WBY, "An Irish National Theatre," *Samhain*, September 1903; rpt. in *Explorations*, 103.

involved what Kenneth Burke calls "the stealing back and forth of symbols,"[5] the attempt on the part of classes in conflict to appropriate the symbols of authority. The socially transformative work of political literature goes on in the quarrel around certain concepts, central because ambiguous.[6] In Dublin during October 1903 and in the months following, the key terms in literary and political discourse were *national, politics, literature,* and, of course, *Irish,* each of which has a fundamental instability of suggestion. At their widest, such terms are capacious enough to allow for broad agreement among conflicting groups; and at their narrowest, they are susceptible to appropriation by a single group. The group able to fix the meaning of such terms has an opportunity to establish hegemony over others, in defining the way in which they conceive of the culture. This chapter examines the struggle over the power to define these symbols—what motivated it, how it affected the interpretation of *In the Shadow of the Glen* and *The King's Threshold,* and what properties finally were at stake in "the stealing back and forth of symbols."

The controversy that greeted the October 1903 program of the Irish National Theatre Society is sometimes dismissed as part of some irrational miasma of the audience. Andrew Parkin, for instance, says that he is trying "to be fair to Yeats" when he asserts that few writers from any land have faced the terrible forces arrayed against Yeats in Ireland: "obscurantism, ignorance, prejudice, and violence—all springing from a state of mind difficult to comprehend and which could, for instance, be expressed by the actors themselves as well as the

5. The term belongs to Burke, but credit for elaborating its significance in Gramsci's terms of ideological hegemony goes to Frank Lentricchia, *Criticism and Social Change* (Chicago: University of Chicago Press, 1983), 79.

6. See ibid., 80, on ambiguity as a property of revolutionary argument, whereby a "ruling discourse is seized and in the name of ruling discourse, turned against the rulers." For an exemplary study of political language that stresses "the polemical circumstances of its expression" rather than simply its "conceptual character," see also Steven N. Zwicker, *Politics and Language in Dryden's Poetry* (Princeton: Princeton University Press, 1984).

mob."[7] That casually assumed "mob," as if it were descriptive rather than evaluative, shows how completely some Yeats critics assume the ideological stance of the poet on whose behalf they plead. The term *mob*, however derisive, nonetheless suggests the volatility, the collective will, and the readiness for action of the Dublin audiences. The Irish historian George Boyce, qualifying Yeats's 1899 forecast of an audience "uncorrupted and imaginative . . . trained to listen by its passion for oratory," allows that they had such a passion, but, "nobody's fools," they were "enthusiastic, keen, and perceptive political audiences," trained not just to listen, but also to search out the practical implications for their destiny of any speech, and to demonstrate their judgment publicly. The university-educated liberal humanists the Irish National Theatre Society played for at Oxford or Cambridge may have been more sympathetic to the avante-garde elements in Yeats's theatrical technique, but the Irish audiences were nonetheless tolerant of artistic experiment, and far more sensitive to the political implications of language than foreign audiences.[8] The Dublin audiences for Irish drama thought of every intellectual act—plays and manifestoes of art being no exception—as involved

7. Parkin, *The Dramatic Imagination of W. B. Yeats,* (Dublin: Gill & Macmillan; New York: Barnes & Noble, 1978), 89. The remark on cultural history is incidental to Parkin's sensitive appreciation of Yeats's plays as experimental works of the theatre. In *A Reader's Guide to the Plays of W. B. Yeats* (London: Macmillan; New York: St. Martin's Press, 1984), 45, Richard Taylor blames the multiplicity of characters in *The King's Threshold* on the need "to captivate an uninterested audience" that was unable to appreciate the "inescapably meaningful symbolic scheme" of the play.

8. G. B. Shaw called the Irish audience "the most sensitive and, on provocation, the most turbulent audience in the world" (*The Doctor's Dilemma, Getting Married, and The Shewing-Up of Blanco Posnet* [New York: Brentano's, 1911], 404). One example of artistic tolerance may be noted: Arthur Griffith, even after the October 1903 controversy with Yeats, advised his readers that "the production of Mr. Yeats's 'Shadowy Waters' on the stage is an experiment which will excite general interest" (*United Irishman* 11, no. 255 [4 January 1904]: 1), and while he found the psychological development in the hero obscure, he nonetheless thought the play "better heard than read," so that the performance of it was "justified" (*United Irishman* 11, no. 256 [23 January 1904]: 1).

in power in every way, caught up in it, used by interests not at all intellectual, and available for such use even without conscious collaboration by its author.[9]

If drama is considered in the light of rhetoric, as a discourse of purpose played out upon a certain audience, the theatregoing Dublin public was a sensitive, powerful instrument in the hands of a playwright. Indeed, this audience made possible a certain kind of drama, although not the "Theatre of Beauty" Yeats forecast. Instead, "the new form of Irish drama," in the words of the *Leader's* theatre critic "Chanel," was "the political allegory" (to be accurate, not so much a new form of drama, as an element in all drama underscored and highlighted by the level of audience response). Chanel thought that *The King's Threshold* must be an allegory, because otherwise it is "absurd . . . meaningless in the modern world." Irish drama will inevitably, he believes, have an immediate frame of reference: "In a country where so much of the life . . . is intermingled with politics . . . where it has been the cause of so many crimes and so many sacrifices, [politics] will form the matter of our tragedies and comedies."[10] Regardless of whether the author ignores national debate, disguises it, or joins it, the play will be received as "political allegory" by an audience with a highly charged consciousness of the political character of all social life.

In *The King's Threshold*, behind the disguise of a historical costume drama, Yeats meant to join battle over the place of art in society. The notes for *Poems, 1899–1905* explain that he wrote the play when the INTS was having "a hard fight for the recognition of pure art in a community of which one half was buried in the practical affairs of life, and the other half in politics and a propagandist patriotism."[11] Through a course of debates between the bard Seanchan and characters from all ranks of society, Seanchan tries to prove that a seat at the

9. I am indebted for some of the language in this particular description of the "sophisticated political consciousness" to Frank Lentricchia's discussion of Kenneth Burke in *Criticism and Social Change*, 87.

10. Chanel, "Plays with Meanings," *Leader*, 17 October 1903, 124–25.

11. Alspach, 315.

king's table is worth more than a gift of lands and money from the king, more than the sorrow his death would give his father and mother, more even than relief to the hungry people of the stony townland where he was born. One can imagine the play carrying its audience through the first lessons—yes, land, family, and food in times of famine are great things, but a principle's a principle, and a man's got to be a man, etc.— but gradually losing the audience as Yeats/Seanchan makes ever more absolute claims for art, passing from powerful assertion through hyperbole to delirious megalomania. After Seanchan chokes a monk, dashes to the ground dishes proffered by the hands of princesses, curses his coaxing lover Fedelm, and seems ready to let his students go hang, it may well have seemed that the bard's team of opponents had the better arguments, but Yeats rigged the conclusion to literally give the crown to the loser.[12]

Considered as rhetoric, there are problems of effectiveness, not only with the argumentative tropes (which oppose abstract to concrete goods), but with the ethos of the wild, unmannerly hero, especially given the nature of the audience. From the beginning, Seanchan's lying about on the steps of the palace, surrounded by silver dishes, looks dangerously like "a fit of the sulks," as A. S. Knowland puts it.[13] He seems spoiled, pettishly indignant, and desperate for recognition. The court life for which he is willing to sacrifice himself, his family, friends, students, and lover, had its analogue in the modern Irish context only in Dublin's Viceregal Lodge or in some country estate, the exclusive environs of the English and Anglo-Irish. The identification of Seanchan with what the audience would see as a pampered product of the aristocracy approaches the obvious in the scene between the bard and his loyal family retainers, Cian and Brian, who ad-

12. In a Prologue not actually performed but published in the *United Irishman* (9 September 1903), the Old Man admits authorial interference with the conclusion: "He that tells the story now, being a poet, puts the poet in the right" (Alspach, 313).

13. A. S. Knowland, *W. B. Yeats: Dramatist of Vision*, Irish Literary Studies, 17 (Gerrards Cross, Bucks.: Colin Smythe, 1983), 27.

dress him as "your Honour,"[14] in the forelock-tugging, obsequious fashion of a nineteenth-century Catholic peasant before a Protestant on a horse. The relation of Seanchan to his servants—charitable noblesse oblige on one side, trust and respect on the other—is actually glorified in the play by comparison with the relation of Seanchan to the mayor, who, with heavy farce, is characterized as pushy, blathering, craven, and uncultured, the very stereotype of the new Irish Catholic politician Yeats hated in the Bantry Gang. In short, the play respects what the audience would ridicule (deference to gentry), and ridicules what it might well respect (natives as local politicians). These aspects of the way in which Yeats dramatized his defense of "pure art" lessened the appeal of his argument to an Irish audience and raised resistance to perception of the play's intent.

Arthur Griffith also tellingly misreads the play when he scorns Seanchan for seeking the "soft life in a King's bosom instead of an eternal one in a people's heart." In fact, in the play the king, monk, and chamberlain all say that the "people" hold the bard high in their affections; should he die, they may well revolt against the king.[15] This bond between the people and Seanchan, however, may have appeared to some in the audience to be inconsistent with his characterization as an aristocrat of the court, contemptuous of clergy.[16] Griffith's misreading edits out qualities Seanchan enjoys only by ascription (claimed by the author, but not properly belonging to the character), and reads into him a more deeply inscribed aristocratic pursuit of privilege.[17]

To the reports of spectators we must add our own look at the text of the play, but if we reject the responses of the Irish audience out of hand, while assuming the attitudes of the au-

14. Alspach, 277, lines 325qq, 325ooo.

15. Alspach, 260, lines 59–62; 285, lines 441b, 445.

16. The historical accuracy of a reference to the medieval rivalry between Irish bards and monks is less pertinent for the audience than a contemporary reference to Ascendancy contempt for Catholic clergy.

17. Knowland observes that the people's love of Seanchan is undeveloped (*W. B. Yeats: Dramatist of Vision*, 29); Griffith goes one better by acting as if it is nonexistent.

thor, as some have done, we not only throw away the benefit of testimony by richly informed, acutely sensitive witnesses, we also lose the opportunity to conceive of Irish dramatic literature as a force in the world, wielded as such and felt as such. It is true that *The King's Threshold* can be read for its evidence of Nietzsche's influence, its record of Yeats's engagement with Greek or Miltonic models, its reflections of Yeats's feelings after the marriage of Maud Gonne, its sentiments about the genetic powers of art over population (prophetic of attitudes more fully developed later),[18] but it can also be grasped, with these additional elements, as part of the artist's struggle in the world. The "high endeavor" of art can be an adventure of the will to power, an attempt to gain a purchase on the mind of the public, to throw it under the dominion of a new way of looking at a state of affairs. Surely *The King's Threshold* is a case of such an assertion of will. It is only in light of the character of the audience over which Yeats sought to assert his will that the assertion itself has its fullest meaning.

2

The philosopher Charles Morris presents a lucid analysis of the process of communication as a five-term relation—*v*, *w*, *x*, *y*, *z*—"in which *v* sets up in *w* the disposition to react in a

18. The influence of Nietzsche on the play was noticed by contemporary observers, such as "Chanel" in the *Leader* (31 October 1903), who regarded it as forgivable, because irrelevant to the plot. It has since been discussed by Richard Ellmann in *The Identity of Yeats* (New York: Oxford University Press, 1964), 96; by Harold Bloom in *Yeats* (New York: Oxford University Press, 1970), 149; and most impressively by Frances Oppel in *Mask and Tragedy: Yeats and Nietzsche, 1902–10* (Charlottesville: University Press of Virginia, 1987), 134–47. Peter Ure gave the first, and still the best, account of the models for the play in *Yeats the Playwright: A Commentary on Character and Design in the Major Plays* (London: Routledge & Kegan Paul, 1963), 31–43. In *Yeats: The Man and the Masks* (New York: Macmillan, 1948), Ellmann attributes Yeats's adoption of a public mask, a sort of stylistic distance, to his reaction to Maud Gonne's marriage to Major MacBride. Though it is not part of my subject, material for a more intricate psychological reading awaits a critic so disposed in the scenes between Fedelm and Seanchan, in which she cares for his needs and worships at his feet, and he curses her with a rather unmotivated violence—a revealing transformation of the real relationship of Yeats and the woman he loved.

certain kind of way, x, to a certain kind of object, y (not then acting as a stimulus), under certain conditions, z."[19] In this system, v would be the *interpretant*; w, the audience; x, the received meaning; y, the play; and z, the conditions of performance. What is particularly useful in Morris's account of communication is that it has three terms rather than the usual one for "context." Usually, we mean by context nearly every historical dimension of a work excluding the author and the text. Morris clarifies theatrical communication by sorting out the audience from the conditions of performance, and both of these from a critical v factor, the interpretant, which sets up in a specific audience the disposition to interpret in a certain way.

As A. P. Foulkes develops Morris's use of the interpretant, many things—not just the text—can dispose the audience to interpret a work in one way rather than another. An audience can, of course, be *predisposed* to react in a certain way to a certain sign. The 1903 Molesworth Hall audience for *The King's Threshold*, for instance, being largely Catholic, would have been predisposed to find fault with a character who snatches the habit of a monk and mocks his God; while for an Edinburgh audience the same gesture might well stand for manly virtue, an anti-papist homily of the Scottish kirk.[20]

An audience not already prejudiced can be disposed to interpret a work in a certain way by the promotion to consciousness of some element in the conditions of performance, an element that becomes the interpretant for the work as a whole. The first performance of *The King's Threshold* and *In the Shadow of the Glen* provides several illustrations of the function of an interpretant derived from the setting in which the audience saw the play. On the evening of the first night, W. G. Fay was surprised to receive a request for six reserve seats from George

19. Charles Morris, *Writings on the General Theory of Signs* (The Hague: Mouton, 1971), 401–2. A. P. Foulkes calls attention to the value of Morris's work to the interpretation of literary texts in *Literature and Propaganda* (London: Methuen, 1983), 23.

20. Alspach, 293, lines 573–79.

Wyndham, the current British chief secretary of Ireland. The theatre at the time was closely identified with the nationalist movement, so it had not drawn much of its clientele from the Ascendancy and was unaccustomed to make provision for special seating. Fay hastily collected six armchairs, and, we are told, "the one assigned to the Chief Secretary chanced to be covered in red."[21] As a result, Wyndham seemed to have been provided with a royal British throne; the command performance was for his eyes first, for Irish eyes second. On the same evening, across the aisle from Wyndham, and to the side, sat the great-bearded, white-haired Fenian John O'Leary. Padraic Colum reports that the nationalist players felt "the wrong man was in the red chair"; O'Leary "had in his hands the succession we looked for."[22] For some in the audience on that particular night, the seating arrangements in Molesworth Hall became the interpretant by which the plays of Synge and Yeats were understood. Consequently, the theatre seemed to have turned away from its nationalist origins and to have become something for the entertainment of the upper class. Suspicious and resentful, some spectators looked for meanings in the plays themselves that supported their impression. In this light, Yeats's hero Seanchan was a blue-blooded scoundrel who "contend[ed] for a soft life in a King's bosom," and Synge's Nora was just a creature out of Ibsen preoccupied with "transpontine" "modern sex problems" of little relevance to Ireland.

This interpretant accounts only for the response of some of the audience at one of the performances. Other spectators on other nights were disposed to interpret *In the Shadow of the Glen* in a certain way by the acting: Maire nic Shiublaigh's erotically charged Nora made some see the character as a "bad wife" rather than as a noble, spiritually profound hero-

---

21. David H. Greene and Edward M. Stephens, *J. M. Synge, 1871–1909* (New York: Macmillan, 1959), 145. In this account, *assigned* seems to contradict *chanced to be covered*, and one may doubt whether a stage-designer like Fay would be insensitive to the symbolism of decor.
22. Padraic Colum, *The Road round Ireland* (London: Macmillan, 1927), 295.

ine, oppressed by circumstance.[23] W. G. Fay's low comic Dan Burke left some spectators, such as Maurice Joy, unprepared to engage the deeper levels of association that emerge in the play's conclusion.[24] Thus, now one actor, now another, can seize upon the imagination of the audience and influence interpretation of the play as a whole. Perhaps even more effective than performance qualities, reviews control the way in which audiences respond. Lord Ardilaun's Unionist *Daily Express*, for example, in denying that *In the Shadow of the Glen* ("the gem of the evening") had "any polemical significance"—just "agreeable fooling" "with a convincing ring of truth"—tried to suppress political rebellion by encouraging the audience to regard the work as light entertainment.[25] John Butler Yeats did not try to pull off the trick of getting the audience to laugh at adultery in a peasant's cottage; he followed the first performance with a letter to the *United Irishman* describing the play as an "attack on that Irish institution, the loveless marriage," a formulation that indeed established terms by which the play was discussed for some time.[26] Alive to these various interpretants—seating arrangements, casting, acting styles, and reviews—many were left uncertain whether to regard the play as farce, light comedy, problem play, tragedy, or travesty of the national character. Synge's "harsh and strange" genius for destabilizing conventions left the play open to this invasion of interpretative forces, but it was the fact that there was something close to a state of open ideological war that gave the conflict over the play its explosive force.[27]

---

23. C. E. Montague, *Dramatic Values* (London: Methuen, 1911), 54; Greene and Stephens, *Synge*, 153.

24. Maurice Joy, "The Drama," *United Irishman* 11, no. 273 (21 May 1904): 3.

25. The *Daily Express* review is quoted in Greene and Stephens, *Synge*, 147.

26. John Butler Yeats, "Ireland out of the Dock," *United Irishman* 10, no. 241 (10 October 1903): 3.

27. WBY, "J. M. Synge and the Ireland of His Time," in *Essays and Introductions* (New York: Macmillan, 1961), 312.

3

At some point, after learning that Horniman had money to spend and might well spend it on one of his theatre projects, Yeats came to know that she would never spend it on the Irish National Theatre Society until he could demonstrate that she would not thereby be making a contribution to an Irish uprising. If he could assure her the theatre would not tolerate nationalists—the sort of people, she said of one (D. P. Moran), that a gentleman couldn't take to a club—then the money was his.[28] So with the first production of *The King's Threshold* and *In the Shadow of the Glen*, Yeats published an essay redefining the meaning of "The Irish National Theatre," now no home to propaganda, he declared, but a place where the "half-dozen minds" of any significance in the nation were granted the privilege of seeing life in their own way. He declared he did not want any financial assistance from nationalists or from Unionists, for that would tie his hands; the only help he would accept would be that of those "who love the arts so dearly they would not bring them into even honorable captivity."[29] And on the evening of the first performance, Yeats came before the audience to drive the point home. He proclaimed the audience must grant the artist the right to "show life, instead of the desire which every political party would substitute for life." His biographer, Joseph Hone, tells us Yeats expected a donation of £20 from Horniman; surely the poet would not thus have sold himself short.[30] If he was going to make a parade of apolitical principles, he deserved to get the £13,000 Horniman eventually spent rather than twenty

28. Horniman to WBY, 2 December 1907; National Library of Ireland, Ms. 13068.

29. WBY, "An Irish National Theatre," *United Irishman* 10, no. 241 (10 October 1903): 2; the expanded version from *Samhain*, speaking of the "unconditioned millions" of a king "who loved the arts and their freedom," is reprinted in *Explorations*, 103.

30. Joseph Hone, *W. B. Yeats: 1865–1939* (New York: Macmillan, 1943), 205: "When he came down from the stage [after his appeal for 'life' as opposed to 'politics'] Miss Horniman, from whom he had been expecting a contribution of twenty pounds, said to him, 'I will give you a theatre.'"

quid. At the end of the evening, Horniman came up to him and offered to give him a theatre.

Horniman did not simply hand over title to a building for the sake of a speech; she had him put it in writing. Specifically, she requested that he reprint his essays on the "Reform of the Theatre" and "The Irish National Theatre" in the 1904 *Samhain* along with the announcement of her offer. In an extraordinary way, these publications formed Horniman's legal contract with the directorate of the Irish National Theatre Society. "The Samhain Principles" come up again and again as the point of contest in negotiations between the owner of the Abbey and its writer-directors.[31] Ultimately, they led to the legal arbitration at the time of Horniman's sale of the building.

Some of these principles are strictly dramaturgical. Yeats advocates poetry before the actor, the actor before the scene, and the decorative scene before the realist one, in a general assault upon histrionically colored prose realism. No doubt, these particular principles were important to Yeats's own attempts to make his mark as a playwright, but one wonders how important they ever were to anyone else, not only to the audience, in whom they were never to stimulate a durable passion, but even to his confederates—Synge and Lady Gregory—with their versions of prose realism in a folk mode, or even, at last, to Horniman herself.

What "the Samhain Principles" meant to Horniman, the single principle to which she clung, was the one Yeats most grandiloquently uttered in the 1905 *Samhain*, but campaigned for throughout the October 1903 controversy: "So long as I have any control over the National Theatre Society, it will be carried on in this spirit, call it art for art's sake if you will; and no plays will be produced at it which were written not for the sake of a good story or fine verses or some revelation of character, but to please those friends of ours who are ever urging

31. Horniman's letter to WBY of 21 June 1907 is one of many instances in which she threatens to stop everything and close the theatre if it is used for political purposes, in violation of the "Samhain Principles." See ch. 6 below.

us to attack the priests or the English."³² Or, as Horniman later put it in an official dispatch to Yeats, bold-faced, double underlined: "<u>**NO POLITICS.**</u>"

4

Yeats's redefinition of the Irish National Theatre in speeches, letters to the press, and the pages of *Samhain* became the major interpretants for all of the performances of October 1903, underpinning other interpretant tending to a nationalist critique, and overriding interpretants that would have led to a consensus of aesthetic appreciation. Debate about *The King's Threshold* concerned the degree of a writer's responsibility to the nation; debate about *In the Shadow of the Glen* ultimately concerned its appropriateness to the repertoire of an Irish National Theatre—issues raised by Yeats's proclamation of policy.

Annie Horniman's patronage of Yeats was not itself an item in the public discussion, because at this stage her promise was known only to Yeats himself. It is true that Arthur Griffith had warned about "the danger of the theatre falling into foreign and hostile hands"; true that he regarded the Irish National Theatre Society as "*our* Irish theatre," the property of nation-alists in spirit, title, and deed;³³ and true that in the bitter con-flict of October 1903, he paid Yeats the somewhat sinister compliment that he knew the poet to be "a Nationalist *who cannot be bought* though he may be misled."³⁴ However sen-sitive to the secret affiliations of capital, Griffith still had no reason to suspect a connection between Yeats's new policy and the fresh promise of finance from Horniman.

It was apparent to nationalists, however, that the October performances were the point of application of a shift in policy for the theatre as a whole. At the time of Frank Fay's public

32. WBY, *Explorations*, 200.
33. Arthur Griffith, *United Irishman*, 8 November 1902; rpt. in Hogan and Kilroy, 2:37.
34. *United Irishman* 10, no. 243 (24 October 1903): 2; emphasis added.

critique of the timid, coterie aestheticism of the Irish Literary Theatre, Yeats—as discussed above—had apparently begun to write plays for the Fay brothers' Irish National Dramatic Society according to their orders: simple, popular, national, and observant of Catholic sensibilities. Fay had asserted in an October 1901 article for the *United Irishman* that Yeats at last recognized "that an Irish theatre would be worthless if it were to be in the hands of people who could in any way prevent it from acting outspoken plays."[35] After they had begun their collaboration, Fay discussed with Yeats the desirability of having a theatre of their own, because "one could only be outspoken in one's own hall."[36] By *outspoken* Fay meant "politically transgressive," and presumed that the author was of one mind with the actors on this score. Fay had reason to believe that Yeats also was disgusted with "this fear to touch politics" and would therefore throw no obstacle in the path of the Irish National Theatre Society's becoming an openly nationalist organization.[37] However, whatever he may have permitted Fay to imagine, Yeats had always had other fish to fry. He never wanted the job of speaking out on political issues in his plays.[38] Before October 1903, however, his personal attitude was not the policy of the Irish National Theatre Society, which regularly produced agitational propaganda, such as Yeats and Gregory's *Cathleen ni Houlihan* and Fred Ryan's *The Laying of the Foundations*. The new INTS by-laws, in fact, prohibited the production of plays offensive to Irish national ideals.

35. Frank Fay, *Towards a National Theatre: The Dramatic Criticism of Frank J. Fay*, ed. Robert Hogan, Irish Theatre Series, no. 1 (London: Oxford University Press; Dublin: Dolmen Press, 1970), 75–77.

36. Fay's letter of 17 February 1902 is reprinted in Finneran, Harper, and Murphy, 2:93–95.

37. Frank Fay to WBY, 25 July 1902; quoted in Hogan and Kilroy, 2:30–31.

38. Yeats's 1902 article on "The Freedom of the Theatre" declares that "art is always a disturber" and society should extend its tolerance to the idiosyncrasies of great natures (Frayne and Johnson, 2:295–99). This is really the same position he took in October 1903, but at that time he was speaking, not just for himself, but for the Irish National Theatre Society.

Against this background, the 1903 *Samhain* principles and Yeats's remarks in defense of *In the Shadow of the Glen* seemed to many like an abrupt transformation of the nature and purpose of the Irish National Theatre Society. Griffith complained that if the society had "no other propaganda but that of good art," it was "no more Irish and National than the Elizabethan Stage Society."[39] Furthermore, under the new policy, part of the company's repertoire would become tabu on its own stage.[40] Week after week, Griffith demanded that Yeats give some reason why the Irish National Theatre Society had any right, with this new policy, to call itself either Irish or national.[41] The war had begun in earnest for ownership of the tribe's symbols of authority.

In the Shadow of the Glen, a riotous comedy by a mischievous writer, had the added misfortune of coming before the public for the first time as an apparent instance of the new policy to disregard the political considerations of Irish nationalists. Given the governing interpretant, the main question about Synge's play was, "Does it represent the Irish national character?"

5

In the Shadow of the Glen dramatizes the tale of a young woman, Nora, living at the end of a long dark Wicklow glen, whose husband, Dan Burke, has apparently died.[42] At the beginning of the play, a passing tramp knocks at the cottage door, and Nora, with no fear of strangers, invites him to come in and be the first guest at the wake of her husband. After he settles down with a pipe and a drink, Nora goes out under the cover of fetching mourners, but actually to speak with a young shepherd, Michael Dara. Once she is clear of the cottage, the

39. This was an intimately cutting thrust since the Elizabethan Stage Society was one of the London dramatic societies through which Yeats had tried to mount his "Theatre of Beauty" in 1902.
40. *United Irishman* 10, no. 242 (17 October 1903): 1.
41. *United Irishman* 10, no. 243 (24 October 1903): 2.
42. Synge, 3:29–59.

"corpse" rises up from under his sheet, terrifying the tramp, and demands a drink, for he's "destroyed with the drouth" and "there's been the devil's own fly itching [his] nose."[43] He tells the tramp he was only letting on to be dead in order to catch his wife with her lover, Michael Dara. He asks the tramp to hand him a big stick, then lies back down under his sheet before the return of Nora and Michael Dara. Michael, it turns out, is no very fiery lover; he is preoccupied with counting out pieces of money and thinking of how much his sheep will prosper on Dan Burke's pasture once the body is buried and he and Nora marry. Nora, however, lets it out that she may be in no hurry to marry Michael, for he will soon be as old, crabbed, and ugly as Dan; anyway, he is not such a fine man as ones she has known in her time, men such as Patch Darcy, a great wild shepherd who used to visit her, but who had since gone mad on the hills and, dying, been left out for the crows to scavenge. In the midst of a speech by Nora on the miseries of mortality, and the hideous sight of the aged, such as Dan Burke, the corpse again rises up from his sheet behind Nora, repeating her words with terrible sarcasm. He orders her out of the house, praying that she may go mad like Darcy or wander a woman of the roads until it is she who is old and crabbed. The tramp then puts his oar in. Saying that such a fate is too hard on a single woman, he suggests that Michael take care of her. But Michael loses interest in Nora once she loses her pastures. For his interference, the tramp is also ordered from the cottage, and, in a lyrical final speech, he invites her to come along with him for a free life on the hills, with all its beauty and its hardship. Acting as though she has a choice, Nora "decides" she will go with the tramp, because he has "a fine bit of talk." Once they leave, at the end of the play, Michael Dara, the former lover, and Dan Burke, the jealous husband, sit down together for a drink of the whiskey laid on for his wake.

Some of the most popular texts for historians of the Literary Revival are taken from the contemporary editorials cen-

43. Ibid., 43.

tering on the infidelity of an Irish wife; for some Yeats critics, these texts are self-evident proof of Irish chauvinism.[44] Irish women—"the most virtuous . . . in the world,"[45] it was claimed—were not properly represented in a national theatre by an adulteress; if so represented, it was no laughing matter. There are apparently no statistics kept on the nations with the most virginal brides and chastest wives, but later Irish literature is full of the agonized satirical confessions of poets condemned to chastity by Irish prudery. One thinks of Patrick Kavanagh's "The Great Hunger," one long scream of sexual frustration, or Austin Clarke's "Pity poor lovers who may not do as they please." It is not at all ridiculous that some should claim Irish women were chaste; it may, however, be questionable whether they should be proud of the claim, Irish Jansenism amounting to something like a mass neurosis.

Arthur Griffith led the reaction against the play by claiming that the plot did not derive from Irish experience or folklore; Synge had taken the story, Griffith suggested, from a tale found in Petronius and Boccaccio, "The Widow of Ephesus," in which a young widow hard upon the death of her husband takes a soldier for lover.[46] Yeats, as Synge's "able lieutenant,"

---

44. The list of literary historians defending Synge against his audience begins early and continues long; it runs from Cornelius Weygandt's *Irish Plays and Playwrights* (London: Constable; Boston: Houghton Mifflin, 1913) and M. Bourgeois's *John Millington Synge and the Irish Theatre* (1913; New York: Blom, 1965) to a kind of crescendo in Alan Price, who says that the "deplorable" "fierce assaults upon Synge" "are not, in any sense, literary comment or criticism that merits consideration" (*Synge and Anglo-Irish Drama* [London: Methuen, 1961], 21). More recently, several critics have been less committed to the enterprise of making a reputation for Synge, and have taken into account the response of the audience and contemporary critics. Weldon Thornton uses contemporary reviews to support his thesis that Synge succeeded in an intent to cause "perceptual—specifically aesthetic—shock" (*J. M. Synge and the Western Mind* [Gerrards Cross, Bucks.: Colin Smythe, 1979], 107). In "Demythologising Cathleen ni Houlihan: Synge and His Sources," Eugene Benson takes a stronger line, justifying nationalist opposition to Synge by arguing that Synge "distorts the folk materials that he dramatizes"; the defense by Synge of his play is, according to Benson, "disingenuous" (*Irish Writers and the Theatre*, ed. Masaru Sekine, Irish Literary Studies, 23 [Gerrards Cross, Bucks.: Colin Smythe, 1986], 1).
45. Arthur Griffith, *United Irishman* 10, no. 243 (24 October 1903): 2.
46. *United Irishman* 10, no. 242 (17 October 1903): 1.

counterattacked that Synge had borrowed the tale from the
Aran storyteller Pat Dirane; that the story had gone through
all countries and perhaps been picked up by wandering Irish
bards in the middle ages;[47] and finally that "everyone knows"
that Irish wives "do sometimes grow weary of their husbands
and take a lover" ("I heard one very touching tale this summer," gossiped Yeats, both the concerned friend and connois-
seur of the bawdy).[48]

For years, most literary historians gathered support for
Yeats's case on behalf of Synge against the "ignorant," "ob-
scurantist" censorship of the "mob." The issue of the folklore
basis of the play, however, was finally authoritatively settled
in the nationalists' favor by Sean O Suillebhain in "Synge's
Use of Irish Folklore."[49] The ecotype of the play is "The Loving
Wife," in which a credulous wife is ready to take for lover the
one who brings the news of her husband's death. No variant
of this tale is found in Ireland. The motif relevant to Synge's
plot, and found in Irish folklore, is "Feigned Death to Test
Wife's Faithfulness." The story that Pat Dirane told Synge is a
perfect example of this motif: among various frightening ex-
periences, the narrator tells of going into a house where a
man has pretended to die in order to catch his "bad wife."
The tale always ends with the wife and lover being terribly
beaten ("and her blood leapt up and hit the gallery") by the
enraged husband, while the narrator flees the scene; it never
ends with the wife going away scot-free with a tramp.

47. Yeats makes the argument about "medieval travellers" during a new
inflammation of discussion about *In the Shadow of the Glen* in January and February 1905. See, for instance, *United Irishman*, 29 January and 4 February 1905.
48. WBY, "The Irish National Theatre and the Three Sorts of Ignorance,"
United Irishman 10, no. 243 (17 October 1903): 2.
49. Sean O Suillebhain, "Synge's Use of Irish Folklore," in *J. M. Synge,
Centenary Papers, 1971*, ed. Maurice Harmon (Dublin: Dolmen Press; New
York: Humanities Press, 1972), 18–34. According to Nicholas Grene, this article "has finally laid the ghost of 'the Widow of Ephesus'" (*Synge: A Critical
Study of the Plays* [London: Macmillan, 1975], 191. Indeed, O Suillebhain
shows the Aran folktale and "the Widow of Ephesus" belong to different tale
types, but he also demonstrates that the play's plot belongs to none of the
many Irish variants of the tale. Thus the question of whether the play is "native" or "foreign" remains alive.

The question of the plot's derivation was crucial, because Irish folklore was universally accepted as the incorrigible record of the national genius. Griffith was willing to allow that the play showed signs of talent; that Ireland, like other countries, had a problem with the custom of arranged marriages (he published several inoffensive plays attacking the institution); that Irish wives were often frustrated, even unhappy, with their husbands; he did not deny that some of them possibly committed adultery. What he would not allow is that it was representative of the Irish, a part of their fireside wisdom, to show a wife making a better bargain of her life by walking out with a tramp.[50] Presumably, if Synge had made Dan cast out Nora alone on the roads, or beat her with his big stick, or even if he had made the tramp and Michael beat Dan for his jealousy, in any of these cases, the play might have passed muster as Irish theatre. The play would then have been clearly one genre or another, as well as consonant with Irish social attitudes, patriarchal, puritanical, and house-proud.[51] But when Synge had made a heroine of a rebellious wife, called her Nora, and sent her triumphantly out the door at the close of the play, the Irish audience smelled a rat: Ibsen. *A Doll's House* had gone through its London furor some years earlier; Ibsen had been played in Dublin. The audience knew that the theatre was being used to stage "problems," especially the matters of sex and the position of women. Synge was evidently trying to introduce this "morbid" obsession to Ireland by marrying a national folk plot and a modern realist plot: "an evil compound of Ibsen and Boucicault," in the sharp phrase of the *Leader*.[52] Synge had defiled the well of

50. "Men and women in Ireland marry lacking love, and live mostly in a dull level of amity. Sometimes they do not—sometimes the woman lives in bitterness—sometimes she dies of a broken heart—*but she does not go away with the Tramp*" (Arthur Griffith, "All Ireland," *United Irishman* 10, no. 242 [17 October 1903]: 1).

51. For readings of the problem of mixed genres in the play, see Thornton, *J. M. Synge and the Western Mind*, 97–107, and Grene, *Synge: A Critical Study of the Plays*, 84–103.

52. "Plays with Meanings," *Leader*, 17 October 1903, 124–25.

Irish spirit, its folklore, and, in light of the theatre's new policy, the nationalists would not have it.

6

This part of the controversy, well-rehearsed in the critical tradition, may be taken as not only shop-worn but essentially irrelevant. The question of whether Nora is a "type" of the Irish wife, representative of the Irish nation, does not lead us, we complain, to a closer examination of what she is as an "individual" or as an "expression" of Synge's mind.[53] In this respect, Yeats has won the argument over critical method and the proper definition of a "literary type." In the 1904 *Samhain*, the poet explained that the "propagandists" had completely misunderstood the terminology of "men of letters." Men like Griffith thought that "types" were "personifications of averages, of statistics, or even personified opinions." In fact, a character was "typical of something which exists in all men because the writer has found it in his own mind." In a noble sentence on Shakespeare, Yeats declared that "Richard II is typical not because he ever existed, but because [Shakespeare] has made us know of something in our own minds we would have never known had he never been imagined."[54] This critical approach gratifies our individualism, our belief in the universality of literature, and our scientific urge to create anatomical classifications of literary archetypes.

Examine, however, the assumptions behind this method: is it obvious that what a writer finds in his own mind is necessarily representative of all humanity? What we find in our minds might just as well belong to any one of the "little platoons" in which we march—our family, sex, class, nation, race, and so on. Of course, a "great" writer is different; he (yes, it must be a male) will speak for all, all white people anyway, doubtless in one European language or another. But

53. See, for example, Price, *Synge & Anglo-Irish Drama*, 125–26.
54. WBY, *Samhain* (A. H. Bullen & Sons: Dublin, 1904), 14–15; rpt. in id., *Explorations*, 145.

putting aside the question of whether or not great writers can express human universals, it still remains in doubt whether or not Synge is such a great writer. Yeats's defense seemed like a blank check with which any writer could draw on the treasury of national values; it is no surprise that the other litigants in this dispute were not persuaded to endorse it.

Yeats's theory of the type belongs to a Platonic school of criticism, reinvigorated by expressive theories of poetry characteristic of romanticism. There is, of course, another school of theory concerning literary types, the one belonging to the tradition of realism. This tradition opposes observation to romanticism's imagination, objectivity to its subjectivity, and impersonality to its celebration of individual expression. Balzac was a student of "social types," found not in his mind, but on the streets of Paris in the 1830s; Taine distinguishes between "types" that are better and worse as "models" for society; and in the Marxist versions of realism, types are conceived as crystallizing points of social change, reflections of contradictions of social development, both representative of the present and prophetic of the future.[55] In short, there is a pedigree for the nationalists' opinion that a type was a reflection of a social norm and an epitome of the national character. Indeed, when Griffith asseverated that it was no business of a national theatre to dramatize exceptions if doing so would hurt the morale of the Irish movement, he was working at the living core of the concept of type, what René Wellek calls its "tension between description and prescription, truth and instruction."[56] One has to conclude, however, that "the typical Irishman," whether in the romantic or the realist tradition, was, in D. P. Moran's tart phrase, a figure "whom, like the banshee (bean-sighe), everybody has heard of, but nobody has seen, or ever will see."[57] It is nonetheless worth noting

55. René Wellek, "The Concept of Realism in Literary Scholarship," *Concepts of Criticism* (New Haven: Yale University Press, 1963), 242–46.
56. Ibid., 242.
57. D. P. Moran, *The Philosophy of Irish Ireland* (Dublin: James Duffy, n.d.), 79.

that the first sort of type appeals for its authority to the writer; the second, to the society.

The audience was initially prepared by the INTS to interpret *In the Shadow of the Glen* as realism, not as romanticism. Press advances announced that Synge was a Gaelic scholar, who spent much time among the peasantry in order to gather material for folk plays. The dialogue showed that Synge had made an original attempt to exploit the literary possibilities of peasant dialect. The producers had spared no pains in seeking to recreate authentic peasant dress and furniture on stage. All these elements were the calling cards of a realist. And it was as an inaccurate realist that Synge was criticized. But the defense Yeats provided for the play was based on entirely different presuppositions about literature. This was a fact recognized by Griffith when he rejected Yeats's comparison of the outcry over *In the Shadow of the Glen* with that over *The Countess Cathleen:* "When Mr. Yeats drew the countess Kathleen he drew her as a being apart . . . Mr. Synge—or else his play has no meaning—places Norah Burke before us as a type—'a personification of an average'—and Norah Burke is a lie."[58] Griffith's definition of a type is a recipe for a drama of the dismal, but he shows that he is sufficiently sophisticated to distinguish the genre of *In the Shadow of the Glen* from that of *The Countess Cathleen* and to recognize that the different genres make different claims to truth.

The critical quarrel over the proper use of literary terminology (the *representative,* the *typical*) is not a pedantic matter; it goes to the heart of the struggle over symbols of authority in the culture. The dispute ultimately concerned whether authors could delegate to themselves the audience's right to political representation. The writer, the lawyer, and the government official are alike in that they all "represent" others. Indeed, the writer, while not under contract to a client, and not subject to rules of evidence or jury trial, can argue a brief in public sessions; moreover, when he states his case, he can

58. *United Irishman,* 10, no. 242 (17 October 1903): 1.

at the same time claim, although not elected, that he is standing for his nation. Indeed, the colors under which Yeats and Synge sailed—"The Irish National Theatre Society"—made this claim for all their work. In this fashion, representation is the fundamental move in the literary struggle between classes: each class, as Marx writes in *The German Ideology*, "is compelled, merely in order to carry through its aim, to represent its interest as the common interest of all members of society . . . ; it has to give its ideas the form of universality, and represent them as the only rational, universally valid ones." [59] The realist critique made by the nationalists impeached Synge's claim to spokesmanship; it charged him with fabricating evidence useful to the opposition, the alien class of the English who happened to be born in Ireland.

John Butler Yeats, an admirer of Synge, intervened in the controversy with a remarkable essay entitled "Ireland out of the Dock." [60] In a trenchant history of Irish literature, the poet's father said that at one time the country lay under an accusation of unworthiness, and writers were either too proud to plead, or did nothing but plead; now, however, Ireland had won her own dignity; she did not need to defend herself against foreign criticism. In this event, a play was not a trial, and no legal representation by Synge was in order. If he turned up a flaw, it was not a matter for defensiveness; no final judgment of national guilt or innocence was going to fall from a foreign court. The metaphor J. B. Yeats develops is true to the generally litigious state of Irish affairs; his use of it, however, comes to the wrong conclusion. Ireland, still a province, with the fate of landownership mulled in the courts, was no less in the dock in 1903 than during the nineteenth century. Furthermore, when W. B. Yeats sued for control of the national theatre society and reinterpreted its charter, Synge's play became a major article in evidence in a new public proceeding.

59. Lentricchia, *Criticism and Social Change*, 28; Marx, *The German Ideology*, ed. C. J. Arthur (New York: International Publishers, 1972), 65–66.
60. J. B. Yeats, "Ireland Out of the Dock," *United Irishman* 10, no. 241 (10 October 1903): 2.

7

The dispute over the meaning of a literary type follows from Yeats's "morning cockcrow" in the October 1903 *Samhain* heralding an Irish drama that would be an "impartial meditation on character and destiny," not "indentured to any political cause."[61] After the reaction to Synge's characterization of Nora, Yeats further pressed his separation of literature from propaganda. He understandably complained that "our propagandists" would make it impossible for artists to show life or speak the truth if they forced playwrights to employ only "the ideal young peasant . . . or the happy Irish wife, or the policeman of our prejudices, or . . . some other of those invaluable generalizations, without which our practical movements would lose their energy."[62] In his guiding similitude, literature, in love with the minute particulars, was happily wedded to life; propaganda was contracted only to a set of barren opinions.

The statement of the difference between literature and propaganda is one of the most impressive and influential aspects of Yeats's critical writings. Its definition of literary values is impressive, richly exemplified, and altogether profound in its expression of those things that cannot be codified by ready understanding, but can be embodied in works of art; its definition of political values, however, is occasionally narrow, polemical, and dismissive. In fact, in these writings, literature and politics are different worlds in different orbits: the literary one is luminous and large; the political, feisty, pinched, and skeletal. For the modern reader, the social origins of this panegyric on art may well be lost; for the Irish audience, however, it was not difficult to dig away at the roots of Yeats's aesthetic. It was, moreover, a Dublin rule of thumb

61. WBY, "The Reform of the Theatre," *Samhain,* October 1903 (Sealy Bryers & Walker, and T. Fisher Unwin: Dublin, 1903); rpt. in *Explorations,* 103.

62. *Samhain: 1904* (Dublin: Sealy Bryers & Walker, and T. Fisher Unwin, 1904); rpt. in *Explorations,* 146.

that where a doctrine of no politics was affirmed with fervor, one should look for its politics.[63] Of those whose catchcry was "Politics are the curse of Ireland," a contributor to the *United Irishman*, "Soerib," explained: "Needless to say, these persons are invariably Unionists. Obviously, if politics are dropped, Ireland's connection with England will not be endangered, nor will the garrison be endangered in losing their Ascendancy."[64] Yeats was certainly no Unionist; but to his contemporary readers it may well have appeared that the privileges of class he enjoyed may have made him willing to acquiesce a little longer in the continuation of the Union, under the complacencies of a thoroughgoing aestheticism.

Yeats's exclusively aesthetic definition of literature seemed likely to promote public tolerance of the intolerable. He spoke of pure tragedy, but would such plays lead to Irish resignation before British fate? He spoke of pure comedy, but such comedies—purified of political intent—might well promote further acquiescence by their belittlement of human problems. Finally, the "joy" of art that Yeats urged against the purposes of art might simply distract the audience from the historical pain of foreign domination, making it possible for them to bear such domination without complaint. Surely there is an appeal in a celebration of Life with a capital *L*, in Art with a capital *A*, but Dublin life in 1903 was for nationalists a matter for lamentation, harangue, rousing calls to action, and embittering nostalgia, not celebration. One nationalist who finally came out and admitted that, yes, he wanted "Art for Ireland's sake," "the handmaiden of Irish nationalism," said that for him there was only one question: "How are we to preserve ourselves from annihilation?"[65] The mild narcosis of aesthetic pleasure would, for this citizen, simply anaesthetize the Irish to the progressive mortification of their national

63. Kenneth Burke, *A Rhetoric of Motives* (Berkeley and Los Angeles: University of California Press, 1969), 28.
64. "Soerib," "Ireland's Danger," *United Irishman* 9, no. 216 (18 April 1903): 3.
65. "Cuguan," "The Play's the Thing," *United Irishman* 10, no. 246 (14 November 1903): 2.

being: the death of their language, their moral habits, and their spirit of resistance to Anglicization. Yeats consistently spoke of the intrinsic values of art; his critics, however, replied with reflections on the motives of the author and the consequences for the audience.

No one who has read through the plays printed week after week in the *United Irishman*—presumably, inspected and certified nationalist products—can fail to feel sympathy with Yeats's sense that although Ireland was a poor country, it was desperate indeed if it could afford no better literary showing than such plays offered. After Synge's play was performed, Griffith published a skit entitled *In a Real Wicklow Glen,* in which a wise old peasant woman discusses life in the Burke household many years after the tramp's visit. Nora has a string of children; she has grown to love old Dan Burke (how couldn't she love him, living together all those years? she explains); the once-young shepherd Michael Dara comes on the scene, ragged and bitter, but still lovelorn. Nora admits that once she preferred him, but since her parents would not bless their marriage, she feels she did right to put him out of her mind altogether. He is the bigger fool for not making something of his life. End of play. The author offhandedly sacrifices the conditions that created the original conflict—Nora's childlessness; her passionate nature; the terrors of the lonely glen; and the wild appeal of the tramp—in order to make his inevitable point: Irish women are virtuous. Even the nationalists who patronized performances of such dramas sometimes complained of their emptiness. Michael Blake wrote to the *United Irishman* a few months before the performance of *In the Shadow of the Glen* to lament that the authors of Gaelic plays "regard their work not as an art or craft, but as propagandism pure and simple." [66] *Ta na Francaighe ar an Muir,* for instance, was a playlet in the form of *King Lear:* it took ten minutes to read, was in five acts, with five years elapsing between the fourth and fifth act, and a cast of crowds. Alice Milligan and

66. Blake, "Two Irish Plays," *United Irishman* 10, no. 232 (8 August 1903): 6.

James Cousins, Griffith's staff writers for his weekly episodes of Irish Masterpiece Theatre, took longer dramatic flights, indeed, interminable ones, as act after act, brave Gael after vicious Saxon, they ground out Celtic Twilight dramatizations of Gaelic literature, fragrant of holy water and mouldy costumes. If Yeats's "pure art" lay under the suspicion of promoting acquiescence to political oppression, the "applied art" of the nationalists often accommodated the audience to sheer ineptitude.

As long as the problem is conceived as a choice between free "literature" and slavish "propaganda," literature will be obviously preferable, from both an artistic and any farsighted patriotic point of view. But Yeats's absolute distinction forces upon the reader an unreasonably limited choice between a writer with no conscious purpose and one with a single political purpose. Frank Lentricchia finds in Kenneth Burke's *Rhetoric of Motives* a passage that opens up an intermediate area of expression "that is not wholly deliberate, yet not wholly conscious."[67] This area "lies midway between aimless utterance and speech directly purposive," between, that is, art with no end but art, and art with the one end of a political message. A complex intellectual creation such as a play, it seems obvious, is going to be overdetermined. The writer will not simply be led by the forceless force of his imaginary characters' needs or guided by the purposiveness without purpose of aesthetic design. He will be pulled by a constellation in the night, unperceived forces and dimly seen lights, as well as by the single guiding star of Art that Yeats hails.

Yeats fashioned a statue of Synge as the ideal artist, "by nature unfitted to think a political thought,"[68] but Synge, though he had no wish to "get mixed up with a revolutionary and semi-military movement," had an interest in politics, deep political passions, and a fairly clear political philosophy.[69] As

67. Lentricchia, *Criticism and Social Change*, 159; Burke, *Rhetoric of Motives*, xiii.

68. WBY, *Essays and Introductions*, 319.

69. I have relied in this paragraph on Robin Skelton's "The Politics of J. M. Synge," *Massachusetts Review* 18, no. 1 (Spring 1977): 7–22.

Robin Skelton has shown, he was disposed by his reading of
Marx and William Morris to regard himself as a socialist with
an appreciation of traditional ways of life; in the Irish scheme
of things, he put himself down as a "temperate Nationalis[t]"
in a notebook from the late nineties. A member of a Protestant landowning family, Synge was obliged by his political beliefs to renounce his class when antagonism arose between
nationalists and Unionists, throwing in his lot with the poor,
the ignorant, and the Catholic; he was, however, disposed by
his whole training in life to find the neighborhood unpleasant. He was at once enamored with the traditional sanctities
of peasant life and disgusted by the "cruder powers of the
Irish mind." He hoped that the "half-cultured classes" of the
towns would come under the sway of the truly cultured writers expressing themselves in English,[70] but he recognized
that, in John Eglinton's words, "the interest of the whole nation lay in extirpating the conditions which produced" Irish
Protestant literature.[71] Out of these sharp divisions between
his public commitments and private hopes, his recent political sympathies and vestigial social snobbery, Synge fashioned
the attitude of mind expressed in his works. Like the characters of Anatole France whom he admired, he kept himself
healthy by an ironical attitude to his own distress, "a humor-
ous optimism" as answer to a frankly bleak forecast. His ironical appetite for incongruity was especially excited, as Yeats
allows, by nearness to his Irish audience.[72] Their shibboleths
delighted his sarcasm, inflated his capriciousness, and drove
him to make mischief in the camp of true believers. Synge
had the artistic temperament of a satirist who thrives on conditions of possible censorship; he flirted with punishments,
flaunted his boldness. He wanted, as he later said, to "make
them hop."[73] When writing *In the Shadow of the Glen*, Synge
knew he was needling the Catholic Irish about their sexual

70. J. M. Synge, "The Old and the New in Ireland," *Academy and Literature*, 6 September 1902; rpt. in Synge, 2:382–86.
71. John Eglinton, *Irish Literary Portraits* (London, 1935), 26.
72. WBY, *Essays and Introductions*, 327.
73. Synge, 2:283.

"squeamishness"; writing to his friend Stephen MacKenna, he as much as admits the play is, among other things, an attack on Irish marriage customs, in an anarchic celebration of "volcanic forces."[74] This is not to imply that Synge's play is doctrinaire in any sense of the word, only to suggest the political complexities of motive in the author and the degree of oppositional force within the play itself.

8

Just as "literature" is not so pure an entity as Yeats proposed, the "propaganda" nationalists expected of the Irish National Theatre was not as strictly defined as he claimed. Both Griffith and Moran, while glad of nationalist propaganda when it was provided, were satisfied with national entertainment of any kind. Plays such as *The Pot of Broth, The Racing Lug, Broken Soil,* and *The Hour-Glass*—former INTS productions—do not simply dramatize a page from Thomas Davis's *Spirit of a Nation,* but all these plays met with approval from the nationalist papers. Moran in fact made a point of stating that any "National Unity that is worth having, that is not a worse evil than national chaos, must be the flower of a number of movements for the creation and fostering of all the elements, spiritual and material, that go to the making of a nation."[75] Moran wanted to allow each movement liberty to work in its own way, but liberty for him did not mean freedom from criticism. Both he and Griffith explicitly granted Yeats the liberty to write what he pleased; they asked that he grant them the liberty to criticize according to their lights. Moran's version of tolerance was a brawl of opinions: "Papers and people will often hit below the belt, and good men will be misrepresented; steady and necessary work may be unjustly belittled and laughed at, and cranks may become uncomfortably numerous. But for all that, liberty with such drawbacks will go further in a week than

74. Greene and Stephens, *Synge,* 156.
75. Moran, *Philosophy of Irish Ireland,* 78.

one 'strong' organization, bounded . . . by rules, definitions, pedantries . . . will go in a year."[76] It misconstrues the facts to make Yeats the sole apostle of liberty and the nationalists a vanguard of Leninists enforcing party discipline.

What the nationalists expected of the Irish National Theatre was not that it confine itself to agitprop, but that it sail clear of challenges to the overt ideology of its audience, or that it stand the storm when this ideology was offended. Doubtless, this expectation places some constriction on the artist, especially an artist like Synge whose genius fulfills itself precisely in such sailing across the wind through dangerous waters. But it allowed most Irish writers great latitude in what they wrote. Yeats, for instance, who himself had some "genius for making mischief in a small place,"[77] never succeeded in stimulating the audience to make a political attack upon any of his own plays after *The King's Threshold* (which itself simply shouldered part of the blame directed at Synge's half of the double bill). In *Deirdre* (1907), Yeats went further than Synge in making an Irish heroine give utterance to sexual desire. Yeats's Irish queen knows "nothing but this body, nothing / But that old vehement, bewildering kiss"; she revels in the memory that she "woke the passion that's in all"; but it is of the kiss and the passion of her husband Naoise she speaks.[78] After his murder, she promises to be the bed partner of Conchubar, tempting him by promising that he will stir more passion in her than Naoise could, but she only says these things, it transpires, as part of a plot to kill herself and save her virtue. Deirdre may have appeared to be idle, prurient, petulant, and hard to please; but in fact, she was just a good Irish wife trying to keep her man. Because Yeats showed respect for the overt ideology of the Irish by confining his glamorization of "sin" to an exemplum of "virtue," no nationalist threw an obstacle in the play's path to popularity.[79] In

76. Ibid., 70.
77. Frank Fay to Maire Garvey, 26 April 1909; Hogan and Kilroy, 3:308.
78. Alspach, 376, 382.
79. See Lentricchia, *Criticism and Social Change*, 104, for discussion of the concepts of "respect for overt ideology" and the "ideology of form."

Synge's play, however, there is an obvious violation of the ideology of form: Nora is, by Irish lights, a bad wife: she is too easy with strangers, has a young fellow down the hill, does not respect her husband, complains about her life, and does not have any kids—a plain failure as an Irish wife. Her final act, when she departs with the walk of a queen, is therefore "incorrect" because it violates the repetitive structure of "bad wife" examples. The nationalists objected not that Synge refused to write according to their dictation (no dictation was, or could be, provided), but that he offended their sense of what was both politically and aesthetically correct.

Given that there are degrees of conscious intent in all literature, and that nationalists were not requiring all INTS plays to serve the cause, one may question the original dichotomy of literature and propaganda. Yeats originated his distinction by a classification on the basis of artistic purpose. In a rejoinder to Yeats, "Sarsfield," writing on "The Artistic Value of Propagandist Poetry," classified plays according to their inspiration and effects, claiming that propaganda was not a separate category from literature, but a kind of literature inspired by love of country, just as love poetry was inspired by romantic attachments, religious poetry by love of God, and speculative poetry by academic interests.[80] Propaganda, Sarsfield claimed, might express an idea, convey a lesson, or make an impression just as well as any other type of literature, often better, since love of country was a more general feeling among the people than, for instance, love of academic speculation. Ceann Maor leapt on Sarsfield's bandwagon with his own curse on "the Slobbering Lyric" of the Celtic Twilight and an anthology of quotations condemning "the Anaemic School of Criticism" raised up to dignify feminine, obscure, and ineffectual literature.[81] Ceann Maor, speaking up for "the plain people of Ireland" against the pale hierophants of "Art," even

80. "Sarsfield," "The Artistic Value of Propaganda Poetry," *United Irishman* 14, no. 350 (11 November 1905): 4.

81. "Ceann Maor," "The Artistic Value of Propaganda Poetry," *United Irishman* 14, no. 351 (18 November 1905): 6.

prints his own version of the true stuff: a bold prophetic ballad in the manner of Thomas Davis. While Sarsfield and Ceann Maor originally claimed only that propaganda was one kind of literature, they gradually give the clear impression that, for all true Irishmen, it is the only kind that counts. What is missing in the debate is the realization that any single work can be classified with respect to its form, motives, or consequences. Classified by form, all plays are "literature"; by consequences, they are "propaganda." If we examine more closely the motives of the author and the embeddedness of the play in history, we are forced to overcome the dichotomy of literature/propaganda and address the politics of form and the aesthetics of struggle. Yeats knew better than anyone that his own plays and poems, and those of all writers of the Irish Revival, arose because their "moral nature [had] been aroused by political sacrifices, and [their] imagination by a political preoccupation with [Ireland's] destiny."[82] It is a paradox that one of the most vigorous twentieth-century defenses of literature against propaganda came from the modern poet with the most intimate sense of the political character of contemporary life and letters. Yeats, however, had a theatre on the condition that he could show Horniman that the INTS was not a "political sideshow"; he had mastery within that theatre if he could demonstrate that "literature" was a thing unto itself, high and holy, justified and needing no justification.

9

It is remarkable that Yeats was left defending a position he agreed to call "art for art's sake" when his own play offers a meditation on a passage from Nietzsche profoundly criticizing this very slogan.[83] Frances Oppel argues persuasively the pertinence of Nietzsche's "Skirmishes of an Untimely Man" in *Twilight of the Idols* to Seanchan's defense of his poetry in

82. "The Irish Literary Theatre," *Beltaine* 1, no. 2 (February 1900): 23.
83. WBY, *Explorations*, 200.

The King's Threshold. Nietzsche says that the "fight against purpose in art is always a fight against the moralizing tendency in art," but it does not follow, he claims, that when moral preaching is removed from art, art is therefore "purposeless, aimless, senseless—in short, *l'art pour l'art.*" In fact, all art praises, glorifies, chooses, prefers, and in this way "strengthens or weakens certain valuations." Nietzsche concludes that "art is the great stimulus to life."[84] According to Oppel, "This argument is the central theme and subject of Yeats's play."[85]

Even if this claim is extravagant, it must be allowed that Seanchan gives a host of examples of how poetry *strengthens or weakens certain valuations* and, all in all, stimulates us to life. First, he leads his student Senias to speak memorable lines on why poetry is honored:

> . . . the poets hung
> Images of the life that was in Eden
> About the child-bed of the world, that it,
> Looking upon those images, might bear
> Triumphant children.[86]

In Nietzsche's terms, the poet makes images of human perfection that show people the limits of the possible; without such images, future humanity would be disadvantaged, like the cripples who linger on stage in Yeats's play. Poets make the "golden cradle" in which basic values are born and nurtured.[87] Because poets "christened gold," Seanchan tells the chamberlain, the king's golden crown consecrates his office, and his money has purchasing power. Had not poets praised courage, men would not dare fight in battle; had they not sung of beauty, young people would not have been stimulated to love, and to love a certain kind of beauty most.[88]

84. Friedrich Nietzsche, *The Case of Wagner, Nietzsche contra Wagner, The Twilight of the Idols, The Antichrist,* trans. Thomas Common (London: H. Henry, 1896), 186.
85. Oppel, *Mask and Tragedy,* 141.
86. Alspach, 264; lines 129ff.
87. Alspach, 266; line 172.
88. Alspach, 290; lines 519–35.

Nietzsche's arguments and Yeats's examples express a fundamental truth of the power of literature and culture as a whole: the idea of what it is to be human—to love, fight, and rule—is historically shaped in a process by which artificial symbols become natural truths.

At the same time, however, the struggle over Synge's play and Yeats's theatrical policy was itself a part of this historical process of self-definition. Those who objected to Synge's Nora also believed that art "strengthens or weakens certain valuations"; they simply objected to strengthening the value of erotic fulfillment and weakening the value of marital fidelity. Should such deeds as Nora's departure with a lively young tramp be performed on stage, indeed celebrated there, what would be the consequences for Irish households? For Nietzsche and Yeats, this might be a tonic for exuberant "life," but for an Irish Catholic public, "life" is not necessarily made up of emotionalism, sexual desire, individualism, and attachment to this world. Confronted by his critics, and awaited by Horniman, Yeats retreated several steps from a Nietzschean understanding of the thoroughgoing effectuality of art, and was finally thrown into the position of defending "pure art," "art for art's sake."

10

Yeats's distinction between literature and propaganda served another purpose as well: if propaganda was not literature, then it was, obviously, not Irish national literature, and no part of the INTS program. Arthur Griffith, finding this rhetoric of terminology confusing, expressly took issue with Yeats when he pigeonholed certain obviously propagandistic works as "political": "We should call them National," Griffith rejoined. "The people in this country are not yet marshalled into Liberals and Conservatives. They are still the Irish Nation and the English Garrison." [89] In the idiom of Dublin na-

89. *United Irishman* 10, no. 242 (17 October 1903): 1.

tionalists, "political" was often limited to its most narrow and pejorative denotation. After the fall of Parnell, many Irish patriots—Yeats included—had turned away from parliamentary politics to labor on behalf of Ireland in other ways. Groups such as Douglas Hyde's Gaelic League, Horace Plunkett's Irish Cooperative Association, and Griffith's own Sinn Fein all insisted that they were not "political" organizations, they were "national." By the use of this vague language, Hyde, Plunkett, and Griffith aimed to escape government repression, to distinguish their movements from the bankrupt shenanigans of the Parnellites and anti-Parnellites, and to invite both Home Rulers and separatists, Irish-Irelanders and Unionists to come together and make common cause.[90] Politics was just a name, in this idiom, for the activity of eighty-six members in Westminster, along with a few hundred rebels sent to jail, and some thousands who occasionally marched in processions to a drum and fife band; there were other ways, beyond politics, for the rest of the population to show that they were Irish.[91] They could be marshaled to speak Gaelic, wear tweed, improve the dairy system, or support the theatre. It is obvious that these cultural organizations—the Irish National Theatre included—were political in every respect except party affiliation. Under the cloak of adherence to no party, they aimed to form policy, spread propaganda, infiltrate existing organizations, lay the groundwork for local government, and prepare for national independence. While for the impartial observer, *all* the activities of cultural nationalism were political, and for Griffith, Hyde, Plunkett, and others, *none* of them were "political," Yeats created confusion by saying *some* national plays were "political" and some were not.

This was not playing the game. By blowing the cover of a

90. For discussions of Irish usage of the term "political," see Nicholas Mansergh, *The Irish Question, 1840–1921* (Toronto: University of Toronto Press, 1965; 3d ed. 1975), 269; Oliver MacDonagh, *States of Mind: A Study of Anglo-Irish Conflict, 1790–1980* (London: George Allen & Unwin, 1983), 62, and D. George Boyce, *Nationalism in Ireland* (Baltimore: Johns Hopkins University Press, 1982), 295.
91. Moran, *Philosophy of Irish Ireland*, 66.

broadly tolerant patriotic movement, it tended to expose irreconcilable versions of the political future of Ireland held by
the different participants. Hitherto, some members of the cultural organizations had looked forward to a republic, some
to a dual monarchy, others to a preservation of the current
union with Great Britain; all these worked side by side with
members envisioning socialist, capitalist, or semi-feudal economic systems; Catholic and Gaelic, Anglo-Irish, British,
or continental societies. Once the cultural movement was
opened to directly political discussion, the broad coalition
was bound to break into factions along the lines of religious,
class, and political stress. The debate over the aims of "The
Irish National Theatre" did not, of course, halt the progress
of the massive movement of cultural nationalism, but it exploded the appearance of silent consensus on what Ireland as
a nation was and ought to become. In order to highlight
Yeats's own definition of a national theatre, a survey follows
of seven definitions of an Irish national theatre, all put on the
table for discussion in Dublin, 1900–1905, and most of them
represented in the quarrels following the October 1903 INTS
productions.

In September 1900 the sharp-tongued D. P. Moran characteristically supplied both the most hard-headed definition of
the actual national literature of Ireland and the most extreme
definition of its ideal literature. "A Nation's literature," he argued, "is no more and no less than what the people read."
The National Library of Ireland, therefore, was not the collection of books shelved in the institution of that name on
Kildare Street; not the series of titles published by Fisher &
Unwin, mostly favorites of Young Ireland; not the works of
the "Celtic Renaissance"; instead, "The National Library
of Ireland is simply Eason & Sons' warehouse, the railway
bookstalls, and the newsagents' shops." Similarly the national theatre consisted of musical comedies, melodramas,
variety shows, pantomimes, and itinerant Shakespeare productions.[92] Moran was not happy about the fact that Irish

92. Moran, "A Nation's Literature," *Leader*, 22 September 1900, 54.

literature was "mostly of a gutter kind, and partly indecent," neither Irish nor literary. That was simply the way things were among the denationalized throng of modern Ireland. The way things ought to be, to his way of thinking, self-respecting, moral, Gaelic-speaking citizens would support an Irish literature that was just what the name said: literature in the Irish language. To realize this ideal, the Gaelic League had to educate the entire nation in its largely lost tongue, the Irish Ireland movement had to turn the people away from English customs, and the "English who happened to be born in Ireland" had to accept the fact that Ireland was a Catholic country.

Between the extremes of Moran's actual deracinated Ireland and his potential Catholic, Gaelic Irish Ireland, other groups entered their candidates for Ireland and its theatre. The third definition comes from William Martin Murphy, capitalist owner of tramways and Catholic nationalist dailies, and Yeats's bête noire. Murphy had his own scheme for the theatrical entertainment of the Irish. He noted approvingly that films and plays were provided by the state in Russia, so that with a cheap ticket peasants could escape their distress. This would be better, Murphy thought, than the "strange, weird one-act metaphysical meanderings about ghouls and faeries in blank verse" that the INTS "thrust upon a suffering people."[93] In addition, the entertainment of the Irish Catholic masses could then be supervised to prevent their being corrupted by indecency and foreign decadence, without putting them to the trouble of learning Gaelic. From this program for "national" entertainments spreads a vision of a petty capitalist Irish nation, with a thoroughly exploited lower class gulled by patriotism and kept in line by clerical supervision.

In the fourth definition of Irish National Theatre, Maud Gonne showed the sentimental side of the physical force republican movement. She was also concerned with the threat

---

93. William M. Murphy, Daniel Tallon, Joseph Mooney, and Count Moore, letter to the editor, *Evening Herald;* rpt. in *United Irishman* 9, no. 212 (21 March 1903): 3.

of foreign influence on workers and peasants. The peasants, in her rapture, are "the hidden spring from which flow the seven springs of Gaelic inspiration:"[94] what arises from peasant life, and returns to it, is for her Irish national theatre. The literature of towns is foreign to them, thus to the nation; the literature of art is too difficult for them, thus for the nation. But unlike the aim of abject escapism of capitalist Murphy, with his plan for the factory production of a national opiate, the ruling principle of Maud Gonne's program is revolt against British tyranny. *Cathleen ni Houlihan,* in which she played the title role, is her ideal of an incendiary folk theatre; the Paris Reign of Terror, a violent and messianic birth of "democracy," is her vision of Irish government.

Fifth, some Dublin members of the Gaelic League, one generation removed from tillage, were not so enamored of peasant life as Maud Gonne, a colonel's daughter. As G. J. Watson explains, "Paddy and his Pig" was a little too close to home for them.[95] They wanted a Gaelic theatre, but one modeled on the best foreign plays, Ibsen's *A Doll's House* and *Hedda Gabler.* For these intellectuals of the towns, clerical supervision and pantomimes of traditional stories would leave Ireland always a provincial backwater: they wanted to join Europe as a separate, modern nation.

In his response to Maud Gonne's article, J. B. Yeats spoke for Anglo-Irish intellectuals in providing yet another example, to supplement the five already discussed. He refused to see the question as either political or difficult. It was obvious to him that Synge's play was as Irish as the lakes of Killarney, just because it arose on Irish soil from an Irish writer. Everything made in Ireland, by people living in Ireland, was Irish. That much was simple; the hard question was determining if a work was art. As to foreign influences, for JBY the old Brit-

94. Maud Gonne MacBride, "A National Theatre," *United Irishman* 10, no. 243 (24 October 1903): 2–3.

95. Watson, *Irish Identity and the Literary Revival* (New York: Barnes & Noble, 1979), 25ff.

ish liberal policy was good enough: "In art matters, as in the commerce of ideas, there must always be free trade."[96] This open view of a broad, free, and intellectual culture is characteristic of the Home Rule Protestants, whose claim to being Irish was often residence, not religion, language, or race. It is, in fact, similar to the sentiments of Synge on the question of an Irish national theatre. Like J. B. Yeats, Synge thought that if "you do not a like a work that is passing itself off as national art, you had better show it is not art. If it is good art, it is vain for you to try and show it is not national."[97]

The seventh and final definition is provided by the largest group of nationalists, those walking in the path of Thomas Davis's Young Ireland movement, who would have been happy to show that certain plays by Irishmen about Ireland were not Irish. That is just what the whole dispute about *In the Shadow of the Glen* concerned. From the poetry of Milligan, William Rooney, and Eithne Carbery, the novels of Charles Kickham, the memoirs of Wolfe Tone, the historical writings of A. M. Sullivan, and the plays of Seamus O'Sullivan and Padraig Colum, this group gathered a lofty view of the Irish character, in which piety, bravery, love of land and nation, and concern for family predominated.[98] If the characters in a play did not have these qualities, then, according to this group, the play was not Irish. While the Davisite nationalists officially supported the Gaelic League, many (such as Arthur Griffith himself) were never able actually to learn Irish; therefore, they were satisfied with a national theatre that staged plays in English that upheld their lofty view of the Irish character. More a tradition of sentiment than a political ideology, it is difficult to project into the future the Ireland this large audience discovered in its fond look on Ireland's past. Per-

96. John Butler Yeats, "The Irish National Theatre," *United Irishman* 10, no. 244 (31 October 1903): 7.

97. Greene and Stephens, *Synge*, 150–51.

98. Boyce, "The Battle of Three Civilizations," in *Nationalism in Ireland*, 243ff.

haps it was just the Ireland that came to be: a patriotic nation, Catholic by constitution, primarily middle-class, capitalist with light industries and trade (Yeats: "a nation of shop-keepers"), and a paternalist state.

11

After his October 1903 *Samhain* statement that he himself was most interested in an Irish National Theatre Society with "no propaganda but that of good art,"[99] Yeats dealt in turn with very nearly each of the groups supporting the many positions described above. He flattered Hyde's Gaelic theatre, hinted that Moran's moral Catholic theatre was English-imported puritanism, ridiculed the idolatry of Murphy's Catholic newspaper and commended to Irish nationalists the example of Russian revolutionaries, utterly ignored Maud Gonne's letter (allowing his father to speak for him), and treated Griffith's Davisite nationalists to a long critique of the empty rhetoric of the Young Ireland writers.[100] In short, he fought back, delighting in battle, one man against the town, always aiming to get in the last word. Usually, as a matter of fact, he got in the best words, whose only shortcoming was that they were too fine for the occasion. In a few instances, Arthur Griffith bested him, as when Yeats had defined a nationalist as "one who is prepared to give up a great deal that he may preserve to his country whatever part of her possessions he is best fitted to guard," and Griffith rejoined that Yeats parceled himself out with the ethics of an "impeccable grocer," asking if this was the same playwright who had Cathleen ni Houlihan say, "If anyone would give me help, he must give me himself, he must give me all."[101] But these skirmishes did not bring out a full-fledged definition of national theatre from Yeats, only a fierce defense of the freedom of the author.

99. WBY, *Explorations*, 100.
100. Ibid., 114–23.
101. Arthur Griffith, "All Ireland," *United Irishman* 10, no. 242 (17 October 1903): 1.

A year later, in the 1904 *Samhain,* Yeats worked out a definition, but it is clear that in 1903 he was operating on the assumption of the sort of national theatre discussed, not in Dublin, in any of its forms, but in London. Literary men in the English theatre, such as Granville-Barker, had broached the idea of an art theatre subsidized by the state, mainly for literary drama and Shakespeare revivals.[102] In the London discussion, questions of language, religion, or national identity were not at issue; the only concerns were art and a subsidy to free the artists from public taste. Yeats's 1903 notion of an Irish national theatre as a dwelling place "for the capricious spirit that bloweth as it listeth" had its origin in these London discussions and the Horniman subsidy.

In his 1904 *Samhain* statement of "First Principles," Yeats elaborates on his vision of a national theatre, replying to his Irish critics while not offending his English patron's ban on politics. According to *Samhain,* what makes an Irish writer is not that he writes in Irish, pleads the national cause, expresses Irish morality, or creates typical Irish characters; not even that he is inspired by Irish literary traditions; certainly not that he executes in his plays the will of the people, or any will but his own. It becomes difficult to see what is left for a writer to do who wishes to be Irish. For Yeats, however, that person's wish should be to make himself not Irish but a writer. Do that and he would be Irish enough. Ultimately, Yeats says, only five or six people have the right to call themselves Irish, people who usually belong, he believes, to the leisured class (read Protestant population), whose thought is *harder* and *more masterful* than that of others; these have, he adds, an *essential nearness to reality.*[103] The essay goes a step farther than the 1903 pronouncements. They made the author responsible only to himself; this makes a claim for one class—the one that included Yeats, Lady Gregory, and J. M. Synge—having a commanding view of the truth of things. By this time, Yeats

102. Dennis Kennedy, *Granville-Barker and the Dream of Theatre* (Cambridge: Cambridge University Press, 1986).
103. WBY, *Explorations,* 147.

had been given the Abbey Theatre by Horniman; he was president of the Irish National Theatre; his plays, along with those of Synge and Gregory, were its dramatic literature; and he was ready to make the extraordinary claim that he and his friends *were* the Irish nation. The long struggle of "stealing back and forth the symbols of authority" had come to end; Yeats and his friends owned them; they minted the coin of the realm.

The boldness of the poet is breathtaking. It is as if he heard Zarathustra's call: "Out of you, who have chosen yourselves, there shall grow a chosen people—and out of them, the over-man." [104] His virtue was not to serve the people, but to *be* the people, acting on behalf of a constituency yet to be born, his majority having only to go through the formality of becoming fact: "[National literature] is the work of writers who are moulded by influences moulding their country, and *who write out of so deep a life that they are accepted there in the end* [italics added]." [105] But more than any political ambition, Yeats was actuated by what Nietzsche calls "the terrible egotism of the artist, which is justified by the work he must do, as the mother by the child she will bear." [106] It is, of course, not *decent* to act like a superman, and after Yeats had taken the tonic of Nietzschean philosophy, he acted as if he had begun to hang out with a bad crowd—bullies and dandies and a crypto-fascist elite. His father, best friend, and Horniman herself all later complained of his domineering behavior, pinning the blame on Nietzsche. [107] But if we recoil from the Yeats who

104. Friedrich Nietzsche, *Thus Spoke Zarathrustra,* in *The Portable Nietzsche,* ed. Walter Kaufmann (New York: Viking Press, 1954), 189.
105. WBY, *Explorations,* 156.
106. Nietzsche, *On the Genealogy of Morals,* trans. Walter Kaufmann and R. J. Hollingdale (New York: Vintage Books, 1968), 220.
107. See George William Russell (Æ) to WBY [May 1903], in George Russell, *Letters from AE,* ed. Alan Denson (London: Abelard-Schuman, 1962), 46–47; Russell to George Moore [6 April 1916], in ibid., 109–10; J. B. Yeats to WBY [1906], in *J. B. Yeats: Letters to His Son W. B. Yeats and Others, 1869–1922,* ed. Joseph Hone (1944; London: Secker & Warburg, 1983), 97; J. B. Yeats to WBY, 24 March 1909, in *Letters,* ed. Hone, 117; Annie Horniman to Yeats, 23 and 26 December 1909 (ms. 13608, NLI). This issue is discussed below in chs. 4 and 6.

wishes to dominate others, we admire the Yeats who always goes onward to overcome himself, who finds fault with his best deeds or discovers his powerlessness over the woman he loves. Indeed, such moments of self-overcoming in poetry would lack salt had he not first overcome others. What portion of the power of his poetry over us is derived from failure, ours to be better than we are, his to be best of all? The attractions of literature may not always be attributable to Christian or humanitarian or universal ethical values, or to democratic or individualist or traditional political values. Like Nietzsche's spectators at an ancient Greek theatre, perhaps we crowd around the stage with a thirst for violence and for tragedy, to watch a man who would be great articulate the limitations of being.

4

Authors and Actors

The Irish National Theatre Society, Ltd., as a Joint Stock Enterprise

On 27 December 1904, in buildings that had once housed the General Emigration Agent, the Dublin Total Abstinence Society, and a morgue, the Irish National Theatre Society opened the doors of the Abbey Theatre.[1] In a reappraisal of the Irish theatre movement, David H. Greene and Edward M. Stephens conclude that when W. B. Yeats mounted the stage to welcome the public, he had a right to feel proud:

> Standing on the stage of the new theatre, speaking to an audience of six hundred people, Yeats might have felt that he was standing on the threshold of the most considerable achievement of his career. The dramatic movement in Ireland had been his doing more than any other's, and the new theatre was the tangible embodiment of his vision. He had conceived the idea as a patriotic undertaking, but he had not hesitated to alienate it from the environment which gave it its meaning when he felt that that environment threatened to stultify it. He had discovered both Lady Gregory and Synge and directed their undeveloped talents. If he had not discovered the Fays,

1. In 1830 the property housed the Theatre Royal, which gave miscellaneous entertainments, excluding straight dramas. In 1839 the building was burned; after restoration, it opened under various names—Princess's Theatre, New Princess Theatre of Varieties, People's Music Hall, and remarkably, the National Theatre, by which name it was known up to three years before Horniman's purchase. The premises in Marlborough Street housed the General Emigration Agent in 1840; in 1863 the National Brotherhood of St. Patrick (a recruiting organization for the Fenians) took over the premises; following the Brotherhood was the Dublin Total Abstinence Society, for which the Fays sometimes performed in the late 1890s. Gerard Fay gathers this information in *The Abbey Theatre: Cradle of Genius* (New York: Macmillan, 1958), 79.

they at least discovered him. He was ruthless in getting his own way. He had eliminated Edward Martyn and George Moore as soon as the price of living with them had become too high. He had survived the defection of two of his best actors. A theatre had been created for his use, and it was beyond the influence of anyone except Miss Horniman. His plays and players had created an audience and impressed English audiences and critics. Nobody will now deny that he had been right in proclaiming that the only real service an artist can render his country is producing good art.[2]

This summary puts the poet's massive activity on behalf of an Irish theatre under the category of "personal achievements," and, surely, Yeats as much as anyone is entitled to claim the credit involved. He had first had the idea of an Irish theatre in the 1890s; now he stood inside the realization of that idea as president of the Irish National Theatre Society and author of the main event on the first program, the verse-play *On Baile's Strand*. Greene and Stephens balance the achievements against their costs, noting that Yeats froze out his friends, stood his ground against the political complaints of his best actors,[3] put himself under obscure obligations to his English patron, and made every ideal take second place to art; these things, they conclude, are the path to "the most considerable achievement of his career."

There is no better time to admit a generous admiration for the poet than when he is standing on the Abbey stage on 27 December 1904. Seeing history as the biography of a great man, however, has limits even in literary study. Greene and Stephens guard against the biographical fallacy by a careful choice of phrase: the dramatic movement's being "more [Yeats's] doing than any other's" implies that many others did

2. Greene and Stephens, *J. M. Synge, 1871–1909* (New York: Macmillan, 1959), 173.
3. Dudley Digges and Maire T. Quinn resigned in protest against the performance of *In the Shadow of the Glen*. Under the guidance of Maud Gonne (who also resigned from the directorate), they joined the Cumann na nGaedheal Theatre Company, before leaving in the summer of 1904 to perform Irish plays at the St. Louis World's Fair (Hogan and Kilroy, 2:75; Maire nic Shiubhlaigh, *The Splendid Years*, [Dublin: James Duffy, 1955], 41–43).

their part as well, without claiming that all Yeats did was for the best of Irish theatre, or that without his efforts—say, if he had stayed in London with the Masquers in 1903—there would have been no Irish dramatic renaissance. Yeats's involvement, they note, placed the theatre movement beyond the influence of its audience ("alienate[d] from the environment that gave it its meaning") and under the influence of Horniman: a strange position for a national theatre, quaking with its own sort of stress. While the principle Yeats fought for, and Greene and Stephens say no one will now deny— "the only real service an artist can render his country is producing good art"—seems to me an incomplete statement of the complex relations between literature and politics, their vision of literary history through Yeats's eyes is admirably free of both apologetics and moral preaching.

This perspective still needs to be supplemented by others, however grand a view one gets from where Yeats stands, at stage front, looking out at a full house on opening night at the Abbey. There were also those in the lobby, in the wings, and back in the greenroom—all necessary to the movement—who had their own understanding of its nature and purpose, and whose points of view are neglected at the cost of distortion. We know from a close relative of the leading actress Maire nic Shiublaigh, or Mary Walker, that there were five members of the Walker family going about the business of the theatre that night.[4] Two were selling programs in the lobby; one was stitching last-minute repairs in costumes backstage; and the remaining two—Mary Walker and her brother Frank—were waiting behind the curtain to go on stage in important roles. The Walkers, who had been with the National Theatre Society from the beginning, had joined because a flair for acting ran in the family, and because the family was profoundly committed to Irish nationalism. This was something the nation was doing on its own, and, in the spirit of Sinn Fein, they threw themselves into the theatre movement and helped as much as they could.

4. Edward Kenny, preface to Nic Shiublaigh, *Splendid Years,* xv.

The Walkers were not the only family that made a great contribution to the Irish National Theatre Society. The Fay brothers took in hand stage-management, occasional scene-painting, actor-training, and key dramatic roles, with W. G. starring in peasant comedies, and Frank in verse tragedies. On opening night, W. G. Fay would have been barking orders at the Walkers and others, seeing to it that the actors knew their cues and took things seriously; his brother Frank was usually pale, cold, and distant on opening nights.[5] Somewhere backstage, he was exercising his voice as he prepared to go on stage as Cuchulain in *On Baile's Strand*, a role for which he lacked the stature and appearance, but had, abundantly, the powers of elocution. The Allgood sisters—from yet another theatrical family—were playful and excited on opening nights, more stage-struck than professional, more professional than patriotic. For them, this was their moment in the spotlight before a full house. Neither George Roberts nor Maire Garvey had their sort of talent or their sort of ambition; Roberts was the organizer, sometime secretary, supporting actor, and publisher, arranging for printing of the evening's theatre program and the house journal, *Samhain*. On this evening, remembering that he was the one who had first suggested in 1901 to the Fays that they produce Æ's *Deirdre*, George Roberts had reason to reflect that it was his impetus that had brought the theatre opening to pass.[6] His fiancée Maire Garvey was a better actress than he was an actor and was equally committed to the political ideals of the movement.

These people were not a collection of extras and stars on special contract. In the movement at the start, they had been the movement ever since. Although they did not, in general, join in hope of money or stardom, the members of the com-

5. Fay was "anxious" and "irritable" not only on opening nights, or previous to appearing before London critics, but also during rehearsals "when things don't come right," as he explains to Maire Garvey in a letter postmarked 8 November 1904 (ms. 8320 [8], NLI).

6. Hogan and Kilroy, 2:28, records Roberts's claim that the Irish National Theatre Society was founded at his suggestion with a capital of less than five pounds.

pany were moved by a variety of other motives: an interest in
theatre business or theatre arts; out of pure love of performance or commitment to the national cause. On one hand,
there were the Walkers, who, in addition to liking theatre and
having a flair for acting, were profoundly committed to national theatre because of their republican convictions. The
theatre was their way of making a revolution; when there was
a better way in 1916, Maire Walker gave up the stage for the
streets, serving as a nurse in Jacob's Biscuit Factory, one of the
Dublin locations held by the Irish Republican Brotherhood
(IRB). On the other hand, there was W. G. Fay, for whom theatre was a trade, not a cause. He had plied this trade for years
in the local entertainment markets of Dublin and in provincial
towns, getting up tableaus and skits with amateur actors and
an all-purpose drop-scene; opening night at the Abbey was
for him the fulfillment of a business he had started and managed throughout.[7]

As Padraic Colum remembers it, the real fuel on which the
movement operated was national enthusiasm.[8] The actors'
eagerness for political independence gave them the solidarity
and intensity of a sect, and the high spirits of a social club. It
made these, for Mary Walker, worthy of the title *The Splendid
Years.* In the summer of 1902, when they banded together and
before Yeats joined them, they had agreed that all should
work, and all be equal, and that they should not surrender
their amateur status until they had made enough money to
become a professional group independent of patrons. They

7. W. G. Fay and Catherine Carswell, *The Fays of the Abbey Theatre: An Autobiographical Record,* (New York: Harcourt, Brace, 1935), 105–6, and passim.
Fay says the Abbey Theatre "was the creation not of men of letters but of
actors."

8. Padraic Colum, *The Road round Ireland* (New York: Macmillan, 1926),
275. Seamus O'Sullivan (pen name for James Starkey), another original member of the INTS, corroborates Colum in "The National Theatre": "enthusiasm
made up for all defects" of the amateur actors; they were "convinced [their]
enthusiasm was . . . 'making history'"; because of the democratic, amateur
character of the organization, "All had their particular work to do, and all did
it . . . enthusiastically." According to O'Sullivan, the many books on the
INTS had all made one mistake: "attributing the movement to one man
only . . . Yeats" (*The Rose and the Bottle* [Dublin: Talbot Press, 1946], 116–26).

were a nest of families, a workshop of amateurs, and a cell of political revolutionaries.

On the opening night of the Abbey, surely a number of them thought, as several later wrote, that they were what had made the Irish theatre come to be, and not Horniman who had bought the hall or the poet at stage front taking his bows and making grand speeches. That is just what they had got him for: Yeats was to be the figurehead, as Æ told him when the presidency was offered, "the gilding at the prow of the vessel," [9] not its captain, not its crew.

2

According to Padraic Colum, who moved both in the circle of actors in Camden Street and in the company of the authors in the garden at Coole, the original members of the society for a long time regarded Yeats as a "great poet, an influential literateur, and a dramatist more concerned with lyrical lines than with situations. They did not suspect he was an excellent business man . . . and that it was his ambition to be the director of the movement." [10] But as Colum came to realize, Yeats had big plans: at forty, Shakespeare had already had the Globe; Goethe had had the Weimar Theatre; Yeats had to have the Abbey.

In December 1904 it was doubtful just who had the Abbey and who was in control of the Irish National Theatre Society. Although it had surrendered much of its original democracy—members no longer had much to say about who played what parts, or where the company toured, or what program it staged—the society was still constituted under rules of gover-

9. Lady Gregory quotes Æ's letter in *Our Irish Theatre* (New York: Capricorn Books, 1965), 31. When Frederick Ryan wrote to WBY asking him to serve as president of the "National Dramatic Society," he told him that the first order of business was for the president to make a speech on the plans and prospects of the new organization, "and of course there is no one who could do it so well as you." Yeats, it appears, was elected as a speech-maker by members who did not realize what he might say (Finneran, Harper, and Murphy, 2:102).

10. Colum, *Road round Ireland*, 278.

nance. These rules had been drawn up by Æ in February 1903 in order to prevent either a literary or a political veto of a play. The rules guaranteed that plays, usually nominated by the executive, should only be performed if approved by a three-quarter vote of the full membership.[11] The society, therefore, was still its original members, mostly actors, not simply its president, and it was to the society that the use of the Abbey had been given.

What the members did not realize is that Horniman meant the theatre to belong to Yeats. He was her Wagner; the theatre was to be his Bayreuth. When Yeats had granted her, as she put it, "the right to call myself 'artist,'"[12] by designing costumes for *The King's Threshold* and *The Shadowy Waters,* she gave them the richness, cut, and fashion of the operatic getup for a Siegfried or Brunhilda.[13] If she had a dramatic wish of

11. Æ to WBY [February 1903]; Finneran, Harper, and Murphy, 1:119. For the background to Æ's revision of the rules, see Hogan and Kilroy, 2:48–51; James W. Flannery, *W. B. Yeats and the Idea of a Theatre: The Early Abbey Theatre in Theory and Practice* (New Haven: Yale University Press, 1976), 324ff.; and Peter Kuch, *Yeats and AE* (Gerrards Cross, Bucks.: Colin Smythe, 1986), 210–13, 215. The first rules were precipitated by rejection of Colum's *The Saxon Shillin',* suspected of being politically motivated; the second set of rules was made necessary because Yeats successfully blocked production of Cousins' *Sold,* even though Cousins had the support of three-quarters of the society's membership. The new rules, introduced at a meeting on 2 June 1903, and registered in Dublin on 30 December 1903, established a reading committee of Yeats, Russell, Colum, and the Fays (Hogan and Kilroy, 2:65; George Russell, *Letters from AE,* ed. Alan Denson [London: Abelard-Schuman, 1962], 52, 229; note, however, that Denson misdates Æ's letter to Yeats as [April 1904], but it must have been written in September 1905, as explained in Saddlemyer, 79).

12. Quoted in James W. Flannery, *Miss Annie F. Horniman and the Abbey Theatre,* Irish Theatre Series, no. 3 (Dublin: Dolmen Press, 1970), 15.

13. Edward Malins argues that Horniman's costumes were cut to Wagnerian patterns ("Annie Horniman, Practical Idealist," *Canadian Journal of Irish Studies* 3, no. 2 [November 1977]: 21). Malins also argues, less convincingly, that the costumes were successful. Thomas Kettle, reviewing *The King's Threshold* in *New Ireland,* 17 October 1903, treated them with sharp irony, saying the costumes were "of a richness almost barbaric" and "beyond the capacity of any but a society journal to record," though he understood, presumably from Horniman or Yeats, that they were designed according to "a scheme marvellous in its emotional and symbolic value." Lennox Robin-

her own, it seems from all available evidence that it was for Yeats, like Wagner, to create at the Abbey a new kind of dramatic song, a new style of performance, and noble, costumed, heraldic figures for a grand fantastic myth like the *Nibelungenlied*. She did not care, as she was ready to tell anyone, about "hole and corner Irish ideas." "If anyone thinks," she wrote Synge, "that 'Irish' or 'National' are anything to me beyond mere empty words to distinguish a Society . . . they are much mistaken." [14] In fact, her intention is there to read in her open letter to Yeats making the formal offer of the theatre in April 1904: "I have a great sympathy with the artistic and dramatic aims of the Irish National Theatre as publicly explained by you [Yeats, the president of the INTS] on various occasions." [15] James Flannery observes that Horniman's statement "contained a number of ambiguous points and, as time passed and policies became more precisely defined, inevitable conflicts began to arise" [16]—especially because what was taken for language of open generosity and large entitlement was intended as strictly definitive. Horniman's "great sympathy" is with the public explanation by Yeats of his aims, not with the Irish National Theatre itself. In fact, we saw in the preceding chapter that these aims—"The Samhain Principles" of 1903 and 1904—explicitly forbade the production of nationalist propaganda.

At the opening of the Abbey, the difference between the sensations of justifiable pride felt on the one hand by Yeats and on the other by the rest of the troupe was that he knew the fact of the matter and they did not; he knew he had the theatre for "the carrying out of [his] artistic dramatic schemes

---

son, coming upon them years later in a closet at the Abbey, was unfavorably impressed; at the time, the Fays were horrified; and Yeats was merely constrained to be patient, apparently begging Horniman, "No more jewels next time!" (Horniman to George Roberts, 31 October 1903, Roberts Papers, Theatre Collection, Harvard).

14. Horniman to Synge, 7 January 1906, quoted in Hogan and Kilroy, 3:58–59.

15. Horniman to WBY, April 1904, rpt. in *Samhain: 1904*, 53.

16. Flannery, *Horniman and the Abbey Theatre*, 12.

and for no other reason"; they had only a set of rules and their utility to the schemes of W. B. Yeats.[17]

3

One year later, the theatre company was riven in two. The Walkers—every one of them—were gone; the Robertses were gone; Padraic Colum had left. All told, more than half of the company departed because they refused to become employees of the newly incorporated National Theatre Society, Ltd. Of course, they still had the rules of the old society, a legal claim to its name, part of its repertoire, and a little money. They could, as they did, form a rival company and enter the market to compete with the better-financed, better-housed, and more fully established Abbey.[18] It was then that J. M. Synge wrote to Yeats that perhaps, since the defectors were about to divide the audience for Irish plays, the Abbey directors should make peace, at least with the most talented of them, such as Mary Walker, who had proved so useful in plays by Yeats and Synge. But Yeats replied that he was "delighted" that "the enemy" were rehearsing Colum's *The Land:* "A rival theatre," he observed, "would only show the power of ours. . . . We have now 400 pounds a year to spend on salaries and a fine theatre—all we have to do is hold firm."[19] Yeats knew the power of capital and of the ownership of the means of production. When Arthur Griffith delivered the acid obituary—"Everybody will be sorry for the conver-

17. Horniman to Synge, 7 January 1906, Hogan and Kilroy, 3:58–59; and Horniman to Yeats, 9 January 1906, Finneran, Harper, and Murphy, 1:58.

18. In an uncharacteristically acidulous foreword to Nic Shiublaigh's *Splendid Years,* Padraic Colum remarks bitterly on the bad fortune of the dissident actors' Theatre of Ireland. The difference between the Abbey and its rivals, according to Colum, is not in the quality of their work, but in the quantity of their financial resources. The Theatre of Ireland "could only give performances now and again in different places, while the Abbey, even though it was in the doldrums at the time, had continuity and a fixed place." As for the dramatists, "they got nothing, absolutely nothing," not a performance fee, or royalty, or opening night dinner.

19. WBY to Synge, 6 January 1906; Saddlemyer, 98–99.

sion of our best lyric poet into a limited liability company"—
he did not suspect what a natural captain of industry Yeats
would make.[20]

4

It is sometimes said that when the theatre obtained a building
and began to tour, it "inevitably" had to put into effect "more
businesslike relations" than were necessary in the original
voluntary, low-budget, amateur organization. But the theatre
did not simply grow and prosper; its entire character was forcibly altered in a way perceptible to all its members and to the
press. This change was no accident caused by incorporation;
it was its very aim.

Before the crucial meeting of 22 September 1905, when
Yeats proposed turning the company into a joint stock business, he wrote to John Quinn that he was "going to Dublin to
preside at a meeting to put an end to democracy in the theatre."[21] The introduction of coercion was, as Yeats said, "an
extremely complicated business," which perhaps only the
poet fully understood; it involved confidential negotiations
between Yeats and Horniman, Yeats and his future co-direc-
tors (Synge and Lady Gregory), Yeats and both Fays, Yeats
and Æ, Æ and the actors, then Yeats as president and the
actors, Yeats's father and certain actors, Yeats's father and
Yeats. Throughout, the poet held his cards close to his chest,
except when showing part of his hand to one or another co-
conspirator. The whole period was rife with bluffing, bribing,
coaxing, threatened rebellions by the actors, and an actual
coup by the Protestant playwrights. Finally, it appears, there
were really two changes proposed for the INTS; the first was
to issue stock to investors; the second, to put actors on salary.
They both had the effect of bringing to an end the last ves-
tiges of a cooperative democratic theatre society.

20. Arthur Griffith, "All Ireland," *United Irishman* 16, no. 367 (10 March
1906): 1; rpt. in Hogan and Kilroy, 3:62–64.
21. Wade, 461.

Yeats first suggested the plan for a joint stock company to
Æ (then involved in yet another attempt to rewrite the society's rules to set up a business committee and restructure
the reading committee) as a legal device to give the directors
control over the society.[22] Although Æ had earlier been the
actors' advocate and the architect of democratic principles, on
this occasion he went along with Yeats's maneuver. Æ had
apparently had one quarrel too many with Yeats.[23] Having
fought with him a number of times (fights rooted in fundamentally different attitudes to life and art), Æ resigned the
field to Yeats in April 1904 when he withdrew from INTS
membership, striking the attitude of a noble man, his pride
wounded, facing the facts and calling it quits: "I believe in re-
signing I have acted for the interests of the Society. Mr Yeats
has more power to aid the Society than I have. His literary
work in the future is likely to be altogether dramatic in form
and I could not feel justified in opposing any course which he
took, as I believe to a great extent the success of the Society is
bound up with the future of his work."[24] During the summer
of 1905, the victor sought the help of the vanquished in dealing with the actors—"It is a very complicated business,"
Yeats wrote Æ, "and requires a great deal of tact, that is why
we are leaving it to you." Æ apparently "did not feel justified
in opposing any course which [Yeats] took"; indeed, though

22. Russell, *Letters from AE,* ed. Denson, 52–53; Saddlemyer cites a letter
from W. G. Fay reporting to Lady Gregory on 21 September 1905: "By some
good luck Mr Yeats asked [Æ] what of turning it into a limited liability company with Mr Yeats yourself Miss H. and Mr. Synge as a board of directors
and he took to it right off" (Saddlemyer, 82; see also notes on 74–75, 79, 81).
Yeats was blunt about his motives in a letter to Florence Farr: "We are turning
[the INTS] into a private Limited Liability Co. in order to get control into a
few hands" 6 October 1905; Wade, 463; discussed in William M. Murphy,
Prodigal Father: The Life of John Butler Yeats (1839–1922) (Ithaca, N.Y.: Cornell
University Press, 1978), 292.
23. The quarrel that precipitated Æ's resignation concerned his grant of
American performance rights of *Deirdre* to Dudley Digges and Maire Quinn,
the actors who resigned over *In the Shadow of the Glen.* To Yeats, Æ's act was
both disloyal and illegal. The fullest account of the dispute is in Kuch, *Yeats
and A.E.,* 220–22.
24. Russell to George Roberts, secretary, Irish National Theatre Society,
23 April 1904; Denson, ms. 9967, 141, NLI; quoted in Kuch, *Yeats and A.E.,*
222.

Yeats was never sure "how far [Æ] would go in support" of him,[25] Æ collaborated fully with him in carrying through a final settlement that granted Yeats, Lady Gregory, and Synge effective mastery of the society.[26] The plan was then presented to the actors by Yeats as Horniman's wish.[27] She had, he said, made a large investment in the Abbey, and this investment required the insurance of formal incorporation. Indeed, Horniman took up the subject of financial security herself and asked that her voting power in the INTS, Ltd. should correspond exactly to her capital investment, as in the other corporations on the stock exchange in which she held shares:

Dear Mr. Yeats,

I have already spent nearly £4000 in the Abbey Theatre and it is now proposed that I should aid in making the society into a Limited Company. I am most willing to do this but I consider the value of the shares should bear an exact proportion to the voting power. I have always been accustomed to this in the companies in which I already hold shares and in these Companies I obviously hold a position with a very small voting power.

Yours sincerely,
A. E. F. Horniman[28]

Problems of interpretation arising from this letter suggest the web of plots and counterplots, feints and strategems, during this transformation of the society.[29] If it was "now proposed"

25. WBY to Lady Gregory, 27 September 1905; Greene and Stephens, *Synge*, 192; quoted in Saddlemyer, 83.
26. Saddlemyer, 75.
27. Ibid., 79.
28. Hogan and Kilroy, 3:35.
29. Peter Kavanagh suggests that Horniman requested that "the Society assure her of its good faith by becoming a limited liability society, thereby protecting her against any serious financial loss" (*The Story of the Abbey Theatre, from Its Origins in 1899 to the Present* [London: Devin-Adair, 1950], 51). Hogan and Kilroy believe Horniman's 26 September letter contradicts Kavanagh's conclusion. Clearly, incorporation did not in the event protect Horniman from serious financial loss; she lost £13,000 anyway, largely as a result of paying the actors' wages, but that in itself does not mean that she may not have made the request for other reasons. Those reasons were doubtless deeply politic, and we may be sure, if of nothing else, that WBY was "the Machiavelli behind the change" (Hogan and Kilroy, 3:35).

to Horniman that she aid in the incorporation of the INTS, then she could not have demanded it in the first place as a means to protect herself against financial loss. But before taking the letter at face value, one must note the salutation: when Horniman wrote to the poet frankly, she addressed him by his pseudonym in the Order of the Golden Dawn, "Dear Demon"; when she executed an official action, almost always with his consultation, and often at his dictation, she addressed the letter, "Dear Mr. Yeats." Furthermore, the letter was written from the Standard Hotel in Dublin; Yeats was in town at the time for the INTS meetings; beyond a doubt, he met Horniman regularly, so that she need not have relied on the municipal postal service to communicate with him. The letter is addressed to Yeats, but it is plainly for others to read and for him to employ in bringing about an end to democracy in the theatre. It was to Yeats's advantage to have Horniman lay conditions upon his freedom of maneuver; those conditions were themselves a maneuver, part of the plan to end the one-person, one-vote democracy, while at the same time preserving for all members a small share in the business of the society.

Even if she had demanded it, Yeats, Synge, and Lady Gregory were not about to cede control of the theatre to Horniman just as it was wrested from the actors. After getting the actors to agree that the theatre should be incorporated to limit its liability and to raise further capital,[30] Yeats had it registered under the Friendly and Industrial Societies Act, according to which no member could hold more than 200 shares, and members had a vote for each share held.[31] Under this arrangement, Horniman could not keep enough, and the actors could not buy enough, to threaten Yeats, Synge, and Lady Gregory. The writer-directors each held 100 shares, while the actors were given one each. In the future, actors could vote, but they could carry no motions.

30. Nic Shiublaigh, *Splendid Years,* 71.
31. Letter from a former member of the INTS, "All Ireland," *United Irishman* 16, no. 367 (10 March 1906): 1.

Turning the INTS into the INTS, Ltd., was just the first stage of the process of eliminating democracy in the theatre; the second stage was putting the actors under contract. According to Mary Walker, the company members consented to the plan of floating a company, not knowing that the directors would receive more shares than actors, and believing that "if we worked hard enough . . . we would be self supporting within a year."[32] But when they discovered that they were no longer consulted by the directors about the future of the company, they became unhappy with the loss of comradeship and cooperation.[33] Walker remembers Yeats then supporting a motion that at least the leading actors should turn professional, taking salaries from Miss Horniman in exchange for submission to the control of the directorate.

As a matter of fact, the two plans were intertwined from the start. On 12 June 1905, in a letter addressed to Yeats as president, Horniman officially offered the Irish National Theatre Society £500 a year to subsidize salaries for "certain of its members."[34] Early in August, Yeats brought up the idea with Æ of setting up a scheme "which will enable Mary Walker and Frank Fay to get paid."[35] W. G. Fay had begun to discuss the idea with actors by early September, when he wrote to Yeats that it was impossible to "pay anyone for doing certain work and then vote him or her out. . . . In a business . . . there can be no democracy."[36] Yeats was not slow to see an administrative opportunity in this conflict between democracy and wage labor. Although the issue of formal incorporation came before the INTS on 22 September (it was actually registered on 24 October 1905), and the issue of formal employment was presented for a vote shortly afterwards, they

32. Nic Shiublaigh, *Splendid Years,* 71.
33. William M. Murphy quotes a passage from Holloway's journal entry for 25 October 1905 documenting Walker's recollection of a change of spirit: "Since the Society turned into a limited liability company some weeks ago, things have not gone smoothly as heretofore, and a big change in the personnel of the players is likely to occur at any moment" (*Prodigal Father,* 292).
34. Quoted in Saddlemyer, 72.
35. WBY to Æ, 3 August 1905, NLI; quoted in Saddlemyer, 79.
36. W. G. Fay to WBY, 8 September 1905; Hogan and Kilroy, 3:36.

were from the beginning two aspects of a single scheme to gain control.

5

An examination of the way the plan for professionalization was put into effect illuminates its deeper consequences for the actors and the national theatre. When theatregoer Joseph Holloway first heard of the plan on 27 September 1905, he wrote in his diary: "Miss Horniman has offered to pay the artists from this out. . . . Miss Horniman is a wonder!"[37] Certainly, turning professional had advantages: the actors would not have to work two jobs, they could be paid for doing what they did best, and they would be free to take the Abbey's shows on the road to rural Ireland, England, and America. The Fay brothers and the Allgood sisters looked upon the change in this light; in Frank Fay's terms, it was a chance to make the theatre their life work.[38] But there were also disadvantages to turning professional, and, while most of the other actors saw the disadvantages, theatre historians had not given them much weight.

At the general meeting, the actors raised a number of objections to the change.[39] They pointed out that, first, the move was premature, the actors having already agreed to work one more year as amateurs in order to raise money through ticket sales for eventual distribution to actors; second, that it was unnecessary, since they would work as hard without pay as with it, and more enthusiastically as equal members than as subordinate employees; third, that it was ill-conceived, since it might well have the consequence of destroying "the individual character of the movement"; and fourth, that it was in violation of the society's first principle, laid down in 1902: "that its independence as a national movement was to be se-

37. Holloway, 59.
38. Frank Fay to Synge, 14 September 1905; Hogan and Kilroy, 38; and Saddlemyer, 80.
39. Nic Shiublaigh, *Splendid Years*, 70–73.

cured only through the efforts of its members." But in spite of these arguments, and the support of the two Walkers, Padraic Colum, George Roberts, Fred Ryan, Mary Garvey, and George Starkey, the directors easily carried the motion to put actors on salary. After all, they each had a hundred votes to an actor's one.

The deeper disadvantages—far greater than a broken agreement or violated principle—appeared after the plan was put into operation. Once actors signed contracts, they stopped being primarily artists and nationalists; they became employees, valuable according to their walk, their voice, and their general capacity for theatrical dissimulation. They were hired by the directors according to terms, and dismissible with a month's notice at the pleasure of those directors. If before "hard work and enthusiasm had been the measure of the members' sincerity,"[40] after signing a contract the only measures were Horniman's money and their technical skill; enthusiasm and sincerity were qualities of no determinate value. Upon signing a contract, they instantly lost all freedom to direct the destiny of the theatre and establish in their own practice a new kind of society, the extra-artistic, extra-commercial objective that gave the society, in their minds, its "individual character." Turning professional led toward a system of bosses and workers, the breakdown of relations between workers through unequal pay and competition for scarce labor, the alienation of the workers from their work, and reification of their skills.

The actors, of course, were under no absolute compulsion to enter into a contract with the INTS, Ltd. But Yeats had the theatre, a subsidy, the body of dramatic work, the allegiance of the stage manager W. G. Fay, and the custom of the audience they had built up; they had only membership status under revised and irrelevant rules. It is some indication of their awareness of what might be lost through turning professional, and their commitment to another idea of society, that most of the actors refused.

40. Ibid., 71.

The ways in which the terms of the contract were set, and the ways in which they were rejected, illustrate the qualitative change professionalization made in the society. Yeats's essential aim, as mentioned before, was to pay Frank Fay and Mary Walker, no one else, since these two were key players in his verse tragedies. But it must have become clear right away that once one actor was paid, all must be, or else the rest, however valuable they might have been before, would see that they were now to be regarded as comparatively worthless. A wage system is a total system; it overwhelms, encompasses, and ultimately renders obsolete other standards of evaluation.

W. G. Fay was hired by the director as their manager, put on the highest salary, and instructed to bargain with the actors, after counseling with the directors.[41] Next to himself, his brother Frank Fay was given the top rate for an actor— twenty-five shillings a week—with a supplement for his voice instruction. Sara Allgood, the leading comedienne in Lady Gregory's plays, was offered the top rate, a little more than Mary Walker, the leading actress in Yeats's tragedies. But her brother Frank Walker and her lover George Starkey, though sincere and enthusiastic members of the company, were usually cast in supporting roles; therefore, they were to be offered only ten shillings a week (Fay subsequently sweetened the offer to Walker by five shillings at the insistence of Walker's sister, a valuable property). This scheme had rapid effects; the actors began to fear and detest W. G. Fay, once their cohort, now the factor of the executive.[42] Mary Walker was envious

41. In September, before the revision of the constitution, W. G. Fay reported to Yeats his trouble in bargaining with Starkey, Roberts, and Walker, who refused to see the stage-manager as anything more than an equal member of the society (8 September 1905 [NLI]). By December, Fay had still not succeeded in putting enough actors under contract to form the cast for a performance, but he was prepared to hire prospective talents from the reserve army of Dublin unemployed (W. Fay to WBY, 4 December 1905, Library of Trinity College, Dublin [TCD]). The fullest record of documents relating to the contract negotiations appears in Saddlemyer, 85–87.

42. William M. Murphy eloquently describes the change of perspective on the Fays: "Those who had originally worked with the Fays now saw the two brothers as sergeants in a regiment led by three generals who were not

of Sara Allgood, who got paid a few shillings more; Frank Walker was humiliated by the fact that his sister was to be paid double his own salary; and Arthur Sinclair held out for more money, seeing that many veterans were not going to come to terms. Holloway nicely describes the final exodus: "Roberts took his girlfriend Miss Garvey with him when he left. Frank Walker left 'in a hump' at being offered fifteen shillings a week, taking his sister, his sister taking her lover Starkey."[43]

It is significant that the actors left as sisters, brothers, lovers, and old friends. To pay them according to their skill as actors was certainly "rational," but it is not how people value their friends, family, teachers, or themselves. In fact, this is a classic case of "rationalization," in Weber's sense of the term: the rapid organization of society according to a single function, market value.[44] Once the actors compared their separate offers and the different duties spelled out in the contracts, they had the unpleasant vision of the salary list as an inventoried social order, and they saw themselves as commodities of perfectly calibrated values and completely specified functions. Instead of a society in which there were ties of family loyalty, personal affection, political commitment, and theatrical enthusiasm, there was a business in which there were strict divisions of labor and value.

Mary Walker's final break with the Abbey illustrates the powerful effect of the change of status from member to employee. In October and November, she at first bargained on his behalf for a higher salary for her brother (fifteen as opposed to ten shillings a week); then promised to sign, but did not; then signed, then withdrew. Even her brother wa-

even really 'Irish,' while over the generals, a grey eminence in the background, lurked a dictator in the person of a rich Englishwoman who hated the Irish" (*Prodigal Father*, 296).

43. Holloway (12 January 1906), 68.
44. Max Weber, *Max Weber: Selections in Translation*, trans. E. Matthews (Cambridge: Cambridge University Press, 1978), 331–40; see also Robert Nisbet, "The Rationalization of Authority—Weber," in *The Sociological Tradition* (New York: Basic Books, 1966), 141–48.

vered from September to December, bitter at the terms of the contract, but still working at the theatre and talking of going on.[45] On 22 December 1905, however, after a dinner with Synge and Thomas Kettle at the Nassau Club, Yeats and Fay went to the Abbey in order to get Mary Walker to sign her contract, as, with some regrets, she had again agreed to do, with an arrangement that with additional duties in taking care of costumes, her wages would be raised to equal those of Sara Allgood.[46] They found that Miss Walker ("such a goose," Lady Gregory said of her)[47] could not bring herself to "sign [the contract] on the spot but promised to sign and send it before morning."[48] At this new vacillation, a torrent of eloquence erupted from Yeats, "his whole being shaken by fits of the most uncontrollable rage."[49] In his excitement, he threatened her with the law, and left, returning to the Nassau Club flushed, still trembling with exaltation. The next morning, Miss Walker brought in her signed contract, and Yeats dashed off a letter stating the terms of her employment. The letter says that she had been appointed wardrobe mistress at two shillings and sixpence a week, for which she must see that the costumes in the men's and women's dressing rooms were "in good order not out of repair, not eaten by the moths, and to set them out before performances."[50] The letter concludes with something between an apology and a criticism: "I am sorry that I was so emphatic with you last night; but I have been waiting so many days on in Dublin to get the thing settled, that I did not look forward with much pleasure to an-

45. On 19 December 1905 Frank Walker had not yet severed his connection with the INTS, Ltd., but he told Holloway that he intended to do so—possibly to learn what arguments Holloway and other friends present could give for his remaining on with the society (Holloway, 65).

46. Synge to Lady Gregory, 5 January 1906 (Berg Collection, New York Public Library); Saddlemyer, 91; the fullest account of the rough courtship of Maire nic Shiublaigh is in Murphy, *Prodigal Father*, 296–99.

47. Lady Gregory to WBY, 3 January 1906 (Berg Collection); Saddlemyer, 86.

48. Synge to Lady Gregory, 5 January 1906.

49. Nic Shiublaigh, *Splendid Years*, 15.

50. Yeats to Maire nic Shiublaigh, 23 December 1905 (TCD); Saddlemyer, 94.

other period of wasted time." Miss Walker read the letter and resigned.

With Mary Walker, *"extraordinarily white* and languid," taking refuge among the poet's father and sisters at Gurteen Dhas (the Yeats home), the other directors busily tried to find out what had gone wrong.[51] J. B. Yeats offered a number of explanations, most of them laying the blame on his son, whom he called "a mad poet" "in the hands of vulgar intriguers." Mary Walker was upset because her brother was upset, because Sara Allgood was paid more, because Yeats attacked her vanity, because he tried to make her think little of herself, because it was immodest for a woman to examine the wardrobes of the male actors (especially, Lady Gregory remarked in sympathy, the wardrobes of new employees "we know not of what class"),[52] because it seemed that both Yeats and Fay— the whole management—had turned against her. In a long letter of remonstrance to his old friend WBY, Æ summed up the whole business best by telling Yeats to ask himself "whether you did not bully and worry Miss Walker into joining you against her own wish and whether as a gentleman you are right in trying to bully and threaten her whatever your legal rights may be."[53]

There is no doubt that Yeats was a disaster as a diplomat. In fact, he freely admitted what Æ accused him of—that he wanted to be a "general autocrat in all literary and theatrical matters," and looked forward to this occasion as an opportunity to let the actors know that he was a dangerous man who "[knew] his own mind, [had] an intolerable tongue, and delight[ed] in enemies." "This theatre must have," he decided, "somebody in it who is distinctly dangerous."[54] Putting Lady Gregory and Synge on notice that he was assuming the role of strong man, he urged the directors to bring suit

51. J. B. Yeats to Lady Gregory, 6 January 1906 (NYPL); quoted in Murphy, 298.
52. Lady Gregory to Synge, 10 January 1906 (TCD); Saddlemyer, 107.
53. Æ to WBY [January? 1905]; Finneran, Harper, and Murphy, 1:151–55.
54. WBY to Synge [2 January 1906] (TCD); Saddlemyer, 88.

against Mary Walker for damages sustained as a result of her delay in coming to a decision—the lost gate receipts from a possible tour of English theatres. Whatever excesses of personality appeared in Yeats's drive for theatrical authority, the repellent features do not manifest themselves in the letter of appointment to Mary Walker: its language is not perfectly gracious, nor is it absolutely irritable; it speaks with the voice of politely restrained irritability. Although Mary Walker was no doubt upset by many things—her brother's disappointment, her rival's prestige, Fay's bossiness, and Yeats's highhandedness—the underlying problem with the letter is that it is a letter of employment from an executive to an employee, a legal instrument for turning Mary Walker into a menial laborer, a maid at 2/6 a week, to whom the employer may freely speak in whatever tones of severity or command he is disposed to use. In short, it is an eminent example of what relations within the company would be like in the future, a signal illustration of "the binding nature of a contract" that Yeats wanted to establish in the actors's minds.[55] To Mary Walker, such contractual relations seemed improper, cruel, hostile, and finally unacceptable.

6

For the members of the INTS to accept money from Horniman was implicitly to acknowledge her superiority and their inferiority; to accept the dominance of theatre business, the submission of political nationalism. The choice was driven home in the case of Padraic Colum. The directors certainly wanted to keep Colum with the company. He was popular all around—with "the hundred percent nationalists," the "literary coteries," and the general public.[56] Moreover, Colum was Catholic, and without him nearly all of the regular playwrights would have been Protestant, so that a division would have been made between Protestants who wrote plays and

55. WBY to Synge [?3 January 1906] (TCD); Saddlemyer, 89.
56. Padraic Colum, *Three Plays* (Dublin: Allen Figgis, 1963), 6.

Catholics employed to act them. As Yeats had written on an earlier occasion, the loss of Colum "would . . . put [the directors] in an impossible situation."[57]

Colum's plays were popular with good reason. If the plays of Yeats or Synge embody themes of rich intellectual significance in Irish stage scenes, those of Colum embody themes of intimate and recognizable social significance in their real setting. Irish audiences recognized themselves in the farmers of *The Land*, with its setting at the end of the Land Wars, its agonized generational conflicts between father and son about the value of the old rural way of life, its depiction of the desperation of small fields and small futures leading to emigration, and its representation of love as disruptive but not improper.[58] Colum's play did not win favor by public worship of nationalist icons or by chorus-leading of any kind; it fulfills itself in the evenhanded dramatization of a single question: with the Land War won, what after all were those little farms worth? Perhaps the land could not heal the scars—greed, brutal devotion, exhaustion—of the old or satisfy the spiritual hunger of the young.[59] The answers were not comforting; as Cornelius Weygandt noticed, the fit left for America, and the drudges remained behind to do their little best for themselves and Ireland.[60] All these elements suggested to the audi-

57. WBY to Lily Yeats, 25 December 1903; Wade, 416.

58. "Spealaodin" pegged Colum's *Broken Soil* as "immature" and "inadequate" in a 12 December 1903 *United Irishman* review of the performance at Molesworth Hall, but the play was vigorously defended by Oliver St. John Gogarty as "a national drama in a fuller sense, perhaps, than any yet presented," blessedly free of "folk smoke" and mysticism (*United Irishman* 10, no. 251 [19 December 1903]: 6). In a review of the year's performances, "D O'D" praised Colum most highly, christening him "the poet of the dawn" as opposed to the evening twilight of Yeats and Æ (*United Irishman* 11, no. 267 [9 April 1904]: 6). M. C. Joy took up this identification in an essay on the poetry of several generations of Irish writers, saying that Colum offered "the poetry of a new life and a new hope" (*United Irishman* 11, no. 268 [16 April 1904]: 3).

59. Zack Bowen rightly praises *The Land* for its objectivity, "which leaves no character unscathed or appearing to have all the answers" (*Padraic Colum* [Carbondale: Southern Illinois University Press, 1970], 73).

60. Weygandt, *Irish Plays and Playwrights* (Boston: Houghton Mifflin, 1913), 204.

ence the playwright's familiarity with their historical dilem-
mas and his basic good faith in representing them.

Yeats and Synge gave the Irish a piece of their minds;
Colum gave them a piece of themselves. They exploited the
image of the Irish tramp or tinker as a symbol of individualism,
imagination, or freedom; he showed what it was like to have
one in the family when he wrote *Broken Soil* (revised as *The
Fiddler's House*). The wandering fiddler of a father brings his
daughters endless worry, poverty, shame, and a hard outlook
for husbands, as well as heart-rending love for a man full of
the vanity of genius. In Maire's sacrifice of love for family,
Colum drew back the curtain of Irish spiritual idealism to permit a glimpse of Irish erotophobia pulling the strings . . . a
brief glimpse, which the audience could choose not to admit
that it had seen.[61] Synge's plays were themselves a problem
for the Irish, but Colum used the Ibsen problem-play to locate
the audience within its own land. Without his collaboration,
the Abbey, supposedly a national theatre, would take on a
more alien character.

Colum was not in Dublin during the acrimonious events of
late November when contracts were offered, negotiated, and
refused.[62] On 3 January 1906, he wrote to Yeats: "As you are
aware I voted for the establishment of a limited liability company in order to save the Society from a disastrous split. I
come back to Dublin and I find the Society hopelessly shattered. The one thing to be done is to reunite the Society."
Yeats, of course, wanted to smash the old democratic society,
but to retain Colum. Colum himself felt a personal debt of
loyalty to Yeats: Yeats was not only a great poet and an admirer of Colum's work, he had also been Colum's teacher in
the art of writing plays, having helped with the many revi-

61. Weygandt, who interviewed the playwright for ibid., notices this psychological analysis of idealism: "Sacrifice is rare in youth, and if it were not
that Maire is afraid of her love for Brian McConnell, and gives up her home
and takes to the road with her father partly because she fears her love for her
lover, fears her powerlessness with him, it would hardly be in the course of
nature that she would sacrifice so much for her sister" (204).

62. Colum to WBY [3 January 1906]; Saddlemyer, 90.

sions of *The Land*.[63] Yeats himself believed Colum was not
only indebted to him but dependent on him; he told Synge
that without the Abbey, Colum "would be chaos" as an artist.[64] Thus the young Catholic playwright was presented with
a dilemma: he could be an artist without nationalism or a nationalist without artistic opportunity. The directors of the
Abbey were betting that he would think first of himself and
his art when they asked him to sign a contract binding him
to give all his dramatic work for the next five years to the
INTS, Ltd.

It was in this confident, bluff, and hard-bargaining spirit
that Yeats had Horniman write to Colum[65] after he had appealed to her for the use of the Abbey by the old INTS. She
said that she was sorry he intended to "imperil his artistic career for politics."[66] At any rate, she did not intend to grant the
use of the theatre to anyone but Yeats and the friends of Yeats,
as she wrote on 9 January 1906, officially transferring the gift of
the Abbey from the INTS to WBY and the INTS, Ltd.: "The
theatre is a means for carrying out a certain theatrical scheme
and as long as you continue in the same path, the theatre is at
the disposal of you and your friends under whatever title you
choose to use."[67] That scheme, as Horniman understood it,
was a theatre for art, not politics. Horniman, like Yeats, did
not worry that Colum would finally resign from the Abbey; as
she remarked, he knew "which side his bread [was] buttered

63. Even in the midst of the INTS split, Colum wrote WBY, "I can assure
you that you can always reckon on my loyalty to you personally & to my
school"; when he finally resigned, Colum, having stated strongly his differences with Yeats's policy, went on to say that he would "always be proud of
being a contemporary. To you . . . I owe much as a dramatist" (Finneran,
Harper, and Murphy, 1:151, 161).
64. WBY to Synge [? 4 January 1906] (TCD); Saddlemyer, 90.
65. In a letter to Synge [?3 January 1906], WBY let it be known that he had
"dictated one or two letters in connection with the matter to Horniman because I want people to understand that we have her resources behind us—
that will make them feel I am in earnest" (Saddlemyer, 90).
66. Holloway, 13 January 1906, 66.
67. Horniman to WBY, 9 January 1906 (NLI); Finneran, Harper, and Murphy, 1:158.

on."[68] This remark, penned from London to one playwright, rapidly made its way around Dublin, echoed among the groups of dissidents, and soon reached the ears of Colum himself.[69] His choice at last appeared to be no choice: Horniman's money and Yeats's theatre, or Ireland's independence and a theatre for the people. Angry, embarrassed, reluctant, he resigned.

7

Yeats succeeded: he established control over an Irish theatre, kept it in operation, and put before the public plays he thought good, whether the public liked them or not. But the INTS, Ltd. was recognized as his theatre, or even Annie Horniman's, not as an Irish national theatre. On 10 March 1906 an "Irreconcilable" from the old INTS wrote the *United Irishman* to inform the public that an impostor was afoot in Ireland: "The National Theatre Society, Ltd., is a body run in the interest of one person, Mr. W. B. Yeats, who has proved himself capable of absorbing for his own personal ends the disinterested work of a large number of people given on the understanding that they were aiding in a work which was devoted primarily to the development of the highest interests of nationality in the country."[70] This absorption of the work of others is a good case of what Foucault calls "colonization"—the encompassing of local structures of power by larger ones of a different type.[71] A native, democratic, collective, and nationalist cultural movement was subsumed by a British-owned and

68. Padraic Colum, "Ninety Years in Retrospect: An Interview Conducted by Zack Bowen," *Journal of Irish Literature* 2, no. 1 (January 1973): 24.

69. Holloway (13 January 1906), 68.

70. "All Ireland," *United Irishman* 16, no. 367 (10 March 1906): 1; Hogan and Kilroy, 3:62–64; Synge suggests the author is "one of the 'Irreconcilables'" in a 10 March 1906 letter to Lady Gregory (Berg Collection); Saddlemyer, 119.

71. Michel Foucault, *Power/Knowledge: Selected Interviews & Other Writings, 1972–77*, ed. Colin Gordon (New York: Pantheon Books, 1972; rev. ed., 1980), 99ff.; Barry Smart, *Foucault, Marxism, and Critique* (London: Routledge & Kegan Paul, 1983), 82–83.

Protestant-operated enterprise that was hierarchial and capitalist in character. "Sound business principles" were clearly not the only objective of this colonization. The struggle in the theatre was a struggle for the nature of a future Ireland, and the issues of the national debate were the same issues argued within the Irish National Theatre Society. The first issue was Home Rule: would the Irish get it or not? If they did, would it be by English permission, under the leadership of the Anglo-Irish, or through the participation of the entire citizenry, directed perhaps by the Gaelic League? Second, the issue of property ownership, made prominent by Michael Davitt and the Land League, and by James Connolly and the Irish Socialist Republican Party: could a nation of renters and employees be free, or was the nationalization of the land a condition of full nationality?[72] Third, the issue of production, given importance by Æ and the Irish cooperative movement: could the Irish be economically self-sufficient, making out of their own resources products for their own markets, or would they be dependent on British capital in producing commodities for the British market?[73]

In the directors' takeover of the INTS, all these issues were

---

72. T. W. Moody supplies a complete history of Davitt's interest in Henry George's concept of private land ownership as the "root cause of poverty," with "no . . . justification in morality or reason." Although this position had little appeal for the mass of Irishmen, Davitt nonetheless held to it to the end of his political career; in 1902, he wrote: "I still hold . . . to this great principle, and I believe a national ownership to be the only true meaning of the battle-cry of the Land League—the Land for the People" (*Some Suggestions for a Final Settlement of the Land Question*, 6–7; quoted in Moody's *Davitt and the Irish Revolution* [Oxford: Clarendon Press, 1982], 540). Connolly did not succeed in making the Irish Socialist Republican Party a popular party either, but, since he was a close friend of Arthur Griffith, Maud Gonne, and Frederick Ryan (all deeply involved in nationalist theatre), his ideas cannot have been unknown to the players. See Ruth Dudley Edwards, *James Connolly* (Dublin: Gill & Macmillan, 1981), 21–42.

73. For recent accounts of the Irish Agricultural Organization Society, see Trevor West, *Horace Plunkett: Co-operation and Politics* (Gerrards Cross, Bucks.: Colin Smythe, 1986), and Henry Summerfield, *That Myriad-Minded Man: A Biography of George William Russell "AE," 1867–1935* (Gerrards Cross, Bucks.: Colin Smythe, 1975).

focused on the question of property. Oliver MacDonagh has described the introduction to Ireland of modern British concepts of property, which granted owners absolute control, "untrammelled *legally* by social obligations," free of all liens and entailments, and entitling owners to buy up holdings, eject residents, and dictate the use made of their property.[74] As John Stuart Mill realized—in a passage that deeply influenced Davitt—the Irish had a traditional view of property that was less individualist and more qualified than the modern free market definition of the British:

> Before the conquest, the Irish people knew nothing of absolute property in land. The land virtually belonged to the Irish sept; the chief was little more than managing member of the association. The feudal idea, which views all rights as emanating from a head landlord, came in with the conquest, was associated with foreign dominion, and has never to this day been recognised by the moral sentiments of the people.[75]

That this communal idea was alive among the twentieth-century Irish, and among members of the original INTS, is shown by a Colum essay in the intellectual monthly *Dana* entitled "Concerning a Creamery."[76] This excellent piece of journalism describes the reaction of farmers to a priest's proposal that they build a cooperative creamery, under the guidance of Horace Plunkett's Irish Agricultural Organization Society. Colum believes that cooperation is not "something outside, something foreign" to Ireland; it is part of the Gaelic tradition of *meitheal*, a party of workers brought together for mutual aid, for example, when cutting turf, weaving cloth, or building a house. More recently, Colum goes on, peasants have had a custom called a "join": many farmers, each unable to buy a spraying machine or cream separator, put their money together to purchase one that all will use. This is not, for Colum, merely a matter of necessity; it springs from "the feel-

74. MacDonagh, *States of Mind: A Study of Anglo-Irish Conflict, 1790–1980* (London: George Allen & Unwin, 1983), 35–36.
75. J. S. Mill, *England and Ireland* (London, 1868), 12–13, quoted in Moody, *Davitt and the Irish Revolution*, 38.
76. Padraic Colum, "Concerning a Creamery," *Dana* 7 (November 1904): 205–8.

ing of mutual aid," or what Mill calls "the moral sentiments of the people." This felt sense of a usufructual right to joint tenancy, this disposition toward mutual aid, and the belief that even the chief leader is no less a member of the association (his supremacy on loan from the group, for the sake of the group) were just what gave the INTS "its individual character" for many of the members; it *was* the meaning of their collective productions, an aspect of Ireland's "subterranean challenge to the formally dominant theory of property" in the nineteenth and twentieth centuries.[77] The political economy of the INTS was an experiment in the establishment of an Irish state, one that was traditional rather than modern, communal rather than individualist, egalitarian rather than hierarchical, and democratic rather than autocratic, in a wholesale Gaelic alternative to contemporary Britain.

In this struggle, Yeats acted decisively and successfully to repeat and restore the colonial ascendancy of the Anglo-Irish. With the assistance of an antinationalist English woman, who enjoyed complete power of purse, in effect he established a Home Rule government under Protestant leadership, dedicated to enforcing respect for "the obligations of contract" and acknowledgment of the untrammelled freedom of the executive. Under the colors of art, the executive shaped the social character of Ireland, so that it produced works, and produced them in a fashion, basically acceptable to Anglo-Irish landlords and English customers. That this is the narrowest estimate of the "Literary Revival," and by no means a sufficient one, does not make it the less fitting as one judgment of the Abbey enterprise.

8

Clearly, Yeats did more "for his country" than "produce good art."[78] But one may wish to distinguish the man from the artist: on one hand, in his capacity as an artist, one might say that he could only produce art, good or bad; in his capacity as

77. MacDonagh, *States of Mind*, 39.
78. Greene and Stephens, *Synge*, 173.

a man, on the other hand, he could produce many other things—journalism, joint stock companies, charters for the National League—that also affected the country's future. Walter Benjamin observes that one cannot fix the political tendency of writers by their social class, by their behavior in matters of public politics, or even by the doctrine in their works of art, since left-wing doctrine, for example, is easily assimilated by capitalist methods of distribution and sold as an object of enjoyment, novel sensations in a stream of sensations.[79] Benjamin prefers to analyze artists' positions with respect to the social relations of production and their works' positions with respect to these relations. As a man, Yeats may have been deeply affiliated to British capital, committed to the subordination of workers, and even alert to a chance for the reascendancy of the Protestant class in Ireland. But there is the question of the artist: how do his works stand in "the social relations of production"?

According to Benjamin's calculus of literary ethics, a work is good insofar as it puts "an improved apparatus" at the disposal of a multitude of consumers who are encouraged by it to become producers. The more readers become collaborators, the better the work. In fact, even by this radical standard, Yeats's dramas were often "politically correct." His restless invention of dramatic forms and exploration of new territories of Ireland's people and past put before the Irish the shapes in which their national life might be expressed. He showed how folk stories could be made into folk dramas (*The Pot of Broth*), how the tradition of "rebel songs" could be turned into propaganda plays (*Cathleen ni Houlihan*), how periods of Irish history before the arrival of the English could be used as a source of purely Irish drama (*The King's Threshold*), how Irish stage characters could be made to speak in realistic, poetic, and non-comic idioms (*Cathleen ni Houlihan, Countess Cathleen*), and how the saga cycles of the Red Branch could bring forth

79. Benjamin, "The Artist as Producer," in *The Essential Frankfurt School Reader*, ed. Andrew Arato and Eike Gebhardt (1937; rpt., New York: Urizen, 1978), 254–69.

relevant examples of Irish majesty and heroism (*Deirdre, On Baile's Strand*). Although a close analysis of several of these works would reveal a doctrine quite hostile to some ideas dear to some nationalists—such as egalitarianism, democracy, Catholicism, and communitarianism—the doctrine is not what matters. It is obvious that his plays caused a number of those who had been spectators to become authors. James Cousins, J. M. Synge, Lady Gregory, Padraic Colum, Seamus O'Sullivan, Maud Gonne, and many others made use of "the improved apparatus" Yeats put in their hands. In many ways, Yeats the artist was an innovator and therefore a liberator, even if Yeats the man was not.

9

In the various conflicts between nationalism and art, many of those who saw their way to becoming playwrights by a study of Yeats's plays were shut out of the Abbey Theatre and forced to take their plays to hastily assembled casts for occasional performances in hired halls. It might well be argued that the world lost no great playwrights in Cousins, Ryan, Seamus O'Sullivan, or even Colum; that, indeed, Yeats stood up for the interests of "good art" even when the backstage door was closed to these young writers. But what was the "good art" for which he stood? George Moore, interviewed at the time of his removal to England, was asked how he could leave Ireland when the Irish renaissance was going on. Moore replied that there was no renaissance; there was only J. M. Synge and his few, short, brilliant plays.[80] With his blunt judgment, generations of readers have concurred: neither the plays of Yeats (at least the pre-Noh plays) and Lady Gregory nor those of any other Abbey playwright until O'Casey in the 1920s reach the standard set by Synge. If only works of the quality of Synge's best dramas were to be played, the Abbey Theatre

80. "Mr. George Moore on Dublin," *Dublin Evening Mail*, 6 December 1905, 3; Hogan and Kilroy, 3:55.

would have opened its doors only a few evenings a year, and then to small audiences. The grounds on which plays were judged worthy of production, as a practical matter, could not strictly be whether or not they were great works of drama. It is clear from the case of William Boyle's fortunes with the Abbey that the working definition of "good art" was broader than "art of high literary merit and permanent interest" and narrower than "art of sound construction, current interest, and general popularity." Boyle's first play, *The Building Fund,* was an extremely popular satire of small-town types of the Irish Midlands. When Boyle submitted a second play, *The Eloquent Dempsy,* in August, 1905, he had the strong support of W. G. Fay, who saw a great acting opportunity in the "miles gloriosus" figure of the boastful, double-talking political poltroon Dempsy. Yeats, however, thought the play "impossibly vulgar in its present form," and wrote to Synge asking his help in preventing the play's acceptance by the reading committee (abolished a few months later, in the fall 1905 revision of the constitution).[81] He impressed upon Synge the seriousness of the issue, since Horniman had spent £4,000 on the Abbey on the condition that they "keep up the standard" of artistic quality. At present, the poet went on, they were at great risk of offending her taste and losing her money, but "when the revision of the constitution is through those of us in the know will be in authority." It is doubtful that Yeats really feared Horniman's disapproval. She objected to many things at the Abbey—from George Moore's presence at rehearsals to sixpenny seats—but not to Boyle or his plays (more "virile," she thought, than those of Yeats and Synge); indeed, these plays were part of the cargo she wished to salvage from the Abbey shipwreck for her Manchester theatre in 1906.[82] Regarding *The Eloquent Dempsy,* as on other occa-

81. WBY to Synge, 15 August [1905] (TCD); Saddlemyer, 74–76.
82. On 13 July 1906 Horniman advised Yeats that if "Dublin efforts lead to nothing," she meant to offer Boyle help getting his plays produced in Manchester (Hogan and Kilroy, 3:73–74); she found "a certain virility" in his work "which is missing in Yeats and Synge work [*sic*]" (Horniman to Yeats, 10 December 1906; Hogan and Kilroy, 3:89).

sions, Yeats used Horniman's money to give authority to his own taste.

In order to define the Abbey conception of "good art," it is necessary to discriminate between two kinds of taste: the delicate palate of Yeats and the larger appetites of the Abbey audience. To the audience, Synge was vulgar, and Boyle was "fair"; to Yeats, Boyle was vulgar, and Synge—more than fair—was the perfection of art. Many explanations have been given for why the satire of one was felt by the audience as pleasant, and that of the other as painful and intolerable. Holloway went home after a performance of Boyle's *Building Fund* to record in his diary one view of the difference between Boyle's truth and Synge's beauty:

> Every word [of *The Building Fund*] rang true, and though the dramatist chose his types from most unsympathetic and unlovable specimens of our fellow-countrymen, there was no denying their truth to life. . . . The great literary quality of Mr. Synge's work cannot be denied, and as literature must rank immeasurably above Mr. Boyle's homely, real, flesh and blood talk; but nevertheless, there is no denying that much of his work rings false to Irish ears.[83]

—a view William M. Murphy perhaps rightly translates to mean that Boyle told the right truths, Synge the wrong truths:

> Boyle's characters were slippery politicians and glib funny men committing venial sins. If they pocketed a dubious shilling here or there, broke an oppressive law or two, or confused people with doubletalk, they were merely displaying the charming weaknesses of the lovable Irish. Synge, on the other hand, showed Irishmen as not always faithful to their marriage vows and occasionally as anticlerical, Irish ladies as untouchable in theory but not in fact.[84]

According to W. G. Fay, the popularity of Boyle's satire had nothing to do with its critique of Irish life, true or not; Boyle's works "played well"—that is, offered good parts, strong curtains, vivid stage "business"—establishing "a fellowship with

83. Holloway, 25 April 1905.
84. Murphy, *Prodigal Father*, 288–89.

the audience."[85] Yeats's explanation can be seen as a refinement of Fay's: he thought Boyle's work went over well because
his plots and characters were the old standbys of nineteenth-
century Irish novels and the popular stage (miserly women,
rakish sons, grasping priests; plots based on wills and mistaken identities); Boyle was popular, by this logic, just to the
degree that he was unoriginal; indeed, it was a Yeats adage
that the Muse whispers only to the outcast: "The more they
cry against you, the more I love you."[86] Boyle often claimed
Yeats hated his work simply because the audience liked it
better than his own;[87] or did they like it because Yeats hated it,
conflicts of taste echoing class war? Certainly some loved
Boyle as one of their own, not part of the Protestant clique
running the Abbey. But Robert Hogan and James Kilroy offer
the most interesting explanation: they find the reason for
the audience's distinction of Boyle's satire from Synge's to
be that Boyle's "easily apprehensible realistic dialogue aroused
laughter and the rich embroidery of Synge's difficult language
did not so much arouse laughter as demand admiration."[88]
Synge's style, and Yeats's too, advanced imposing claims to
greatness and demanded that such claims be recognized.[89] An

85. Fay and Carswell, *The Fays of the Abbey Theatre*, 173; Saddlemyer,
74–75; for a fuller discussion of the Fays' preference for "theatrical theatre,"
see Flannery, *Yeats and the Idea of a Theatre*, 185–90.
86. WBY, *Samhain: 1905*; rpt. in *Explorations* (New York: Macmillan, 1962),
184; WBY to John Quinn, 4 October 1907; Wade, 495: The people "never
minded Boyle, whose people are a sordid lot, because they knew what he
was at. They understood his obvious moral." The sentence about the Muse is
taken from *Samhain: 1904*; rpt. in *Explorations*, 163.
87. Boyle's hatred of Yeats was obsessive; every letter to Holloway mixes
rage with ridicule of the INTS, Ltd. directorate, as in this 2 February 1910
assault: "If the Directors wanted another play from me, do you fancy they
wouldn't ask for it? As long as [Yeats and Lady Gregory] have money enough
to run unpopular pieces they'll continue running them. When the fund runs
out, they'll chuck the show. 'The advancement of drama' means to them their
own drama" (Holloway Manuscript, ms. 13267–69 [2], NLI).
88. Hogan and Kilroy, 3:54–55.
89. As Conor Cruise O'Brien suggested in conversation (24 April 1988),
the Abbey directorate imagined the theatre as a sort of school through which
Protestant author/teachers could fulfill a proselytizing mission to their Catholic middle-class spectator/students, teaching them to admire works of high

audience attempting to struggle free of ancient habits of sub-
servience was not disposed to grant such peremptory, authoritarian claims in the style; moreover, an audience that
had given the price of admission for two hours' oblivion of
fabled laughter or tears felt cheated if forced to ponder an os-
tentation of idiosyncratic intellect.

To collate these extracts, we can say that, according to the
taste of the audience, good drama is drama that entertains the
audience, invites them to a full understanding, and reflects
with some (but not too much) truth the qualities of their lives,
but accommodates itself to the patterns of their popular fic-
tions. But none of these things is necessary to good drama, at
least according to Yeats's taste. For him, good drama may be
obscure, unpopular, even painful to watch; what it must be is
drama of egregious literary quality. Conrad says that a good
novel must carry its justification in every line; for Yeats, a
good play must show its literary ambition in every phrase.
His first principle is that "our plays must be literature"; his
second, third, and fourth, that they should be little else but
literature. He would put the actors in barrels, model their gestures after marble statues, allow the scene-painter shades of
but one color, jealous of anything more theatrical than the
language itself, which, next to that dullness, should seem, he
hoped, extravagant, fantastic, and noble.[90] The suppression
of "common life" was the condition for the expression of
literature; the theatre was to be a mirror of reverie, not reality—reality had to be "checked":

> In all drama which would give direct expression to reverie, to
> the speech of the soul with itself, there is some device that
> checks the rapidity of the dialogue. . . . The dignity of Greek

culture. It is true that the plays on the Abbey syllabus were better literature
than what the audience would itself have chosen as entertainment, and that
the directors had better taste than spectators without their advantages of
higher education and broad reading, but the audience nonetheless resented
the pedagogical presumptuousness of the INTS management, and of the literary style itself.

90. WBY, "The Play, the Player, and the Scene," *Samhain: 1904*; rpt. in *Explorations*, 164–79, esp. 170.

> drama, and in a lesser degree of that of Corneille and Racine, depends, as contrasted with the troubled life of Shakespearian drama, on an almost even speed of dialogue, and on a so continuous exclusion of the animation of common life that thought remains lofty and language rich.[91]

Yeats sought this "check" in versified dialogue, choric speaking, and ritualistic movement; Synge found it in the "long and meditative" cadence of dialect, an elaborately decorative screen rather than a window of words, for the audience to look at, rather than see through. Yeats admires the fact that this cadenced dialect "makes the clash of wills among his persons indirect and dreamy, it helps him . . . to preserve the integrity of art in an age of reasons and purposes."[92] Surely it is true that from Synge's plays we do not remember most clearly characters, situations, or human problems; instead, we recollect first the filter of "fine language" through which all these dramatic elements make their impression. Great plays may be written according to Yeats's definition of good drama (it is a feat, but Synge proved that it can be done); however, drama so relentlessly literary, so deeply at war with its own materials, can never make up more than a small portion of the best works of the living theatre.

A form of drama that compels the audience to admire the playwright is not just "authorial" drama, but autocratic drama. The audience is forced to admit, or outright to reject, the privilege of the author's point of view and his right not just to show life but to make it after his own will. The genius of Yeats is magisterial, and his highest love is for the art of other magisterial geniuses—for Blake, Nietzsche, Synge, and Pound. Talents less noble, those of another kind, tend to draw his contempt. Æ, taking Yeats up on his rough treatment of Marie nic Shiublaigh, went on to treat him to a full-dress lecture on the intolerant, authoritarian bent in his nature, connecting his style of writing with his style of leadership:

91. WBY, "John Synge and the Ireland of His Time," in *Essays and Introductions* (New York: Macmillan, 1961), 333–34.
92. WBY, "The Well of the Saints," in *Essays and Introductions*, 300.

There is probably not one of the younger people of whom you have not said some stinging and contemptuous remark. They may have been justified. But if you wish to lead a movement you can only do so by silence on points which irritate you or by kindly suggestions to the people. A man without followers can do nothing and you have few or no friends in Dublin. . . . You are committing the great mistake of so many people about Ireland "the twenty years of resolute government" theory. Irish people will only be led by their affections. . . . Compare Hyde's power with your own and you have twenty times his ability. Fall out of their circle of affections and they will turn on you like Healy o[n] Parnell. You may lose all your present actors who are not paid, as they will probably meet continually the young men in the clubs who will say you are confessedly not a Nationalist, and if a new company was formed it would get all the old group of actors except the two Fays, Miss Allgood and Wright. You who initiated the theatre movement in Ireland will be out of it. . . . You will be as out of everything in Ireland as Dowden & with as little influence. . . . There have been greater artists in literature than yourself but it is not always recorded that their position impelled them to speak contemptuously of everyone not their equal. The fact is the position you wish to hold of general autocrat in literary, dramatic and artistic matters in Dublin or Ireland is a position accorded through love and cannot be assumed without a press to back you up.[93]

Æ rarely wrote better than when writing of his best friend's faults; he had a fatherly way of putting "the soul in uncomfortable places."[94] Yeats in response could choose between being demolished as a person, and being utterly unmoved, above the attack. His answer, an unrepentant page from Nietzsche, has a graceful superiority:

I desire the love of a very few people, my equals or superiors. The love of the rest would be a bond and an intrusion. These others will in time come to know that I am a strong and capable man and that I have gathered the strong and capable about me. . . . The antagonism, which is sometimes between you and me, comes from the fact that though you are strong

93. Æ to WBY [late December? 1905]; Finneran, Harper, and Murphy, 1:151–55.
94. WBY to Æ, 19 September [1905] (NLI); Kuch, *Yeats and AE*, 225.

and capable yourself you gather the weak and not very capable about you, and that I feel they are a danger to all good work. It is I think because you desire love. Besides you have the religious genius to which all souls are equal. In all work except that of salvation that spirit is a hindrance.[95]

The friendship of Yeats and Æ could not bear this degree of plain-speaking; the exchange of letters was their last for many years.[96] From it, we can see not only that others felt Yeats to be imperious and domineering, but also that he embraced that description. Both his high standards and his particular taste for literature with qualities of power put him into constant conflict with his actors and audience, and drove him to seek dominion in that conflict. One of Yeats's sayings that Lady Gregory preserved gives this lordliness marmoreal expression:

In questions of taste, it's no good to use argument, one must use force.[97]

10

Once Yeats succeeded in colonizing the Abbey, a dialectic between repression and domination came into play.[98] Aspirations on the part of the Irish to national self-expression were repressed by the rule of "no politics" and the practice of wage labor; on the other hand, the consciousness of the people was dominated by a conception of theatre as a grace of cultivated society and an expression of individual, as opposed to social, will.

The dominating and repressive effects of a narrow definition of "good art" can be illustrated by an analysis of *The*

95. WBY to Æ [8 January 1906]; Wade, 466.
96. For a fuller account of the quarrel between Yeats and Æ, and their reconciliation, see Kuch, *Yeats and A.E.* 225–38.
97. Lady Gregory, *Seventy Years: Being the Autobiography of Lady Gregory*, ed. Colin Smythe (Gerrards Cross, Bucks.: Colin Smythe, 1973), 351.
98. For a fuller account of the distinction between domination and repression, see Smart, *Foucault, Marxism, and Critique*, 81. The roots of Foucault's theory of repression are in Reich, those of his theory of domination in Nietzsche.

Shadowy Waters, first performed on 4 January 1904. Yeats had worked on various scripts of this play since his youth: it is doubtless deeply entangled in his ways of conceiving the world, so deeply that it was difficult for him to articulate his intention in a way that would be understood, even by his friends.[99] But he nonetheless soldiered on, finally making a stage version, partly in prose, which he mounted on 8 December 1906 with the greatest care for lighting, costume, and vocal delivery. Though Yeats was right enough when he wrote Frank Fay that a drama like *The Shadowy Waters* would "prove itself the worst sort possible for our theatre,"[100] during the struggle for control of the Abbey, he regained interest in the play, trying to remake it into something "strong" and "simple."[101] It represents one attempt to embody his dream of an Irish "Theatre of Beauty."

In all versions, the story centers on a romantic and mystical pirate, Forgael, who has set his ship's course to the north, steering by the voices of human-headed birds that give him messages, much to the fear and discontent of his crew, who are only interested in a happy outlaw life of booty and stolen brides. Immortal, insatiable longings have come upon Forgael; he won't

> Be satisfied to live like other men,
> And drive impossible dreams away,[102]

99. See George Moore's hilarious account of his attempts to help Yeats chisel away a few poetical passages from *The Shadowy Waters*, which ended with Moore finding himself "inside a prison-house with all the doors locked and windows barred." To Moore, the thought in the play is like a carriage wheel spinning off the ground: it works beautifully, but goes nowhere (Moore, *Hail and Farewell!* vol. 1, 1911; *Ave* [London: Heinemann, 1937], 186–87). David R. Clark's early essay, "W. B. Yeats: *The Shadowy Waters* (MS. Version): 'Half the Characters Had Eagles' Faces'" still provides the best brief, sympathetic account of the play's origins, phases, and intentions (*Irish Renaissance: A Gathering of Essays, Memoirs, and Letters from "The Massachusetts Review,"* ed. Robin Skelton and David R. Clark [Dublin: Dolmen Press, 1965], 26–55).

100. WBY to F. Fay, ?20 January 1904; Wade, 424.

101. See for instance WBY's 15 July 1905 letter to Florence Farr (Wade, 453).

102. Alspach, 321; lines 103–4.

as his friend Aibric counsels. Forgael is sure that

> What the world's million lips are thirsting for,
> Must be substantial somewhere.[103]

They come upon a merchant galley, massacre its crew, and capture Queen Dectora after killing her husband. Dectora is forced by spells, shed from the strings of a harp made of apple wood, into a love for Forgael so overwhelming that she consents to follow him in his quest for the ultimate kingdom of Love in realms beyond the Pole—beyond mortal life. After Forgael recovers from his distress that Dectora casts a shadow (he was hoping for an immortal, disembodied beauty), and his guilt over drugging her with his Druid crafts, the rope is cut that has tied them to the now mutinous crew, and the pirate captain and his love set off alone into magical seas.

On the one hand, the play is full of symbols of primarily personal significance to the poet, and Yeats was happy to let people know that more was meant than would be understood—something was "kept back . . . for instructed eyes."[104] On the other hand, the play is basically an allegory of the rejection of the pursuit of wealth for the pursuit of values beyond those of the exchange—beauty, knowledge, love, and so on—though it is not clear whether Love is one of those values, or a way of finding them. In fact, interesting questions arise for Forgael as to whether the queen is that for which he thirsts, a means to finding the goal of life, or a possible distraction for it. In its origins, the play is very much the troubled fantasy of a young man who has not yet found happiness with a woman ("The play . . . came into existence," Yeats explained to Florence Farr, "after years of strained emotion, of living upon tip-toe"),[105] but in its extensive later development it became a screen on which Yeats projected interests of a technical, mystical, and, I would argue, political kind.

---

103. Alspach, 322; lines 122–23.
104. WBY to John Quinn, 16 September 1905; Wade, 462.
105. WBY to Florence Farr [? July 1905]; Wade, 454.

One might hypothetically subject all the ostensible meanings of *The Shadowy Waters*, both personal and allegorical, to a sociological revision. It is certainly important that the hero be rich, but not committed to riches; that he be outside the law, indeed, above it. It is even important that the captain of the pirate ship is a lonely man under the threat of mutiny from his men (who have in common only the pursuit of gain), because if the ship is construed as Ireland, the loneliness of the captain would be the loneliness of the Protestant. The Protestant—soldier, buck, and planter—is a sort of pirate: someone who has taken a voyage across the Irish channel for the sake of booty. The handsome thing about the pirate is that he romanticizes illegality. When debates in Parliament dwelt upon the forms of legal justification for the booty of Protestants, Yeats produced a play that adds glamor to lawlessness. The pirate is both a revelation and criticism of the merchants upon whom he preys. Both are engaged in the transportation of wealth from the small to the strong, though merchants do it in the name of a nation, the pirate for the sake of denationalized outlaws. By attacking the legal system of expropriation, the pirate can become a hero to common people, as the merchant never can.

Perhaps Forgael is not an analogue to the Irish Protestant; perhaps he is no more than Axel on a boat; one is eager nonetheless to construe significance where so much is suggested and so little is spelled out, and it would be a familiar surprise if this most aesthetic of playlets were a dark design of unconscious propaganda, an occult transfiguration of class conflict. But however the play is read, it must be conceived as in some sort a celebration of exalted individuality, Alastor at the Abbey. While *The Shadowy Waters* may have been just the ticket for a 1905 Convention of London Theosophists,[106] to those Irishmen who paid to see it performed in 1906, the whole conception was an impertinence. They had come because it was on the

106. "The first version of 'The Shadowy Waters' was performed at the Court Theatre, London, for a Theosophical Convention on July 8" (Wade, 451).

stage of the Abbey Theatre that the emergent life of Ireland was to be enacted, only to find that space had been taken up by a prospectively beautiful, but to them incomprehensible, piece of poetic self-indulgence. Forms of social life were announcing themselves in which the individual as one who lives for love, who creates exquisite values beyond the exchange, who sails to uncharted seas, who acts alone outside the law, would be more and more impossible. To speak of the individual's harmony, culture, and ideal aspirations was to base one's hopes on an idea of man as he had existed in the past. The task for the Irish people was not to harmonize the isolated individual, but to realize the nation as a whole. *The Shadowy Waters* is in its way another triumph by Yeats, of a piece with his victories as president of the Irish National Theatre Society: it is an instance of the repression of explicit politics and the dominance of the implicit politics of beauty. In *The Shadowy Waters*, big business and high culture take the stage in place of national theatre.

Miss Annie Horniman. Oil painting by J. B. Yeats, 1904, reproduced by kind permission of the Abbey Theatre. See chapter 5 for a discussion of this picture.

W. B. Yeats. Sketch by J. B. Yeats, 1899, courtesy of Michael Butler Yeats.

Lady Gregory. Sketch by J. B. Yeats, 1905, courtesy of Michael Butler Yeats.

J. M. Synge. Sketch by J. B. Yeats, 1905, courtesy of Michael Butler
Yeats.

Mary Walker [Maire nic Shiublaigh], actress in the Irish National Theatre Company. Sketch by J. B. Yeats, 1906, courtesy of Michael Butler Yeats.

Sara Allgood, leading actress for the Irish National Theatre Company. Sketch by J. B. Yeats, 1911, courtesy of Michael Butler Yeats.

Frank Fay, actor and one of the founders of the Irish National Theatre Company. Sketch by J. B. Yeats, 1904, courtesy of Michael Butler Yeats.

Padraic Colum, playwright. Sketch by J. B. Yeats, 1907, courtesy of Michael Butler Yeats.

Foyer of the Abbey Theatre. Sketch by Raymond McGrath, by kind permission of the Abbey Theatre.

Stage of Horniman's Abbey Theatre, looking out over the pit. Photograph from the Abbey Theatre Collection, National Library of Ireland.

5

Authors and Patron

The Self-Expression of Capital

In the lobby of the Abbey Theatre hangs a portrait of Anne Elizabeth Fredericka Horniman by the poet's father John Butler Yeats. The sitter is not of the type that inspired the painter's most famous work; this is not a "friendship portrait" of a person with the soul of an artist.[1] Miss Horniman had no such soul, and there is nothing in J. B. Yeats's letters to suggest he cherished her company; he found her, in fact, "fatiguing": she talked all the time of the sins of the Irish and threatened them with a sudden stoppage of funds.[2] Insofar as he characterized the owner of the Abbey Theatre, JBY referred to her as "the Quaker Lady."[3] Nonetheless, the Horniman portrait is a chronicle of her character, told with the "broad sympathy and human interest" of J. B. Yeats's best pictures.[4] His society portraits of great men's wives often disappointed in their representation of clothes and jewels, but in this portrait the jewels, if not the best thing in the picture, do signify. Their mere size is a frank assertion of wealth; their outlandish design is Horniman's declaration of her freedom to do as she

1. J. B. Yeats described himself as a painter of "friendship portraits" in a 15 December 1920 letter to John Quinn, quoted by Murphy (*Prodigal Father: The Life of John Butler Yeats (1839–1922)* [Ithaca, N.Y.: Cornell University Press, 1978], 285).
2. Lily Yeats to WBY, 2 February 1904; quoted in Murphy, *Prodigal Father*, 276.
3. J. B. Yeats to WBY [25 May 1906]; quoted in Murphy, *Prodigal Father*, 300.
4. Douglas Archibald, *John Butler Yeats* (Lewisburg, Pa.: Bucknell University Press, 1974), 54.

likes. the painter's interpretation, however, is not in the jewels, clothes, or dark enclosure; it is in the face, about which there is something overstrained: the skin around the eyes, along the hairline, is pulled tight, almost as if in terror, so that the subject's reclining position does not suggest lassitude; it suggests a cat before it strikes.[5] Most telling, however, is the mouth: this mouth, slightly pouting, slightly drawn, looks as if its lips are quivering. The painting does not show an especially likable person, but nonetheless it finally applies the portrait painter's "balm of sympathy and tenderness."[6] The picture first gives the facts of the face, but then adds a comment, with the comment insinuated, not with underhanded irony, but with a most telling kind of understanding. Behind the terrifying person, it shows the terrified one; behind the imperious middle-aged would-be queen of an international art theatre, it shows a thin, desperate, and suffering woman.

J. B. Yeats's portrait brings before us as a person the "grey eminence in the background," the "dictator" behind the three "generals" who stood over the ranks of INTS, Ltd.[7] In chapter 2, it was seen that the prospect of her money gave W. B. Yeats freedom of political maneuver at the time of Queen Victoria's visit to Ireland in 1900. In chapter 3, it was implied that her promise of a theatre in 1903 (broached in April 1903, privately offered in October 1903, and officially declared in April 1904)[8] called from WBY his *Samhain* distinctions between literature and propaganda in the dispute over *In the Shadow of the Glen*. In chapter 4, finally, it was shown that her June 1905 offer to pay salaries to actors led to the split in the Irish National The-

5. The feline image is perhaps appropriate to a woman nicknamed "Tabby," who purred when pleased and when angry stretched out her fingers like catclaws, while from her lips there issued a low-pitched hiss. See Ben Iden Payne, *A Life in a Wooden O: Memoirs of the Theatre* (New Haven: Yale University Press, 1977), 78.

6. Dr. James White, *John Butler Yeats and the Irish Literary Renaissance* (Dublin: Dolmen Press, 1972), 16.

7. Murphy, *Prodigal Father*, 296.

8. James W. Flannery, *Miss Annie F. Horniman and the Abbey Theatre*, Irish Theatre Series, no. 3 (Dublin: Dolmen Press, 1970), 8; William G. Fay and Catherine Carswell, *The Fays of the Abbey Theatre: An Autobiographical Record* (London: Rich & Lovan; New York: Harcourt, Brace, 1935), 152.

atre Society. In each of these cases, the "generous gift" of Miss Horniman did more than propel the development of Irish theatre; the motivation of the gift, its origin, and the conditions placed upon it determined the shape of the history of Irish theatre. The issue is not that the Irish dramatic movement was floated for many years upon the capital of an Englishwoman, or that the plays written were underwritten by Horniman; the key issue is the extent to which her capital made Irish drama her form of self-expression rather than the embodiment of national feeling. W. B. Yeats was not the only one to make the INTS the instrument of a secret agenda; another was Miss A. E. F. Horniman.

If Yeats thought Horniman was that sort of patron from whom (he claimed in 1903) the Irish National Theatre Society would accept him—"a mad king [*queen* would have been more to the point] who loved the arts and their freedom," offering "unconditioned millions"—then he could not have been more wrong. Horniman loved the arts well enough, but her thousands, not millions, were never given unconditionally.[9] From the beginning, Horniman realized the political tendencies of the theatre society sufficiently to attach her formal offer to Yeats's public explanations in *Samhain* that a literary theatre precluded political engagement.[10] The first sentence of

9. WBY, *Samhain: 1903;* rpt. in *Explorations,* 105. I do not possess Horniman's bank records, but some idea of her fortune may be gained by her 7 December 1910 letter to W. A. Henderson: "You may as well be told that my income of £2400 made the £1000 a year (at best) to the Abbey a heavy burden" (ms. 1733, Henderson Collection, NLI; quoted in Flannery, *Horniman and the Abbey Theatre,* 35). Her capital was likely to be fifteen times her income, or £36,000. The death of her father in 1906 had brought her £25,000, in addition to monies inherited earlier from her grandparents, but she spent part of the capital in setting up the Manchester Gaiety Theatre. According to Rex Pogson's version of the "bare facts," Horniman spent a total of £13,000 on the Abbey and its company (Pogson, *Miss Horniman and the Gaiety Theatre, Manchester* [London: Rockcliff, 1952], 13).

10. Although Maire nic Shiublaigh doubts that Horniman "fully realised the basis upon which the National Theatre Society had been established," Horniman claimed she had made it clear to all the members of the company when she offered them free use of the Abbey Theatre that she had no sympathy with their politics (Nic Shiublaigh, *The Splendid Years* [Dublin: James Duffy, 1955], 48; Horniman to Synge, 7 January 1906; Hogan and Kilroy, 3:58–59.

Horniman's April 1904 letter—published in the Dublin news-papers, and reprinted in the 1904 *Samhain*, along with a letter of acceptance signed by all members of the INTS—states that Horniman has "great sympathy with the artistic and dramatic aims of the Irish National Theatre as publicly explained by [WBY] on various occasions." Horniman's formal letter pre-sents a condition in the legal sense of the term: if Yeats had not expressly stated that the INTS policy excluded Irish pro-paganda, and if the other members of the company had not signed a letter of acceptance binding them to his state-ment, Horniman's offer of the theatre would have been void. Horniman subsequently proved herself capable of prose-cuting her claim according to the letter of the deed of gift: not content to offer a theatre in which the aims for which she had sympathy might be realized, she was determined that only these aims and no others should be pursued on the premises of the Abbey Theatre. What some might think an open-handed, generous gift—"a gambler's throw"—was in effect a closely worded contract of purchase.

"She regarded our group," Maire nic Shiublaigh reflected, "as yet another small company in which by her aid she would receive a governing interest."[11] Lady Gregory hated to admit the power of Horniman's proprietary interests, complaining in 1921 that Horniman "made the *building*, not the theatre," but Lady Gregory earlier had occasion to reflect with dread that when the directors of the theatre fell out with its owner, Horniman was in a position of command. Lady Gregory pleaded with Yeats that in a showdown, Horniman "would have a very strong hand, theatre, renewal of patent, and money"; all the directors had was the plays and the players—and the players, she might have admitted, were only theirs by contract, their salaries being paid out of Horniman's sub-sidies. Horniman was never backward in her awareness of just how strong her hand was and what she had a right to expect. Indeed, Lady Gregory once conceded that Horniman possessed not only title to the building but power over what

11. Nic Shiublaigh, *Splendid Years*, 48.

happened on the premises: when Horniman turned down
the Theatre of Ireland's request for use of the Abbey, Lady
Gregory remarked to Synge that while "a propagandist theatre would be very useful," "it is not what [Miss Horniman]
spent her money for."[12] In this case, the difference between
giving and buying, between empowerment and disenfran-
chisement, is obvious: for all the talk of the rights of artists,
Horniman had in mind consumer rights and the rights of
property.

Yeats often thanked Horniman publicly for her complete
generosity, and he even assured nationalists that she "never
attempted to interfere with our policy in even the slightest
things,"[13] but the fact of the matter is that she harrowed the
directors of the Abbey constantly, Yeats especially, with an
escalation of daily letters that climbed from allegations to
complaints, complaints to incitements, incitements to requests, requests to demands, demands to threats, and threats
to ultimatums. If Horniman did not interfere in the affairs of
the INTS, why did Yeats beg her to stop doing so? One such
plea called from her the wounded, exaggerated, and fundamentally false reply, "I do not remember ever having wished
to sacrifice your work or ambitions to any idea of my own."
But Horniman throughout continued to assert that INTS affairs "concern[] my property and as such [are] my business
and I ought [to be] considered."[14] When Horniman decided to
start a second front in the more hospitable environs of Manchester and employed Ben Iden Payne to manage the Gaiety
Theatre there, the young director dropped by Yeats's rooms in
Woburn Buildings. The poet offered him the benefit of his experience with Horniman in suggesting that Payne draw up an

12. Lady Gregory to Synge, 20 February 1906; Hogan and Kilroy, 3:61.
13. Nic Shiublaigh, *Splendid Years*, 48–49; Lady Gregory, *Journals*, ed.
Daniel J. Murphy (1947; rpt., New York: Oxford University Press, 1978), 247;
quoted words are from WBY to D. O'Connell, n.d., Coole Park (taped in
copy of WBY, *Ideas of Good and Evil*; ms. 1742, NLI).
14. Horniman to WBY, 16 February 1910. Citations from the letters of
Annie Horniman, when not otherwise noted, are drawn from the Horniman
Papers at the National Library of Ireland, ms. 13068.

agreement with her very carefully: "He advised me that, when the subject came up, I should make the contract a tight one, laying down definite limits beyond which Miss Horniman should have no authority to interfere. *'You know,'* Yeats explained, *'she is a vulgarian.'* This attitude surprised me greatly for the moment . . . [but] I took Yeats's advice, and learned to be grateful for it [emphasis added]."[15] By the time of his discussion with Payne in the summer of 1907, Yeats had reason to believe that even if he had already gotten £7,000 out of Horniman (purchase of theatre, actor salaries, subsidies for tours of England), he had not driven a hard enough bargain: having to hand over the reins of the theatre movement to a rich vulgarian was more than he had counted upon.

Brief and conclusive evidence of the fact that Horniman laid down significant prohibitions upon both the directors and actors of the Irish National Theatre Society appears many years later, in 1909, in the joint understanding that Horniman's sale of the Abbey would release the theatre from a host of obligations. Horniman offered Yeats and Lady Gregory easy terms, sweetened by the prospect that once they had paid £428 down and a £1000 quittance, the new owners could rent the theatre to the Gaelic League, sell sixpenny seats, end their quarrel with the Theatre of Ireland, and reap the rewards of popularity that would follow from dissociation from Horniman herself.[16] Horniman here provides a short list of her imperatives as owner of the Abbey: it could not be used to advance the Gaelic language, to proselytize for nationalism, to entertain the sixpenny public (that is, the mass of Dublin Irish), or to direct its destiny unhindered by the veto power of the English owner. The motives and consequences of these prohibitions remain to be addressed; at this point, suffice it to say that without Horniman the Abbey was free to be a popular, nationalist theatre led by the Fay brothers; with her it was forbidden to be so.

Not only were Horniman's thousands consigned upon a

15. Payne, *Life in a Wooden O*, 80.
16. Horniman to directors of the NTS, 9 September 1909.

"no politics" clause, and on her understanding that they implied rights of property in the theatre society, they were also "conditioned" by every quality of her character, certain powerfully independent proclivities, but mostly antipathies, which Yeats was later to describe as "stops of an organ":[17] years after an offense had been given her, some accident would reawaken the memory, and groans of contempt, shrill denunciations, and scherzos of hatred would all voluminously sound forth, with strict warnings that if her voice were not heeded, she would soon stop all cheques and hang a *For Sale* sign on the door of the Abbey. In order to take a reading of her determinative role upon the history of Irish drama, it is first necessary to analyze in more detail the character of the frail woman in rich brocade painted by John Butler Yeats.

2

John Butler Yeats described Horniman as "the Quaker Lady"; indeed, her grandfather, John Horniman, the first man to put tea in bags for retail sale, was a Quaker, but her father converted to the Church of England as a faith more fitting to the conservative proprietor of what had become a major firm, Horniman Tea.[18] The family nonetheless laid down principles of education derived from their former faith: they forbade their daughter to play cards or frequent the theatre. Showing the independence of a Quaker, if not the beliefs, the young Annie Horniman soon made theatre her private passion, and it was not many years before she was searching for her fate in a deck of Tarot cards.

Even as she became more Rosicrucian, Horniman kept the character of a Quaker: she was a plain speaker, hated subterfuge in others (and often tried to expose it), thought the difference between right and wrong a clear one and hated the wrong, expected cleanliness in others, smoked cigarettes, be-

17. WBY to Florence Farr [? July 1907]; Wade, 490.
18. The information in this paragraph is taken from Pogson, *Horniman and the Gaiety Theatre*, 1–16.

lieved nothing was achieved by violence, thought the sexes equal, but did not approve of suffrage campaigns—they involved the illegitimate use of force. She was also proud of the mercantile virtues of Low Church petty capitalists. Hard work, work for "honest" money, prompt payment of accounts, neat bookkeeping, the building up of a name in the eyes of the public, the conduct of oneself according to what is required of one's position in life, determination to provide satisfaction to the paying public, the "right" to get value for money—these were all ideals of character for Horniman, and she was highly indignant when the Irish insinuated there might be something spiritually demeaning about these "commercial" characteristics.[19] The "transcendental" Irish, she raged, were like feebleminded madmen at the Townsend Asylum, "better under care and guard"; if they were on a high plane, she preferred "rather a lower plane where a sense of Honor & Self-Respect find a home."[20] Home, righteousness, honor, self-respect, solid success: this is the design embroidered in the Quaker's sampler.

It is to Horniman's credit that as an unmarried woman in turn-of-the-century English society, she refused to retire from life or offer any apology for being single; she was instead a proud, passionate spinster. Her belief in the equality of the sexes took many forms: she wore bloomers, rode a bicycle, and traveled unchaperoned around Europe and North Africa; she bravely played a part in public life. But her belief that she

19. See for instance Horniman's letter to Florence Darragh of 18 August 1906, where she warns Darragh that "a lot of nonsense will be talked to you against 'commercial drama,'" by which Willie Fay simply means "the distinct intention to act, to work for a living honestly, to have ambition . . . to look and behave with knowledge as to what is required on stage." A few days earlier, she urged Yeats to accept as a definition of theatrical "Art" as "the commonplace professional idea of earning a living and getting a bigger salary," which is "at any rate, honest" (Horniman to WBY, 14 August 1906). In a later dispute over Abbey business matters, Horniman wrote Yeats that because she was a shopkeeper's daughter, and proud of it, she would not immediately stop the subsidy; and because she was a shopkeeper's daughter, she would stop it when the termination date of her promised support came due (Horniman to WBY [? April 1907]).
20. Horniman to WBY, 4 August 1906.

could do anything she cared to do, just as a man might, did not imply any degree of sexual freedom. She regarded the sex life of humanity as one great scandal. Indeed, she generalized upon her own role as spinster and applied it to others, believing that in most cases no offer of sexual relationship could be decently accepted. When W. G. Fay fell in love with the young actress Brigid O'Dempsey, Horniman went on the warpath, even though Fay wanted to marry the girl and soon did marry her.[21] When Yeats was meeting with Mrs. Patrick Campbell, the famous London actress, concerning the title role of *Deirdre*, Horniman's reaction was again overstrained. She rather unnecessarily pointed out to Yeats that he was already too old for "Mrs. Pat"; the leading lady "might well go in for someone young."[22] (In fact, Beatrice Campbell had been born in the same year as Yeats—1865—and five years after Horniman herself.) Perhaps this remark was meant as a joke among intimates, but if so the meagre covering of humor is a dress code to permit the introduction of naked panic about sexual relations.

Horniman's feelings about sex took the shape of disgust when John Synge fell in love with the young Abbey actress Molly Allgood. Synge accompanied the players on an English tour for which Horniman did the publicity, and she found the "spooning" almost more than she could bring herself to mention, but having brought herself to that point, she then could not stop making it a bone of perpetual contention. She frequently wrote to Yeats first to report Synge's misbehavior, and, after the tour, to seek out tidbits of gossip about its further progress: "As to Mr. Synge—he too has proved himself to be no good. Any holiday can be put off for a few days when necessary [to the business of the theatre]. Has he had the courage to take Mollie Allgood with him? Or has he gone to escape from her? Is the man content with what he has

21. Horniman to WBY, 1 October 1906. Fay's romance was a matter of concern to the directors as well, because Brigid O'Dempsey was under age and her father was initially not in favor of the union (Saddlemyer, 148–50).
22. Quoted in Flannery, *Horniman and the Abbey Theatre*, 13.

done already or does he think he can get along without the [help] of the theatre?"[23] John Millington Synge's love for Molly Allgood—his queerly romantic, parsonical letters to her, his plays inspired by her, his marriage to her prevented by his Hodgkin's disease, his legacy to her, her starring performance after his death in *Deirdre of the Sorrows*—makes up one of the great popular "real life" love stories of the age, but Horniman could not countenance the possibilities that a director could fall for an actress, a Protestant Anglo-Irish gentleman for a Catholic working girl, or any man for a woman of lower social rank. The only reason could be passing lust, demeaning to both the man and his social peers; in her book, Synge was written down as a callow male of no morals, and time would show that "three months of one girl on his knee doubtless leads him to wish for a change."[24] In these relationships—Fay/O'Dempsey, Yeats/Campbell, and Synge/Allgood—two features come to the fore: first, a threat of open sexual relations; second, a misalliance between the partners. Whenever it becomes possible that a man and a woman might have a sexual interest in each other, for Horniman there always appear overriding reasons—age, class, financial position, business interests—why such an imputation is unthinkable, much less something upon which the couple might like to act.

In light of her pattern of response, the sparsely documented ruckus in the Order of the Golden Dawn during 1896 takes on fuller significance. On that occasion, Horniman was apparently the subject of what she took to be a sexual overture from one of the Order's leading warlocks, Dr. Berridge.[25] The meetings of secret societies like the Golden Dawn served for at least some of their members the function of an experience of heightened eroticism under the cloak of communication with the sublime. It is true that there was more robing than disrobing, but the meetings in darkened chambers of numbers of female adepts with a few powerful mages, where

23. Horniman to WBY, 3 September 1906.
24. Quoted in Flannery, *Horniman and the Abbey Theatre*, 22.
25. Harper, 14.

participants underwent rites of passage from an outer temple to an inner temple, with considerable blindfolding of the women, while male mystagogues sometimes evoked images of fire and spear, cups and water, were an exquisite theatre of the erotic. Altogether, such secret societies offered the excuse, the occasion, and the crypto-language for late Victorian men and women to enter upon a subject for which they lacked other means of expression.[26] It is not known how Horniman distinguished between the generalized eroticism of the Order's carryings-on and the particular advance of Berridge, but he must have made an attempt on her person for which no mystical rationale could be found. It may indicate the general character of sublimated license in the Order that other members took Miss Horniman's violent rejection of Berridge's offer, and her demand for action, to be a case of "intolerance, intermeddling, and self-conceit."[27] Other members, it appears, refused to meddle in the private rituals of consenting adepts. Horniman forced so much undesirable attention upon the question of insidious impropriety in the society that its head, MacGregor Mathers, delivered an ultimatum to all members, but aimed at Horniman in particular, to submit themselves without question to his authority. Horniman refused, and in the ensuing ructions she cut off Mathers's annual subsidy; he promptly kicked her out of the Golden Dawn. From this early incident in Horniman's womanhood, a profile of her psychic economy begins to emerge. The Golden Dawn's "Soror Fortitor et Recte," our sister straight and strong, manfully perpendicular in her propriety, Horniman was a passion-

26. The coincidence of the bodily and the disembodied is, in fact, never more frankly explicit than in the automatic script of George Yeats when she communed with daemons to find answers to the poet's questions about the ideal frequency of sexual intercourse and the connection between his sexual interest in Maud Gonne's daughter and the proliferation of his poetic impulses. If sex is an all but explicit agenda of the automatic script, it is implicitly one impulse gratified by meetings of the Golden Dawn as well. For information on Yeats's automatic script, see George Mills Harper's fascinating *The Making of Yeats's* A Vision (Carbondale: Southern Illinois University Press, 1987), pp. 31ff. 88, 92, 101–2, and passim.
27. Harper, 14.

ate puritan—passionate so long as passion was not named, and indomitably puritanical when it raised its head.

3

Miss Horniman was certainly drawn to Yeats by something more than approval of his poetic drama; she was, in fact, in love with him. There is an embarrassment of evidence for this attachment. She kept a lighted portrait of the poet in her rooms at H1, Montague Mansions, London; she was pleased to claim that she served as his secretary in the 1890s; she made him a present of the Abbey Theatre, which is an expensive sort of gift to make to a mere friend; she was watchful for rivals, and jealous of Maud Gonne, Lady Gregory, Mrs. Patrick Campbell, and Florence Farr. Horniman's almost daily letters to Yeats are addressed to her "Dear Demon" or even her "Dear Demonical Director" and signed "Affectionately." She let herself into his London apartment when he was absent, and in a fussy wifely way, spoke of moths in the curtains, dust on the bookshelves, papers on the floor; she even looked into his wastepaper basket (on a search for a parcel wrapper, she said), which suggests the sort of surveillance even a wife might reconsider.[28] All this evidence bespeaks, on her side, love in name and spirit.

Yeats, on his side, kept company with her, sometimes answered letters, and in general permitted her to devote herself to him. William M. Murphy and James Flannery are correct that there is no evidence that he "encouraged her suit" only if her suit is understood to have been for either a sexual relationship or a marriage proposal.[29] For Horniman to believe her affections in some part not unwelcome, it may have been enough that a poet like Yeats comported himself a great deal like a man in love.[30] He talked about his feelings, and few men

28. Horniman to WBY, 7 July 1907.
29. Murphy, *Prodigal Father*, 271.
30. Edward Martyn spitefully attributed Yeats's theatrical success to his high-handed way with women: "The qualities by which Mr. Yeats has made the theatre are Napoleonic and consummate. A fine poet and subtle literary

not in love did such an "effeminate" thing; he wrote, and even recited, poems, a surefire sign in an ordinary man of an approaching proposal. Yeats's letters to women—especially those to Florence Farr and Olivia Shakespear—show him to have been a wonderfully chatty companion, an easy organ of confidential humor and private revelations. He was often ready to make a woman his cohort; for instance, he worked with Maud Gonne in politics, with Farr in cantillation, with Lady Gregory in playwriting, and of course with Horniman in the management of the Golden Dawn and the Abbey. This habit of respect for a woman's own powers was surely endearing. It would be wrong, however, to treat Yeats's relationships to all these women as equivalent. At one extreme, he desperately sought a sexual relationship with Maud Gonne; at the other extreme, he was oblivious to the possibility of a sexual interest on the part of Lady Gregory. His relations with Florence Farr offered him a relaxed combination of long friendship, professional collaboration, and sexual gratification. His relation to Horniman was like none of these.

The art of managing Annie Horniman involved a perfect balance between dismissing and introducing intimacy. The question was kept alive year after year, with immense assistance from Horniman. Most of Yeats's letters to his patron have not survived and those that have—addressed to "My dear Miss Horniman"—are generally the more public and least familiar of his communications. The type of relationship, however, can be inferred to some degree from Horniman's own letters, such as her 10 December 1906 missive following an incident at the Abbey Theatre. Maud Gonne had sued for divorce from Major MacBride early in the year, alleging bru-

---

critic, he has above all a weird appearance which is triumphant with middle-aged masculine women, and a dictatorial manner which is irresistible with the considerable bevy of female and male mediocrities interested in intellectual things" (Denis Gwynn, *Edward Martyn and the Irish Literary Theatre* [1930; New York: Lemma Press, 1974], 154). Admittedly, Yeats was dictatorial, but his real charm was his romantic, open-hearted, and intimate familiarity with women, which as friendship could be mistaken for love, and as love, for friendship.

tality and drunkenness; after a bitter trial during the summer, separation was granted. Throughout this painful episode, Yeats had supported his old love, and on 20 October 1906 he escorted her to the Abbey premier of *Deirdre*, *The Gaol Gate*, and *The Mineral Workers*. When the couple entered the theatre, with Maud Gonne dressed in black, members of the audience stood up to hiss the woman who had scorned an Irish hero and broken her Catholic vows of wedlock. Maud Gonne smiled, unperturbed, but Yeats "looked bewildered as the hissing went on," and afterwards he was in a fury of contempt for the village nastiness of Catholic nationalists.[31]

Horniman's letter alludes to a conversation she had had with Yeats about Maud Gonne's reception at the Abbey:

> When you get back [from Dublin] I must have a number of questions answered, I'll remove all reading matter from within reach & you will have to give me your full attention whether you are bored or no. You have been too much petted of late years until you have taken to use that crushed pained & distressed look of misery as a means of terrorising Lady Gregory and me whenever we object to anything.
>
> You naturally made no remark when I said that Mrs. Mac-Bride got what she deserved when she came to the theatre. In a case like that your silence is quite right—you know that it is true but of course you object to saying so. But you might remember that continual snubbings when kindly feelings are expressed may in time not only stop their expression but blunt their vitality or even at length destroy them. Yet, as I ought to know well, writing (& even speaking) makes no difference to you when you wish to abstract yourself from life, so I'm not at all cross & trying not be sad & I certainly will not worry you, for I have my own dignity to consider.[32]

These are the words of a woman in love, in love with a man not in love with her, but dependent upon her. It can be inferred that Yeats did not answer her letters as often as she liked, but answered some; that he did not visit her until told

31. Mary Colum, *Life and the Dream* (1958; rev. ed., Dublin: Dolmen Press, 1966), 124. See also Samuel Levenson, *Maud Gonne* (New York: Reader's Digest Press, 1976), 232–33.

32. Horniman to WBY, 10 December 1906.

he must do so; that when he did visit her, he looked quickly for a book to entertain himself, went slightly deaf to inquiry, and finally forced to respond, put on his "crushed pained & distressed look of misery." He did not, in short, do much to sustain his relationship with Horniman, but he did just enough. In this letter, Horniman is in fact giving him instructions as to the degree of disregard she is willing to suffer: a certain number of snubs "blunt[s] the vitality" of her "kindly feelings"; a few more will destroy them altogether. The complicated mix of signals required can be deduced from a letter Florence Darragh (an actress friend of Horniman's) wrote to Yeats: Darragh counsels him on one hand that Horniman stood in need of "all those ridiculous little attentions which she values so much," on the other hand that she would "fling thousands in your lap if she saw you were becoming independent."[33] The delicate art of management this required took its toll, especially when the patron expressed her "kindly feelings" by demanding that Yeats admit "Mrs. MacBride got what she deserved" when she was hissed and reviled at the Abbey. Horniman is bizarrely out of touch with Yeats's true feelings when she says he knows that this is true. On the contrary, Horniman's statement placed her among the group of petty, vicious puritans he loathed. Yeats kept his silence— and it must have been hard to do so—because to speak could only have been to blast Horniman's soul into a cinder, and with her, her money.[34]

Yeats may have paid Horniman insufficient attention at times and ignored her altogether when she slanged Maud Gonne, but he was attentive enough about matters of money. In July 1906 Horniman wrote Yeats that she was ready to give up on Ireland and the Abbey; they had done their best, no one could do more, but it was time to admit defeat and try

33. Florence Darragh to WBY, 22 September 1906; Finneran, Harper, and Murphy, 1:170–72.
34. During December 1906 Yeats was deeply involved in creating a new scheme for the Abbey that would satisfy its owner and secure from her an additional £25,000 investment (WBY to Synge, 2 December 1906, especially the postscript marked "Private"; Saddlemyer, 175). These events are discussed below.

again at a new venue—namely, the Manchester Gaiety. Yeats, she suspected, would struggle onward for a while in Dublin, but when he tired, she welcomed him to join her in Manchester with his "little band of earnest, practised playwrights." [35] In a gesture of extraordinary goodwill to him personally, she told him to "hold tight to the remembrance that [he could] always claim [her] help"; if he needed more cash, she would find a way to send it, adding "but this must not be known to anyone but you." Across the top of the letter, Yeats wrote and underscored the brief comment: "*A letter offering to increase the £800 subsidy if necessary.*" What is revealing here is the contrast between the sentiment of her private message and the strictly documentary, official attitude of his notation. She offers him a life in England and a gesture of her love; he takes it as a promissory note on her bank account.

It would be imprecise to say that Yeats hoodwinked Horniman; he had only to keep his temper while she hoodwinked herself. He also cannot be blamed for not taking the relation to a deeper stage of intimacy: he did not want to, and if Horniman did want a sexual relationship, she was not likely to admit to it. Her extraordinary aversion to the sexual motive— in herself as much as in Fay, Synge, and Dr. Berridge—was essential to her self-deception. It not only enabled Yeats to leave the relationship in a perpetual stall, it caused her to displace her desire in several ways, among them financial generosity. She hated Maud Gonne for "arousing the most animal passions": "the greatest artist on the stage" (by which she meant WBY) was "helpless compared to a beautiful woman screaming from a coal-cart," but it was just her own inability to arouse such passions, and to welcome them, that left a hole in her life, a deep hole into which she cast a great many banknotes. [36] She paid and paid, but what she paid for was never delivered. She aimed to buy the love of Yeats; lacking that, an Irish theatre society; lacking that, the Abbey Theatre building. In the end, she was relieved of title to the building, with

35. Horniman to WBY, 13 July 1906.
36. Horniman to Florence Darragh, 18 August 1906.

£1,500 remaining of a £13,000 investment, and of her relationship to Yeats.[37] The poet did not hoodwink his patron; he exploited her, which is what patrons are for.

4

Four years after the purchase of the Abbey, Horniman told Yeats that she "never imagined for a moment" that he was "practically exploiting" her: "You were a great deal too stupid."[38] It would have been cheaper, she reasoned, to hire a theatre in the London's West End for a week of matinees for Yeats's verse plays if the only purpose of her philanthropy was to build up his reputation as a dramatist. She had something in mind a great deal wider, and so, it may be said, did Yeats. "I felt that I was doing something in Ireland that could only be done by an outsider, by someone with no axe to grind," she told the press, but quite obviously she had an axe to grind, as Yeats had one, and everyone came with axes raised. In fact, this is a classic illustration of the phrase, which, according to *Brewer's Dictionary of Phrase and Fable*, derives from the story of a man who wanted to have his axe blade sharpened, but had no money to pay the blacksmith.[39] So he praises the skill of the smith, suggests that his admiration would be splendidly gratified if he saw that skill practiced on his own axe, and, when it is ground, laughs at the blacksmith. Yeats's axe was his dramatic ambition, and Miss Horniman's money played the part of blacksmith to put an edge on it; Horniman's axe was her desire for self-expression. Horniman came to Dublin with a desire to participate in the production of arty, mystical plays by Yeats; she permitted the

37. On 6 May 1937, meeting with Holloway at the Abbey, Yeats remarked that he had called on Miss Horniman in London "for the first time in thirty years"—an exaggeration of only a few years. Their visits diminished after the summer of 1907 upon Horniman's purchase of a theatre in Manchester; their correspondence ended with Horniman's 5 May 1911 telegram (see p. 238 below).

38. Horniman to WBY, 27 February 1908.

39. E. Cobham Brewer, *A Dictionary of Phrase and Fable*, Classic Edition (New York: Avenel Books, 1978), 78.

Irish to wax proud of their myths, dialect, and natural talent for acting; then having used these blandishments to see *The King's Threshold, The Shadowy Waters,* and other plays into performance, she scorned the workers, denied their desire for national expression, and claimed the credit for their art.

Later in her life, and after several bitter lessons, Horniman learned that she was, as she confessed to the Reverend James O. Hannay, "one of those people who cannot produce anything myself." [40] But as a young woman, she had wanted to be an artist, so she attended the Slade School of Art in London. It was there that she met Moina Mathers, daughter of Bergson and wife of MacGregor Mathers; through Mathers she met Florence Farr and Yeats. She came into association, that is, with creative people of mystical inclination, but no money; she had the money, but the Slade School drawing masters discovered no particular creativity. Without husband or child, with nothing to show for herself, her frustrated desire for the satisfactions of creativity was a torment to her. When Yeats was bringing her into his plans for an Irish theatre, he held out the tempting offer that she would be given a chance to design all the costumes for his own plays. She still had not yet committed herself to buying a theatre when he went ahead and put her in charge of costumes for *The King's Threshold.* She did not exactly buy a business in order to get a job in it, but out of gratitude for getting a job, she bought the business.

Horniman's thankfulness for the opportunity put in her hands is painfully complete. After Yeats introduced her to the acting company in its shabby little quarters in Camden Street, she made a point of staying in Dublin after his departure to become acquainted with the actors and advise them wisely about stage matters.[41] Exalted by the fellowship with artists, she wrote to Yeats that the stars in their courses blessed her new work: "I am so anxious to help as effectually as I may and it seems as if it were already ordained. I'll stay on here next week to see what I am to do. Do you realise that you

40. Horniman to Hannay, 21 February 1907; ms. 2259, NLI.
41. Nic Shiublaigh, *Splendid Years,* 48.

have now given me the right to call myself 'artist'? How I thank you!"[42]

Never was a woman of fortune so happy to be a seamstress. Horniman took measurements of some, but not all, the chief actors, and, upon her return to London, she shopped for the richest possible materials, and she bought them in the greatest quantity, for the costumes of an eighth-century Irish king, bard, mayor, cripple, servant, priest, and so forth. With lectures from Yeats on the symbolic and aesthetic value of decorative staging to guide her, she set about cutting and stitching costumes for actors. Letters were dispatched from London to the company, requesting more information about the measurements, letters that went unanswered.[43] When the costumes and players were brought together on stage, the effect was obviously, embarrassingly, unfortunate. In his review of the play, Tom Kettle, although coached by Yeats, took an arch tone: "The costumes of King Guaire and his Court were of a richness almost barbaric. The cut and colour of each garment was adjusted, I understand, to a scheme marvellous in its emotional and symbolic value, and beyond the capacity of any but a society journal to record."[44] Kettle's "society journal" dig has the true stink of Dublin wit: an Anglo-Irish poet's play, dressed and overdressed by a wealthy Englishwoman, had become a clotheshorse, the dull center of a peripheral discussion of *couture*, etiquette, and the guest list.

Horniman's first attempt at cutting a figure as a theatrical artist was not a success; her second attempt—with the 14 January 1904 production of *The Shadowy Waters*—was no better. Fay was clearly concerned lest his work with the actors be lost in a high-camp fashion show, but Yeats stayed his course. He wrote Horniman "as delicately as [he] could that there ought not to be gorgeousness of costume,"[45] but at the

42. Horniman to WBY, n.d.; Fay, ms. 10952, NLI; Hogan and Kilroy, 3:72.

43. Horniman to WBY, 22 September 1906.

44. Thomas M. Kettle, "The Irish National Theatre Society," *New Ireland*, 17 October 1903; Hogan and Kilroy, 3:72.

45. WBY to Lady Gregory [21 January 1904]; Wade, 427.

same time instructed Fay that Horniman was in the company for the duration: "Miss Horniman has to learn her work and must have freedom to experiment."[46] It was his own fault, Yeats told Fay, that her work failed, because he had told her old stages permitted elaborate dress. Now he would correct her misapprehension by giving her Joyce's *Social Ireland* so that she could make her next costumes more suitable to the scene in which the play was laid.

By December 1904, with the Abbey Theatre in hand, Yeats was prepared to challenge Horniman's right to call herself an artist. He came on stage with Horniman during a rehearsal of *On Baile's Strand*, called all the actors on the stage, and with "an abundance of plain-speaking," spoke of Horniman's costumes as "grotesque," "eccentric," "like Father Christmas's," like "fire-extinguishers." Under this storm of ridicule, Horniman at first could only protest that she had gotten nothing but the best material. Nevertheless, Yeats ordered the actors to rip the fur off collar and edging, to dispense with the vast red cloaks on some, and then the green cloaks on others. But, Horniman interjected, to do so would ruin the archaeological accuracy with which she had reproduced Joyce's descriptions. "'Hang archaeology,' said the great W. B. Yeats. 'It's effect we want on stage.' And that settled it," remembers an astonished Joseph Holloway.[47] The company had been given an object lesson, humiliating to Horniman, that no matter who paid the bills, Yeats ran the show.[48]

This searing incident cauterized the flow of Horniman's creativity, such as it was, at one opening; she was left with another. She had been put in charge of promoting the Irish

46. WBY to Frank Fay [?20 January 1904]; Wade, 425–26. Concerning Yeats's promise of freedom of experiment, William M. Murphy drily remarks: "That was before [Horniman] put her money on the table" (*Prodigal Father*, 296).

47. Holloway, 47.

48. Murphy rightly smells out Yeats's policy in "allow[ing] a disagreement between himself and Annie to arise in the presence of the company"— to "let her know clearly, before the first curtain went up, that no matter who was paying the piper, he was calling the tune" (Murphy, *Prodigal Father*, 278). I would simply add that Horniman did not learn the lesson.

National Theatre Society's performances in England, and, living in London, hoping for réclame with its literary high society, she threw herself into the job with energy and pertinence. For the March 1904 English tour, she wrote 300 letters in ten days, arranging for a theatre and personally inviting acquaintances to attend the performances of "her" traveling players in a work by "her dear friend" Yeats. As a result, on 26 March 1904 the West End's Royalty Theatre was packed with a well-disposed, hand-picked audience for *The King's Threshold, In the Shadow of the Glen, The Pot of Broth, Riders to the Sea,* and *Broken Soil.* The reviewers showered praise on the simplicity and naivete of the INTS style of acting.[49] Perhaps more important still, English critics praised the heroic drama of Yeats and the comedy of Synge—the very plays that had caused a furor at Molesworth Hall in October 1903. A fashionable audience had vindicated what a nationalist audience had vilified, and Horniman's labors as promoter were fully rewarded.

The next English tour of the INTS, in November 1905, was also promoted by Horniman.[50] She showed her pertinacity when Fay's attempts to book theatres in Oxford and Cambridge failed to impress theatre managers. Horniman took charge and hired the Corn Exchange Hall for 23 November in Oxford and the Assembly Rooms for 24 November in Cambridge.[51] These were important dates for the company, because Synge's *The Well of the Saints,* the bleak philosophy of which had soured Irish audiences, won over the more intellectual playgoers of the university towns. The actors played to full houses, and the INTS left England with a sizable balance of ticket sales over expenses.

This tour, however, and Horniman's role as promoter, became the subject of criticism in the Dublin press. For the London performances, Horniman had hired St. George's Hall in

49. C. E. Montague's review for the *Manchester Guardian* is quoted in Fay and Carswell, *The Fays of the Abbey Theatre,* 155.
50. Gerard Fay, *The Abbey Theatre: Cradle of Genius* (New York: Macmillan, 1958), 103.
51. Fay and Carswell, *The Fays of the Abbey Theatre,* 179.

Langham Place, a suburban location outside the theatre district. Furthermore, she had made the cheapest ticket two shillings and sixpence, a price that one disappointed London Irishman ("Padraig") said put the plays out the reach of most of his fellow-countrymen, forcing them to witness Irish drama "through English eyes."[52] Releasing an arrow in Yeats's direction, Padraig concluded, "It will not do to say 'good art' does not draw the 'crowd,' especially when the Irish crowd here are in need of National plays and look to the Irish National Theatre Society to supply the need." Horniman, of course, had no particular desire to make provision for the nationalist appetites of Paddies in London, but she nonetheless attempted to handle the bad press by sending an explanation to the *United Irishman*. Her letter makes three points: first, St. George's Theatre had no gallery, only a balcony; second, the INTS was trying to make money in England for Irish tours; third, they could not therefore "afford to charge 1s. for a part of the hall which will fetch 2s 6d." The final sentence of her letter was a political faux pas—"I am entirely responsible for the arrangements of the English tour"—but her pride in her successful efforts would not let her keep silent.

Sarsfield—a self-appointed journalistic tribune of the people—rose up to face down the English patron and her poet. "The Abbey Street Theatre in London" picked Horniman's letter to pieces in the columns of the *United Irishman*.[53] What was an Englishwoman doing in a supposedly Irish theatre? "Isn't it able to manage its own affairs?" What kind of reasoning was it that one "could not afford" to charge less than the most? Sarsfield reminded Yeats that once he had uttered the sentiment that the upper classes "put everything in a money-measure," but "the poor clerk or shopboy" "writes for the glory of God and country." But that was in the 1901 *Samhain* when the poet was trying to win friends among the nationalists; had Yeats joined the upper classes when he went into business with Horniman? Finally, Sarsfield zeroed in

52. *United Irishman* 14, no. 351 (18 November 1905): 1; *United Irishman* 14, no. 352 (25 November 1905): 1.
53. *United Irishman* 14, no. 355 (16 December 1905): 3.

on Horniman's particular aims as a promoter: the company, he said, would have had no trouble getting sufficient attendance to make a profit if the performances had been "advertised properly and widely" rather than "in a select fashion." "But," he declared, "it looks as if a fashionable audience were wanted, not an audience of the people."

The small scandal over prohibitive ticket prices did not drive Horniman out of her job, nor did it alter her aims as a promoter, but it was surely an embittering perplexity. She went ahead with the next tour in June 1906, and, while reporting to Yeats some painful steps to notify the Irish in England of the performances,[54] she once again tried to select the audience from her own class: she canvassed the London Theosophical Society and secured the assistance of Lady Alice Egerton in reaching out to the haute culture public.[55] For at least two spells in the fall and spring, she would make the players of the Abbey the theatre for her people, not the Irish. It would play for academics, mystics, and titled folk; Miss Horniman's theatre would be the talk of critics, and Dublin would learn it had no taste. On the 1906 tour, however, nothing went right for Horniman: the INTS lost £199 10s. 7d.; the critics, no longer taken with the "simplicity" of the INTS, remarked on shoddy sets and cheap wigs; and traveling in the company of the Irish players proved an unbearable social embarrassment for Horniman. She was finished with promoting such an operation; it was time to transform it.

5

If Horniman's attempts to achieve self-expression as costume designer and impresario ended in failure, there were other

54. Horniman gave in, a little resentfully, to Sarsfield's pressure to advertise the theatre at least partly among the Irish in England. She went so far as to arrange to place an article in the *Catholic Herald;* indeed, "to please your blessed countrymen," she says, "I'm managing for a portrait of Kathleen ni Houlihan to go into that paper." This, she concludes, "will 'fetch' the 1/- public." The sixpenny public, even the one shilling (1/-) people, were a very precise consumption community: the Catholic nationalist Irish. Raising prices was Horniman's way of getting rid of them. Horniman to WBY, 18 April 1906.
55. Horniman to WBY, 18 April 1906.

avenues to take in trying to make her mark on Irish theatre. Her original decisions as owner of the Abbey had a permanent effect on the formation of its audience, and the attitude the audience assumed toward the works staged there. The reconstruction of the Mechanics' Institute under the supervision of Joseph Holloway, at a cost of £1,300, turned it from a common playhouse to a small, but glamorously appointed, theatre.[56] On opening night, 31 December 1904, its ideal patrons would arrive by carriage on Marlborough Street, enter the separate entrance installed for those with expensive seats, shed their wraps at their private cloakroom, come up the stairs into the vestibule before the play, admire John Butler Yeats's portraits of the Fays, Maire nic Shiublaigh, and Horniman herself, take in the Celtic Art Deco of Sarah Purser's three-window, stained-glass design of a tree in leaf, and then pass down into their stalls for Yeats's verse-tragedy, *On Baile's Strand*.[57] The more common visitor to the Abbey would take a tram to the O'Connell Street Terminus, walk down a block on Abbey Street to the entrance of the theatre, step in to stare in wonder at "the complete and beautiful arrangements" inside, nervously check out the pit, only to learn that no gate had been installed to set off sixpenny seats, would then inquire at the box office, and, if he could afford the price of a shilling ticket, would pass into the theatre to enjoy Lady Gregory's *Spreading the News*, the curtain-raiser, before sitting through the splendors of Yeats's blank verse. Because of the ways in which Horniman employed her money (with Holloway, J. B. Yeats, and Purser), the Abbey made the rich feel at home, and the poor—on a first visit—out of place. The Abbey was a lovely little theatre, built and decorated by Irish hands with Irish materials, but its appointments made clear it was intended as a house of gentility—with a door for aristocrats, another door for the middle class, and no seats for the poor. Quite obviously it was not erected to be a factory of revolution.

56. Hugh Hunt, *The Abbey: Ireland's National Theatre, 1904–1978* (New York: Columbia University Press, 1979), 58–59.

57. See John Masefield's review of the Abbey Theatre opening in the *Manchester Guardian*, and the very different review in the *Irish Daily and Independent*, quoted in part by Gerard Fay (*Abbey Theatre*, 92–93).

Horniman's rule against sixpenny seats—declared in her formal offer of the Abbey to the Irish National Theatre Society—caused "great and ever-growing indignation."[58] Maud Gonne wrote a personal note to Yeats, saying he was "lost to nationalism," and in the *United Irishman* Arthur Griffith publicly called the price "undemocratic" and "unpatriotic." It would be wrong to treat the flare-up over ticket prices as mere nationalist hysteria, as if a sixpenny coin were nothing. The wages of workingmen in Dublin were miserable: investigatory commissions suggested that twenty-two shillings a week were required to maintain "merely physical efficiency," but general workers with regular employment made from twenty to twenty-five shillings, casual laborers made from twelve to fifteen, and, in the fall of 1905, some members of the INTS, Ltd. cast were offered only ten to fifteen shillings a week.[59] Other economic conditions exacerbated the problem of low wages: infant mortality was the worst in the British Isles, 20 percent of the workers were unemployed, 30 percent of the population lived in slums and often could not keep up with the rents there.[60] Yet these wage earners were the backbone of the Gaelic League, political clubs, and theatre groups. Effectively, the Abbey was asking of nationalists a half-day's wages for a night's entertainment, when a day's wages barely met, if at all, the needs of food and shelter. Furthermore, there was a national tradition, going back to Daniel O'Connell's "Catholic Rent," that made a small subscription the ticket to full participation in a political movement.[61] Making the most off some was sacrificed to making a little from all, thereby achieving solidarity and popularity for movements. According to D. P. Moran of the *Leader*, Abbey prices placed "the Theatre outside the sphere of utility of the Gaelic League," a remark that

58. WBY to Lady Gregory, 24 November 1904; Wade, 445.
59. See Joseph V. O'Brien, *"Dear, Dirty Dublin": A City in Distress, 1899–1916* (Berkeley and Los Angeles: University of California Press, 1982), 199–240; esp. 203.
60. F. S. L. Lyons, *Ireland since the Famine* (1971; rev. ed., London: Fontana/Collins, 1973), 275–76.
61. J. C. Beckett, *The Making of Modern Ireland, 1603–1923* (London: Faber & Faber, 1969; 1966), 299–300.

must have given ironic satisfaction to both Yeats and Horniman, since they had always resented the assumption that the dramatic movement was to be a branch office run out of nationalist headquarters. The political groups, Yeats observed, "had all got to look upon the Hall as their property," but now they would learn that Horniman's purchase of the Abbey disappropriated them; the new ticket prices were their notice of eviction.[62]

So great was Horniman's desire to regulate the character of the audience at the Abbey that she not only doubled the normal price of a ticket for the pit, she wanted to give away free tickets for the stalls to "respectable" people. After the split in the acting company, Horniman proposed employing a Mrs. Higgenbottom or a Miss Taylor (representative citizens of English Ireland) to "paper the theatre." She wanted the "class of people" who found Irish nationalism abhorrent to "see for themselves" "that the shows are [not] overpolitical."[63] Lady Gregory, who knew her Ireland, nixed the plan: not even complimentary tickets would draw the Castle crowd, and a desperate play for their favor would kill the theatre for its natural audience.[64]

62. In the fall of 1906, Lady Gregory, who "was always against a 1/- pit," prevailed upon Yeats and Horniman to permit the sale of sixpenny seats (announced in *The Arrow*, no. 1, 20 October 1906), although the theatre owner continued to worry that this would "cheapen the house" and lead to "untoward behavior" on the part of nationalists. She sent the bill for the installation of a gate dividing the pit into shilling & sixpenny sections to the directors. When Maud Gonne's Cumann na nGaedhal rented the Abbey and also sold sixpenny seats, Horniman found out and banned them from further use of the theatre, since tenants were ordered to abide by the old rule of a 1/- pit. The National Theatre Society might profit from the new prices (and it did), but she was not going to let an expressly political organization take advantage of them for popular patriotic entertainments. See Lady Gregory to Colum, enclosure in Lady Gregory to Synge, 9 January 1906; Horniman to Darragh, 18 August 1906; Horniman to WBY, 24 June 1906; and Horniman to Holloway, 28 February 1907.

63. Horniman to WBY, 22 July 1906; Finneran, Harper, and Murphy, 1:163.

64. In the long run, as Yeats noted in 1908, the Abbey had "nothing but the pit": "the stalls won't come near us, except when some titled person or other comes and brings guests. All the praise we have had from the most

6

On the spring and summer tour of England in 1906—the last promoted by the owner of the Abbey—something happened that galvanized Horniman to transform the Irish National Theatre Society, Ltd., for good—or so she thought. Before the tour the INTS, Ltd., placed popular plays on the boards in Boyle's *Eloquent Dempsy* and Lady Gregory's *The Canavans;* after the tour, in October, Lady Gregory came back with the moving *Gaol Gate* and Boyle with *The Mineral Workers.* Yeats was at work on what would become in November his most successful tragedy, *Deirdre.* The audiences were the best ever for the November and December program. But Horniman had gone sour on the whole enterprise: "growing popularity in Dublin" was just "a snare."[65] She and the directors should not fall into the trap of an Irish success. The situation, in her opinion, was dire, and called for drastic measures, beginning with the demotion of W. G. Fay from his position as stage manager. Through Yeats, she proposed that the directors hire a new stage manager, begin a star system, broaden the repertory to include foreign and classical drama, and altogether change its character from a national theatre ("an Irish *toy,*" she called it) to a dignified international "Art Institution."[66]

It is difficult to get to the bottom of Horniman's fury over the state of the INTS that made her introduce this plan for transformation of the company. Her letters to Yeats over the summer of 1906 roved wildly from complaint to complaint. She was no doubt disappointed that Yeats's own plays had not made him the Wagner of the British Isles; that the Irishness of the affair would not somehow go away; that the tour of England had not been a great success; that the actors once put on salary became less, rather than more, dedicated to their

intellectual critics cannot bring the Irish educated classes, and all the abuse we have had from the least intellectual cannot keep the less educated away" (WBY to Quinn, [October] 1908; Wade, 512).

65. WBY to Horniman, 22 July 1906; Finneran, Harper, and Murphy, 1:163.

66. Horniman to Lady Gregory, 26 December 1906; Saddlemyer, 200.

work; that her efforts to play a creative role in the company had failed; that Yeats did not love her; that Lady Gregory was doing well as a playwright; that her position in the public eye was not all she hoped it might be. But the complaints of the summer of 1906 whirl around a common center: what Synge called a "regular craze against" W. G. Fay.[67] He did not give her bills, she said, in time to pay them before they came due;[68] he once paid actors money out of the account for the tour rather than the Abbey Theatre account;[69] he failed to provide receipts for the expenditure of £5 she had given him for petty cash; he did not acknowledge by letter receipt of monies. More terrible still, when she sailed around to tell him that the day-bill for the Edinburgh performance contained a mistake, "I was told it did not matter, just as if I were an errand boy."[70] She also complained that the performances were shabby: the actors did not make up properly, they did not use the same stage business in each performance, they did not remove their greasepaint with the proper solvent, and they did not know how to attach their wigs properly.[71] Horniman had retained an English advance agent and an English road-manager, Messrs. Wareing and Bell, to assist her, and they agreed with her that the Irish players did not know their own business. Finally, Horniman brought Mr. Bell—"a profoundly self-satisfied and vulgar commercial man," Synge called him—to the green-room just before a show to tell Fay that Bell would make up the company. Fay exploded at this intermeddling in his job, and Horniman's exit, Fay bragged, was like that of a "cat driven out of the kitchen with a broomstick."[72]

67. Synge to Lady Gregory [4 July 1906]; Saddlemyer, 130.
68. Horniman to WBY, 19 June 1906, from Edinburgh.
69. Horniman to WBY, 21 June 1906.
70. Horniman to WBY, 23 June 1906; from Edinburgh.
71. Flannery draws up a useful list of Horniman's complaints about makeup, wigs, diction, stage direction, and stage-management in *Horniman and the Abbey Theatre*, 20–21. Flannery notes that while many of Horniman's complaints amount to "minute and petty carping," others are "identical with those expressed by Yeats" in a December 1906 memorandum to the other directors on the future of the Abbey.
72. Synge to Lady Gregory [9 June 1906], Saddlemyer, 128; Gerard Fay, *Abbey Theatre*, 105; Flannery, *Horniman and the Abbey Theatre*, 22.

Gerard Fay gives a brisk and accurate narrative of the mael-
strom of Horniman's wrath, blown back across the Irish Sea, a
positive tumult of yellow stationery, to the little post office in
Gort, County Galway, near where Yeats summered out the
storm with Lady Gregory. He is, however, hard put to find
"the slightest reason why Miss Horniman should have any
spite against either of the Fays," much less sufficient grounds
for the malicious campaign she waged against the stage-
manager's job.[73] There are, of course, a superfluity of manifest
explanations—by Horniman, by the Abbey directors, and by
scholars—but the vehemence of her "craze" against Fay calls
for another diagnosis.

Years earlier, in September 1904, the pooka of Irish literary
life, George Moore, had pseudonymously written an article
for the Dublin intellectual monthly *Dana* entitled "Stage Management in the Irish National Theatre."[74] Moore may well
have been, as Yeats thought, "laying pipe to get into" the
Abbey, but if so he bungled the attempt badly by allowing a
sentence in his article to imply that Horniman had fallen in
love with W. G. Fay. Moore had been dispraising Fay's abilities, discounting the good London reviews as just the sort of
condescension given to "any little bushman who came over to
London with his boomerang," but he held up short of full
criticism because Fay had struggled along on his own: "We
were about to say he has received very little support, but that
after all cannot be truly said of *a man who has found an admirer
to buy him a theatre*" (emphasis added). Horniman may have
been the only reader of the article to see a sexual innuendo in
this phrase, but she soon notified the world that she had taken
offense by asking the editors of *Dana* to print the following
correction in the December issue: "The Abbey Theatre . . . has
not been 'bought' for Mr. Fay or anyone else. It has been ac-
quired by Miss Horniman, who has arranged to lend it on
very generous conditions to the National Theatre Society for

73. Fay, *Abbey Theatre*, 104.
74. Paul Ruttledge, "Stage Management at the National Theatre," *Dana*,
no. 5 (September 1904): 150–52. The correction appears in *Dana*, no. 9 (December 1904): 256.

their performances. But she retains herself entire proprietary interest in the Theatre."

This sanitization of Moore's language is so thoroughgoing that it alerts readers to threats of pollution from every phrase. Horniman's second step was to have Yeats dictate a letter, taken in her own hand, stating that "Moore's return to the theatre is out of the question."[75] In February, after Moore praised Synge's *Well of the Saints* in the *Irish Times*, Horniman took a startling third step: Moore's "unbounded enthusiasm" made her so furious, she ordered Yeats not to associate with his "friend" (Horniman's quotation marks), and that if, by any further writings, Synge should appear to be Moore's "protégé," she expected those writings to be "publicly repudiated" or else she would "look upon it as a public insult to me by the whole Society publicly and collectively."[76] Horniman's wealth freed her from the obligation to be rational and enslaved others to her whim: how the lessor chose to see things had to be accepted by the lessees as reality; if one raised questions about the accuracy of her perceptions, she elected to regard *that* as "doubting her word," and she "refused to hold communication" with someone who slighted her honesty.[77] Horniman's prohibition of Moore as a writer for the Abbey was probably no real loss: though a strong talent, he could not work in harness with Yeats or Fay. However, it was damaging that Horniman's wrath against Moore, with the irrationality of bad weather, hung over Synge, and settled heavily on W. G. Fay.

It was loathsome enough that Moore might have been seen to hint that she was Fay's lover—what a violation of purdah, an English heiress and a dirty little Irish former electrician! But Horniman must have realized with humiliation that few would take this slander seriously; after all, they knew she was

75. WBY to Frank Fay, 13 November 1904; Wade, 443.
76. WBY to Quinn, 5 February 1905; Wade, 447; Horniman to WBY, 9 February 1905; Finneran, Harper, and Murphy, 1:147; see also Hogan and Kilroy, 3:55.
77. Horniman to WBY, 9 July 1906; Synge had questioned Horniman's judgment that Abbey performances during the summer 1906 tour were very poor.

in love not with Fay but with Yeats; it was to him she had given the Abbey. It was horrible that so many people in Dublin would be able to make this correction and enjoy a good laugh at her expense and Moore's dottiness.[78] Once the idea had come up, Horniman simply could not lay it to rest. Yeats somewhat mischievously reported to her a sally of Moore's at her expense that cut to the quick: "I cannot write what you told me last Winter what he said to you about me—you said it with a smile I must strive to forget."[79] But forget she could not, because her secret was out and she could read it in the faces of all. She settled on putting Fay in his place, as she put it, bringing him to his senses, that he was just a paid actor, open to dismissal, nothing more than that, but Fay insisted on acting as though he was her equal, even in theatrical matters her superior. In the end, the only way to handle the problem was to get rid of Fay altogether.[80]

Stirred in the witches' cauldron of Horniman's psyche, a snide phrase in a 1904 article on stage management became the "*Dana* Affair," and the *casus belli* of a full-blown assault in 1906 on Willie Fay and the Irishness of the Abbey Theatre.

7

Another cause of Horniman's attack on Fay and her plan for the wholesale transformation of the theatre society had nothing in particular to do with Fay; he was simply a scapegoat for

78. Many years later, Arthur Sinclair, lead actor with the INTS, Ltd., was still gossiping with Holloway on how Horniman and Lady Gregory, both in love with Yeats, fought for their prize (Robert Hogan and Michael J. O'Neill, eds., *Joseph Holloway's Irish Theatre*, vol. 3, *1938–1944* [Dixon, Calif.: Proscenium Press, 1968], 60).

79. Horniman to WBY, 22 September 1906; Finneran, Harper, and Murphy, 1:167.

80. "The *Dana* Affair" remained a thorn in her flesh: on 19 September 1906, to take one instance, Horniman wrote Yeats that she was now pleased she did not have to go to Dublin and be insulted by the company of Moore and the surliness of Fay. As to Moore, by October 1908 she still remembered the *Dana* article against him, refusing to permit his play to be read on the Abbey stage for copyright purposes, or even to answer his letter, though she telegrammed the business manager, Henderson, to bar the door against Moore's arrival (Holloway, 27 October 1908; Hogan and Kilroy, 3:230).

the tribal wrongs of the Irish. The fact is, the woman who loved one particular Irishman hated all the rest. During the *Playboy* riots of February 1907, the playwright William Boyle, after dining with Horniman, confided to Holloway that the policy of the theatre was shaped by her personal antipathy to the Irish:

> It has surprised me that Miss Horniman's name has been kept out of the discussion. As a matter of fact, she is at the back of it. Her hatred of everything Irish amounts to lunacy. She wouldn't allow a word of patriotic sentiment to be brought out in what she calls her theatre! As I gathered this on several occasions at her own dinner table, I can't say it openly, but I know it and know Yeats has not a free hand as he pretends.[81]

Horniman made no secret of her feelings to Yeats. She told him his countrymen were disloyal, slovenly, vulgar.[82] They wanted to destroy everything good and refined. Their folk music was "common," "vulgar"; their country costumes— "clean boots and tidy aprons"—were mere "Gaelic League vanity": everyone knew the Irish were a dirty lot.[83] In time, Horniman realized that her gibes at Irish manners, music, clothes, work habits, temperament, political culture, in fact, her "intense distaste for *any* manifestation of 'national feeling,'" as she called it, were repellent to Yeats.[84] Indeed, they must often have caused him to put on his "crushed, pained, and distressed look of misery." She brought herself to "accept 'national feeling' as a part of [Yeats's] nature," but on his side, she complained, Yeats refused to return the favor and "accept as part of my nature what is personal to me": an equally ardent contempt for the Irish. If he gave her his help, she promised, "we will conquer your country, with the help of mine," hanging fire for one beat before the last well-aimed shot— "not for the first time."[85]

The Irish would be all right, in their place, and that was

81. Boyle to Holloway, 10 February 1907; Holloway, 90.
82. Horniman to WBY, 4 August 1906.
83. Horniman to WBY, 17 July 1906.
84. Horniman to WBY, 22 September 1906.
85. Horniman to WBY, 18 April 1906.

where she, the Londoner who "loved a bobby," meant to keep them. The following anecdote may serve to illustrate Horniman's essential master/servant relation to the Irish: as an employer, she was accustomed to a better quality of service than they provided. On her first visit to Dublin, Horniman came down for breakfast at the Temperance Hotel. A leg of her dining table being short, she spoke with the Irish waitress, who, most apologetically, said, "I'll soon put it to rights, ma'am." The waitress then went to the sideboard, cut a half slice of bread, slipped it under the short leg, remarking cheerfully, "There, that will steady it now!"[86] Clearly, the Irish had to be taught to behave, to serve, to leave off with their damnable familiarity, to work for an honest wage, to play supporting roles, to be manageable, and to provide for the comfort and entertainment of the English. The nationalists were, as she said of D. P. Moran, not the sort of people "a gentleman could take to a club," but at least they could be taught to work in one.[87]

Fay took responsibility for "what she call[ed] the discipline of the company."[88] On the 1906 tour, Horniman drew up in quasi-legal form, witnessed, with dates and places, documents somewhere between a policeman's summons for minor infractions and a schoolmistress's list of demerits:

> Cardiff. Sinclair at station. Music on journey during night.
> Glasgow to Aberdeen, stop at Edinburgh, shouts in Gaelic,
>   good advertisement.
> Edinburgh to Hull . . . talked to crowd who were drunk. At
>   Carlisle with hair down.
>
> > Seen by Mrs. Wareing & Miss Gilden.
> > Notes taken July 8th, 1906.

Nothing she names against the company is a dereliction of their jobs as actors, much less a misdemeanor in their legal duties as citizens. She simply describes in a punitive form the

86. Fay and Carswell, *The Fays of the Abbey Theatre*, 143.
87. Horniman to WBY, 2 December 1907.
88. Synge to Mollie Allgood, 22 May 1907, in *Letters to Molly: John Millington Synge to Maire O'Neill, 1906–1909*, ed. Ann Saddlemyer (Cambridge, Mass.: Harvard University Press, Belknap Press, 1971), 139.

behavior of young people, young people from Ireland, on a trunk holiday in England: carefree, flirtatious, bibulous, full of song and backchat. But English employers had remarkable powers to demand an exhaustive discipline of employees; they could institute, to borrow Foucault's language, "a whole micro-penalty" "of time (latenesses, absences, interruptions of tasks), of activity (inattention, negligence, lack of zeal), of behavior (impoliteness, disobedience), of speech (idle chatter, insolence), of the body ('incorrect' attitudes, irregular gestures, lack of cleanliness), of sexuality (impurity, indecency)."[89] Horniman's outraged eye detected in the Irish actors' conduct literally every item in Foucault's catalogue of minor misbehaviors.

Foucault's *Discipline and Punish* is a key to understanding why Irish ways were a scandal to Horniman, and what motivated her schemes for their improvement. Foucault explains that a rational system, developed in the Enlightenment, of timetables, exercises, penalties, and rewards, derived in part from medieval monastic practises and perfected in the training of students, soldiers, and workers, ultimately shaping the bodies of the population and the architecture of institutions, was fundamental to the establishment of the modern industrial state. The productive capacity of new technologies was, in other words, only half the story of the rise of the state; the other half was disciplining people to operate like automata. The entire mode of being of populations had to run like clockwork; they had to execute tasks in just one way, to accept the system of rank and file without question, to desist from the search for comfort and pleasure, to labor for wages alone. Without the compliant, trained bodies of workers, the modern industrial state would not function. Foucault's work is illuminating of the history of Germany, France, and especially England from the seventeenth through the nineteenth centuries; it does not, however, cover the case of Ireland, which

89. Michel Foucault, *Discipline and Punish: The Birth of the Prison*, trans. Alan Sheridan (New York: Pantheon Books, 1977), 178.

was not a modern industrial state. The people of Ireland were exposed to few of Foucault's disciplinary practises over the centuries: they had no armies of their own, an undeveloped educational system, and few factories.

It was observed by many outsiders—Florence Darragh, Ben Iden Payne, Yeats, and Lady Gregory—that the Irish players had a most "unbusinesslike" attitude to their work. When the young English director Ben Iden Payne took over management of the theatre society from Fay, their casual ways "astonished and infuriated" him.[90] He discovered on his first day at the job that actors were allowed to arrive ten minutes after the hour for the start of rehearsal because the trams sometimes ran late. But some of the Abbey actors dawdled in at twenty past the hour, and then claimed their ten-minute allowance on top of the official grace period. They stopped after an hour of rehearsal for tea in the greenroom and stayed to chat for a long time over a sumptuous plate of cakes. Once the rehearsal was resumed, W. G. Fay quarreled with Frank Fay, striking him; the company then turned on W. G.—not for quarreling, but for taking advantage of the rake of the stage during the fisticuffs. Lady Gregory encountered the same inability on the part of the actors to separate personal life and social relations from the sphere of the workplace:

> I came round before matinee. M. wanted to speak to me to "tender his resignation" in consequence of Miss N. having insulted him during "Cross Roads" last night, before the stagehands, asked me what the devil he meant because he had missed his cue. . . . Also he was knocked down in "Cross Roads" by O. instead of being choked sitting in a chair, and this he seems to think was revenge, because he had at some previous time hit O. with the pipe he throws at him in "Workhouse Ward." I spoke to Miss N. who accuses him of a variety of small offences connected with cues. . . . On my way back to the auditorium I met Miss Q. and asked her about the quarrel. She says M. is desperately in love with N. He has been much worse since Mr. Yeats did her horoscope saying she was to marry a fair man. He walked up and down saying, "I am that

90. Payne, *Life in a Wooden O*, 71.

fair man." She went to him the other day and told him he was foolish and ought to put N. out of his head, but at the end he said, "I know very well that you are in love with me yourself!"[91]

These relations—personal, touchy, inexplicable, and inefficient—were maddening to the English (Darragh, Payne, and especially Horniman); the Anglo-Irish regarded them with a mixture of tolerant humor and apparent concern. Yeats relates an episode during Miss Darragh's adventures with the company that shows the differences between English, Anglo-Irish, and Irish attitudes to social relations at work. Miss Darragh was not popular, Yeats explains, because "she says such things as, 'Why do you not get that castor screwed on to the table leg?' instead of making enquiries and finding out that the castor cannot be screwed on because the woman who washes the floors and the stage carpenter have quarreled about it—and the stage carpenter would sooner die than screw it on. She is considered to lack tact and the finer feelings."[92] Miss Darragh, accustomed to the arrangements of an English professional company, would scarcely have thought that tact was in order. She was a star, a friend of the owner, and an associate of the director. That gave her rank. The stage carpenter was simply a worker, a rung in the hierarchy of labor. His insubordination was for Darragh a cause, not of drollery, but of indignation: to her, they were "'nothing but amateurs,' 'the most ill bred lot she ever met'—'the worst manners,' 'the rudest,' etc., etc."[93]

In the conduct of the acting company, Horniman was up against an alarming case of uneven development between the imperial and colonial economies. For several months following her explosion of antipathy to Fay, she introduced a scheme of disciplinary practices to bring the Irish up to date from a three-century lag. Since "discipline is an art of rank,"[94]

91. Lady Gregory, *Seventy Years: Being the Autobiography of Lady Gregory,* ed. Colin Smythe (Gerrards Cross, Bucks.: Colin Smythe, 1973), 416.
92. WBY to Florence Farr [October 1906]; Wade, 481.
93. Lady Gregory to Synge [6 December 1906]; Saddlemyer, 164.
94. Foucault, *Discipline and Punish,* 145.

her first objective was to put W. G. Fay in his place: "Whatever we do," she wrote Yeats, "will be frittered away until Fay comes to the conclusion that the directors must direct. . . . Fay must be brought to his senses."[95] For the rest of the company, there should be an exhaustive use of time, since time measured and paid for must be (in Foucault's expression) "time of good quality, throughout which the body is constantly applied to its exercise."[96] Horniman proposed that during the weeks when they were neither performing nor rehearsing, the players should take dancing lessons and study "bits of impossible plays."[97] There would be a double advantage to these exercises: the actors would not be paid for idle time, and by repetitive lessons, they might be trained out of their "natural ways," which Horniman considered to be an entirely inadequate basis for acting. She wanted them to execute each performance in exactly the same way, as if a role were a six-step procedure in a manual, like raising and shouldering a musket.[98] The discipline of exercises would give them "backbone," "something to fall back upon." Such training, she said, was her "idea of Art": "the very commonplace professional idea of earning a living and making a bigger salary."[99]

Finally, there should be a more thoroughgoing supervision of the players, both on stage and off, to ensure that the will of the executive was carried out. At present, working with the Irish was futile, Horniman complained to Florence Darragh, because they did not tell the truth, and either nothing she asked was done ("once your back is turned it will be 'forgotten'") or when what she asked was done, it was "done in a slovenly manner."[100] Horniman's solution to these "upstairs/downstairs" exasperations was to keep the players under sur-

95. Horniman to WBY, 21 June 1906.
96. Foucault, *Discipline and Punish*, 151.
97. Horniman to WBY, 3 September 1906.
98. Flannery, *Horniman and the Abbey Theatre*, 19–20.
99. Horniman to WBY, 14 August 1906; Finneran, Harper, and Murphy, 1:165.
100. Horniman to Florence Darragh, 18 August 1906.

veillance. Darragh was sent into the Abbey both as a star actress and as a spy for Horniman, expected to report back to the head office on behavior in the shop.[101] In addition to supervision on the job, Horniman also took an unusual interest in what the actors did on their own time: she reported to Yeats that Brigid O'Dempsey (W. G. Fay's young fiancée) had been seen by a Horniman acquaintance "going into a shop with a common-looking girl."[102] The triviality of the information is an index to the totality of Horniman's surveillance: if she could not see the actors at all times, in a sort of penal panopticon, she wished them to understand that they might be observed at any time and interrogated about any activity. All these disciplinary practices—enforcement of rank, exhaustive use of time, repetitive exercises, and surveillance—may have been necessary if Horniman was to make the backward Irish into the efficient labor force for "the factory—the school—for an International Theatre"; however, it was a mere fantasy of domination for Horniman to think she could run an overseas theatrical empire and make no end of headway against history's figuration of the Irish heart. Still more drastic measures were in order if she were to enter into full possession of her property at the Abbey.

8

After the end of the Abbey's 1906 summer tour, Horniman left for the Continent, where she recuperated from her debacle with the Irish by enjoying the superior arrangements at the Wagner theatre in Bayreuth and at the Prague National Theatre, the high-society sort of affairs she had had in mind all along for Dublin. She realized that "Prague is not Dublin, luckily for Prague," but she nonetheless hatched plans to turn

101. At the time of Miss Darragh's entrance to the acting company, Synge wrote Molly Allgood to be careful to be both "affable, and reserved at the same time," around Miss Darragh, "so that she will not know whether you like her or not." This counsel was necessary because "She is playing her own game," or, in fact, Horniman's (Synge to Molly Allgood [6 November 1906], in *Letters to Molly*, 48).

102. Horniman to [WBY?], [19 September 1906?].

the Abbey into a continental municipal theatre. These matured through the late summer and fall in conversations with Yeats and Florence Darragh and were then presented to the other directors by Yeats in a 6 December 1906 memorandum.[103] The proposals affected nearly every major aspect of the enterprise—the name of the company, its director, actors, repertoire, and schedule. Apparently, Horniman wanted the theatre company to be called simply "The Abbey Theatre Company"; Yeats surrendered the word "Irish" from the title, leaving "The National Theatre Society, Ltd."[104] In view of the further changes, it would indeed become impossible to continue to call the Abbey an Irish Theatre Society: professionals from the English stage were to be called in for starring roles at high salaries; the repertoire was to be enlarged by the addition of classics and foreign plays; and an English professional director would be placed in charge of the company and made a member of the board of directors. In presenting the plan, Horniman used both the carrot and the stick: the carrot was that she had £25,000 to spend on making the Abbey a "distinguished Art Institution"; the stick was that unless the INTS directors elected to make the change within thirty days,[105] the

103. The plan for conversion of the INTS to an International Art Institution should not be confused with an earlier plan, initiated before her European trip, for "Home Rule" at the Abbey. The terms of this earlier proposal were tentatively set forth in her letter to Yeats of 24 June 1906: she would pay a £500/annum subsidy quarterly in advance; the company would then receive the profits from concessions; the INTS gained the right to sell sixpenny seats, but tenants would not; and the directors would be in control of day-to-day operations. The real purpose of this liberal arrangement was to save Horniman the unbearable exasperation of personally writing daily cheques for activities she neither approved nor controlled; the "Home Rule" scheme did not in any way signal the end of her involvement in the theatre, only a change in the method of her involvement. For Darragh's role in the new scheme, see Saddlemyer, 164–65.

104. Darragh to WBY, 22 September 1906: "Surely it would be better to call it 'The Abbey Theatre' . . . if Miss H. had only put her theatre in London even small as it is there would have been none of this silly worry about names & Leagues etc." (Finneran, Harper, and Murphy, 1:172).

105. On 19 December 1906 Horniman issued her formal offer to hire a stage manager at £400–500 per annum to stage-manage all plays except those stage-managed by authors at their request and peasant plays by Fay. The directors had to vote on the offer before 21 January 1907, on which date it would be withdrawn.

offer would be retracted, no money would be provided for tours, and the subsidy would be stopped at the end of the patent period (1910).

There can be little doubt that Yeats was, on balance, in favor of Horniman's proposal; indeed, much of it was of his own making. He made suggestions to her that he knew would redress her grievances while at the same time strengthening his own position in the theatre. Neither Yeats nor Horniman was pleased that the theatre was "accomplished in the performance of Irish peasant comedy and in nothing else," particularly not in the verse-tragedies of Yeats, supposedly the raison d'être of Horniman's investment.[106] Yeats was inclined to lay the blame for the slow growth of his reputation upon the abilities of the company. "Women of the class of Miss Garvey and Miss Walker"—Irish Catholic actresses—he once complained, "have not sensitive bodies," even though they had "high ideals" and "simplicity of feeling."[107] They would not serve as vehicles of his vision of passionate womanhood so well as a Maud Gonne, a Florence Farr, or ultimately, a Miss Darragh.[108] Trying to finish *Deirdre*, he could make little headway so long as he envisioned the plump, sweet Sara Allgood in the role, but once he began to think of Miss Darragh as the hot-blooded queen, bravura speeches rushed into his head. The idea of getting the famous Mrs. Patrick Campbell to draw attention to his play was even more exciting. After worrying with the issue in a letter to his father, in which he could not decide whether to "leap to the advertisement of Mrs. Pat, or keep to my own people," he wedded the alternatives by supporting a new policy of bringing guest celebrities into NTS shows. Yeats also wanted to try his hand at the translation of Sophocles, to stage Maeterlinck in Dublin,

106. WBY to Synge, 2 December [1906]; dictated to Lady Gregory; Saddlemyer, 168.

107. WBY to Synge, 21 August [1904]; Saddlemyer, 67.

108. Yeats again declared the hopelessness of finding "a passionate woman actress in Catholic Ireland" when he presented the scheme for transformation of the company to Synge and Lady Gregory (WBY to Synge, 2 December [1906]; Saddlemyer, 174).

and, in general, to reestablish (or perhaps, invent) a tradition of high, spare, symbolist tragedy in which his own plays would take their proper place, so he saw personal advantages in the proposal to broaden the repertoire of the Abbey. Yeats therefore put forward the elements of the plan involving a star system and an international repertoire partly to satisfy Horniman's insistent desire to "raise the theatre to the dignity of an Art Institution" and partly to advance his own work. The proposal to demote Fay and bring in another director was Horniman's idea, but one that Yeats was not unwilling to second. Fay was essential to the work of Lady Gregory and Synge, but the tough, stunted, capering little man had none of the qualities that would make him useful to Yeats's own plays—"He is not a romantic actor, he is not a tragic actor," Yeats complained [109]—and Fay's cantankerous temperament made him somewhat unmanageable. In the proposals for the transformation of the INTS, Horniman told Yeats, "I think of your advantage and your fame," especially his advantage over the other directors. Yeats not only went along with her, he was her co-conspirator against his fellow directors.

Synge and Lady Gregory were not at all taken with the proposals made to them by Yeats on Horniman's behalf (and by Horniman on Yeats's behalf) even in consideration of the big bribe of £25,000 for the theatre, and the bigger threat that without such a change in the NTS, they would lose the subsidy and the patent. Although they doubtless wanted to protect Fay because he was such an important actor in their own plays, their main concern was not for personal advantage. Lady Gregory, in fact, forthrightly conceded that "the right of first production of Yeats's work is our chief distinction," [110] a concession Synge's own literary judgment would not quite allow him to make, although even Synge was "ready to agree to almost any experiment that [Yeats] thinks desirable in order to ensure good performances" of his own plays. [111] Lady

109. WBY to Synge, 2 December [1906]; typescript dictated to Lady Gregory; Saddlemyer, 170.
110. Lady Gregory to Synge [6 December 1906]; Saddlemyer, 168.
111. Synge to Lady Gregory, 13 December 1906; Saddlemyer, 177.

Gregory and Synge objected instead on the grounds of the national character of the society. To Synge it was a "disastrous policy" to turn a national creative movement into "a highly organised executive undertaking where the interest lies in the more and more perfect interpretation of works already received as classics." The production of more foreign plays would not, as Yeats claimed, educate Irish audiences; it would confuse them. He objected that if Yeats and Horniman brought in foreign stars at high salaries, the Irish actors would have to be paid equally, making the total cost more than even Miss Horniman's £25,000 could cover. Most important, Synge did "not see a possibility of any working arrangement in which Miss Horniman would have control of some of the departments." In his judgment, it would be better for the NTS to pursue a more broadly national policy, in the hope of support from a Home Rule Irish government at the end of the patent period:

> If we are to get a grant from the Government in Ireland—it will [be] a small one only, and we shall never get it if we become too English. I object to giving Miss Horniman any control over the company whatever. If she is given power it ceases to be an Irish movement worked by Irish people to carry out their ideas, so that if any such arrangement becomes necessary I shall withdraw.[112]

Lady Gregory spoke of the changes in still more vehemently national terms, comparing them to great setbacks in the long history of the Irish struggle for independence from England: if foreign actors were imported, she said it would "be a case of calling the Normans into Ireland," so that the Anglo-Irish Board of Authors would be remembered in later days as traitors to their country.[113] Lady Gregory seized upon another nationalist analogy—the famous split in the Parnellite party in Committee Room 15 on 1 December 1890—when speaking of

112. Original draft of Synge's letter of 13 December 1906 to Lady Gregory; Saddlemyer, 178–79.
113. Lady Gregory to Synge [19? December 1906]; Saddlemyer, 181.

the plan to oust Fay from control: if Fay refused to go along with the scheme, "we should all refuse—& not be like Dillon & Co, giving up Parnell to please an English howl."[114] The Anglicization of the theatre was entirely inimical to Synge and Lady Gregory and irrelevant to Yeats's artistic needs. In fact, while Yeats had conspired with Horniman in the scheme for transformation, his part had been to suggest that the company needed more professional actors, trainers, and directors; her part was to make sure that in each case these added workers would be English. Furthermore, Horniman insisted on distinctions of status being made between the English performers and the Irish regulars. When Yeats was enticed by the notion of Horniman's friend Miss Darragh playing his *Deirdre*, Horniman insisted that "she must be billed as a star and there must be extra advertising." The English would be in big letters, the Irish in small print. Furthermore, Horniman was not going to throw her stars in among the rabble; "some rearrangement of dressing rooms [was] implied." Holloway was instructed to go forward with building plans "for a leading lady to have a room to herself."[115] Horniman also made a point of salary distinctions between the English and Irish stage managers. The directors were permitted to hire the man to run the Abbey, but they had to follow certain guidelines: he had to be English (another "Irish Fay" was out of the question),[116] with professional experience of the English stage, someone "young, of good manners, and of such a temper as will make the position possible for him," and with a salary of £400–500 a year—vastly out of line with the Abbey scale, and much more than was necessary to obtain the services of Ben

---

114. Lady Gregory to Synge [29 December 1906]; Saddlemyer, 191.
115. These distinctions rankled with Synge. He respected the talents of Sara Allgood (bumped by Darragh from the roles of "Deirdre" and Dectora in *The Shadowy Waters*); compared with Allgood, Darragh, for all her "West End sophistication," was "an ordinary if clever actress." So for the May 1907 tour of England, Synge insisted that if there was to be special notice given leading ladies, Allgood (in the *Playboy*) should be billed equally with Darragh (in *Deirdre*) (Synge to Lady Gregory and WBY, 7 May 1907; Saddlemyer, 220).
116. Horniman to WBY, 13 January 1906.

Iden Payne, a twenty-three-year-old actor who in his experience with traveling companies had never starred in a play or taken over the complete management of a performance. The purpose of the salary was to declare in emphatic language Horniman's notion of the relative value of being English.

Horniman left Synge and Lady Gregory no room for doubt that she meant to put into effect a plan that would basically change the theatre from an Irish to an English venture, responsive to the interests of its owner. When she came to know of Synge's opposition to English control of the NTS, she was furious: "It carried this to my mind. . . . The lessee has no vote, she is bound by her Saxon sense of honor. It is 'absurd' that her views or desires should be regarded except when she admires or pushes Synge's plays. . . . Fay is necessary to Synge himself but neither are anything but extrinsic to my root idea [*sic*]."[117]

A few days later, she elaborated just what her "root idea" involved: "I understand that I am *ex*trinsic to the Irish idea, but that on the other hand, all that side is *ex*trinsic to my scheme itself."[118] What was clearly intrinsic to the new regime at the NTS was not just that it should be more efficient, professional, or versatile, but that it should be English.

9

At this pass, Lady Gregory and Synge were ready to make a stand against Horniman. Indeed, the deal was all but scuttled on the 5th of January, when Lady Gregory telegraphed Yeats, "FAY REFUSES SYNGE RELIEVED MY INSTINCTS WITH THEM BUT MOST UNWILLING TO GO AGAINST YOU."[119] However, only days later, in a last-ditch effort "to keep [Yeats] and his work for Ireland," Lady Gregory prepared two fallback proposals: the first agreed to accept a new manager provisionally for six

117. Horniman to Lady Gregory, 26 December 1906; Saddlemyer, 196; Hogan and Kilroy, 3:94–96.
118. Horniman to WBY, 28 December 1906; Saddlemyer, 195.
119. Lady Gregory to Synge [5 January 1907]; Saddlemyer, 196.

months and to allow foreign actors, but only in Yeats's plays (or foreign plays already planned); the second rejected the basis of Horniman's scheme, declaring that the NTS was not "an Irish toy," and claimed the right of the company to work in its own way another six months—with tours of England—before a reconsideration of the necessity for drastic changes at the end of this period.[120] The first counterproposal, as being the "easiest," was presented to Yeats for his approval, but before he was able to respond, Horniman again threw a wrench in the works.

In the contest for control of the NTS, Lady Gregory showed a certain amount of pluck in standing up to Horniman, saying that if the Englishwoman did have money, the theatre, and the patent, the Irish authors had the plays and the players. Not all the plays, Horniman shot back; not the plays of Yeats. According to a "secret treaty," she told Lady Gregory, if Horniman left the Abbey, she would take Yeats and his plays with her. This was a deft thrust of the hatpin. Lady Gregory, already deeply troubled with thoughts of treason, now sank under the threat of betrayal by her closest friend. For Synge's benefit, she showed great faith in Yeats, saying she was sure he "never had given this promise consciously,"[121] but she treated Yeats himself to the full force of her disappointment. The letter Lady Gregory wrote to her friend is an appeal "from Philip drunk to Philip sober": it seeks to awaken Yeats to his own sense of honor, or what ought to be his sense of honor:

> You so often talked of independence—even in your letter yesterday—as what [we] are trying for in the end. But if that "promise" holds we go into a fight, either at the end of the patent period or sooner, with our right hand tied. You will have given Miss Horniman one of our strongest possessions or weapons. She can take your plays from Ireland altogether or force you to put them into some movement opposed to your views. You will have betrayed those who have been working for you. You will yourself be in a humiliating position, seeing

120. Lady Gregory to Synge, [7? January 1907]; Saddlemyer, 198–200.
121. Lady Gregory to Synge, 10 [January 1907]; Saddlemyer, 202.

your friends and comrades dictated to and not being able to take their side. Synge and I have a right to protest because we were never told of this supposed bargain at the same time we accepted the subsidy. I certainly should not have done so at that price. . . . I am taking it to heart very much. Those plays were our own children, I was so proud of them, and loved them, and now I cannot think of them without the greatest pain.[122]

Lady Gregory here brought into play the most magnificent qualities of her character—her genius for tact, her profound sincerity, and her fundamental nobility of feeling—and applied their combined forces to the most intimate point of her relation to Yeats, in a magical conflation of lecture and love letter. She could truly speak of Yeats's plays as their children, not just because in their strange affair they had no other offspring, but because of her role in their common parentage: she had both created the environment at Coole in which they had been written and nurtured them with her own scenarios and dialogue. Lady Gregory's letter offers Yeats a wonderfully melodramatic choice: Horniman's money or my friendship and your country's welfare.

Perhaps one might wish the poet had needed less prodding, but, however late, at last Yeats stood the test. Not only did he immediately write Horniman saying he did not recollect entering into any such "Secret Treaty,"[123] but six months later he composed a stirring declaration of his duty to his country:

My dear Miss Horniman,

I have thought carefully over your proposal of yesterday and have decided that it is impossible. . . . I am not young

122. Lady Gregory to WBY, [? January 1907]; Saddlemyer, 202.
123. Horniman replied that there was no "Secret Treaty," only a "well-meant offer" that in a shipwreck of the NTS, she would save "the best part of the cargo" for another theatrical venture in England. She said she had returned to the issue later and asked Yeats to "Promise me yours . . ." "after the Patent has lapsed." Yeats, she recollected, had agreed. Horniman's memory, based on her letter to Yeats of 17 June 1906, was perfectly accurate as to her proposal; no record remains as to Yeats's acceptance of it.

enough to change my nationality—it would really amount to that. Though I wish for a universal audience, in play-writing there is always an immediate audience also. If I am to try and find the immediate audience in England I would fail through lack of understanding on my part, perhaps through lack of sympathy. I understand my own race and in all my work, lyric or dramatic, I have thought of it. If the theatre fails I may or may not write plays—but I shall write for my own people— whether in love or hate of them matters little—probably I shall not know which it is. Nor can I make any permanent allocation of my plays while the Irish theatre may at any moment need my help. At any moment I may have to ask friends for funds with the whole mass of plays for bait.[124]

One can understand why, of all the letters Yeats wrote to Horniman, he made a copy of this document for posterity. It does him as much credit as any letter he ever wrote.

The episode concerning the "Secret Treaty" between Yeats and Horniman did not have an instant effect on Horniman's attempts at self-expression through the Abbey Theatre. Yeats contrived a case of tactical amnesia about any "promise"; Horniman backed down from her absolute claim to his work; Yeats accepted the counterproposal of Lady Gregory and Synge; Fay agreed to step down (with a complimentary salary boost to £100 a year and a promise of no further interference); the young Englishman Ben Iden Payne was appointed stage manager of the NTS; Florence Darragh was retained once again as leading lady; and the repertoire was broadened to include a performance of Maeterlinck's *Interior*. To all appearances, then, Horniman's scheme for the Anglicization of the NTS was put into effect. But the "Secret Treaty" episode gave Lady Gregory the occasion to speak her mind on the diplomatic double game Yeats was playing, approaching Horniman as the "emissary of the other directors' greed" and appearing before the other directors as the ambassador of Horniman's

124. WBY to Horniman, n.d.; Wade, 500. Wade dates the letter to early 1908, after Horniman's opening of the Manchester Gaiety in September 1907, but it actually belongs with other Horniman/Yeats correspondence of June– July 1907 on planning a new theatre; it is mentioned in a Lady Gregory communication to Synge that Saddlemyer dates 20 June 1907 (Saddlemyer, 223).

power. Whether for good or ill, Lady Gregory was always the conscience of the "noble" side of Yeats's character, making him feel to the quick the grandeur of certain aristocratic values: friendship among the strong, oversight of the weak, service to country, and superiority to middle-class money. The "Secret Treaty" episode enabled her to appeal to these values in breaking up the Horniman-Yeats combination and leaguing Yeats with Synge, herself, and the Irish against Horniman. As a result, the plan for the transformation of the NTS was seen as Horniman's, not Yeats's at all. With no support from the Board of Authors, the inherent weaknesses of the arrangement were suffered to take their course.[125]

Horniman soon sensed that the change in her position was not what she had contemplated. She had pictured a situation in which she as owner had her own man in complete charge, a nice English boy who would officially report to the directors, but was under private instructions that based on his reporting to her about progress toward the NTS becoming an International Art Institution, she would decide whether or not to continue footing the bill. Gradually, it appeared to her that as soon as she signed the draft agreements for the new scheme, she was as much as dismissed by the Board of Authors. Alone in London, she suspected constant plots against her by the conspirators in Dublin, now joined by Yeats: they had suckered Payne into a dangerous spot, she charged, by allowing him to cast himself as lead in *Oedipus the King*, and his wife as lead in *Deirdre*; they twisted the language of Fay's

125. Horniman accused the directors of bad faith in carrying out the plan, blaming them (1) for allowing Payne to give himself the lead in *Oedipus the King*, in her opinion a plot to make Payne unpopular; (2) for not changing the Abbey stationery in such a way to make clear that Payne was completely in charge—a copyeditor's mistake, Yeats angrily shot back (Horniman to WBY, 27 March 1907; WBY to Horniman [29 March 1907?]; Horniman to WBY, 30 March 1907); and (3) for allowing Fay to produce *The King's Threshold*, not permitted according to her interpretation of Fay's contract to produce "all plays in dialect, and such other plays as he may be specially selected to produce" (NTS and W. G. Fay, memorandum of agreement; 15 February 1907). Payne sensibly resigned from a company in which he did not belong, and Horniman immediately stopped Fay's increased salary (Horniman to WBY, 6 June 1907).

contract to allow him to stage-manage Yeats's *The King's Threshold*. To a degree, Horniman was simply showing her chronic paranoia and irritability. In fact, although the Board of Authors was happy to let the new scheme fail from its own flaws, they avoided doing anything that would leave them open to the charge of destroying its chance of success.[126] But Horniman was certainly correct that her wishes—for control, for self-expression—were not being fulfilled; and she was also correct in noticing that Yeats had turned (or been turned) against her.

Within months, the curtain fell on the scheme Horniman plotted. Payne resigned, citing as his first reason that "an English manager is out of place in an Irish national theatre."[127] Yeats then floated another dream for Horniman to finance: a second theatre, which he fancied could be in Dublin—either a second company run out of the Abbey or a new theatre building altogether. Yeats even applied a certain pressure on Horniman, arguing that she had given her word to build "a stately home on the banks of the limpid Liffey" in a 1904 interview with the *Leader*.[128] Horniman, however, was obviously

---

126. The measure of their good faith is given by a letter from Synge to his fellow directors written during the NTS tour of England in the spring of 1907. Although Synge hated Payne's stage management, calling his production of Wilfred Scawen Blunt's *Fand* "deplorable," "a bastard literary pantomime," and "the end of all Samhain Principles," he allowed that Payne was doing his best and might "come to understand our methods in time" (Synge to Lady Gregory and WBY, 7 May [1907]; Saddlemyer, 220). Lady Gregory was "sorry . . . but not surprised" at Payne's failure: "He has only the common method, & he doesn't yet believe in our work" (Lady Gregory to Synge, 10 [May 1907]; Saddlemyer, 221).

127. Other reasons cited in Payne's 22 June 1907 letter of resignation are that it was "an impossible task" to train Abbey actors for foreign masterpieces, that he had a distaste for making so much money for so little work, and that his false position in the company "must have the effect of stultifying all my efforts" (Saddlemyer, 225–26).

128. Horniman to [WBY?], 31 July 1907. Even after she had entered negotiations with Payne for establishing a repertory company in Manchester, Lady Gregory and Yeats continued to press the claim that by a remark to the *Leader*—"Yes, I hope to live to see my little theatre in the hands of the housebreakers, torn down to make room for a stately home for drama near 'the limpid Liffey'"—Horniman had incurred an obligation to build her next theatre in Dublin.

done with Dublin. Her second theatre would be safe in England, run by English managers for English audiences. She repaid Yeats for his fantastic pettifoggery over "the vague remembrance of the *Leader*" by bringing up the "Secret Treaty." Yeats then came through with the noble declaration, examined above, that he would write for his own people. The descent of the Horniman-Yeats relation into the nastiness of quasi-legal wrangling (rather like a divorce) plunged Horniman at last into plain recrimination. She seized upon a trivial occasion—the dismissal notice of the business manager, W. A. Henderson, in July 1907—for the expression of her anguish. Horniman suspected that Yeats had asked leave of his fellow directors, and even of Fay, before he had given Henderson a statement of her case; by this consultation, she complained, he had removed the poison from her sting and made her a laughable, ineffectual person: "Don't you see how [prior consultation with others] is very insulting to me? To consult other people—then come here as if it were a private matter *to me* & not tell me of the others at all; that puts me alone against a group of people, all determined to get that legacy money out of me somehow." She thought his new "diplomacy" was Lady Gregory's doing: "You are ceaselessly victimised on the score of your gratitude for her kindness." But Lady Gregory's motherly care for Yeats's comfort at Coole Park was really, Horniman warned, a terrible, delicate trap: "You are under the nets again. The poor little strawberries will soon be eaten and you will starve amongst the leaves & the gardeners won't come to let you out when they understand that nothing more is to be got out of me." [129]

If the tone is vile, the tenor is true: Horniman knew Yeats would miss her money; the little boy loved his strawberries. But Yeats was "touched by that vampire Kathleen ni Houlihan": the kiss of nationalism had made him "bond-slave" to the gang of Irish ghouls. This desperate language is the seal of Horniman's defeat: in the struggle for the soul of Yeats, she turned at last to scratching and biting.

129. Horniman to WBY, [19? June 1907].

10

It would be inadequate to portray the dispute over the scheme for foreign management at the Abbey as simply a struggle between two older women for the love of W. B. Yeats. Of course, Annie Horniman loved Yeats, but both the scheme and the poet meant much more to her than an affair of the heart. She wanted to achieve self-expression, through her money, through Yeats, through transformation of the Abbey Theatre. Her jealousy of Lady Gregory was as much an aspect of her thwarted desire for self-expression as it was of unrequited, stolen love. Lady Gregory wrote plays, Florence Farr cantillated, Maud Gonne orated, but Horniman could not simply have the Abbey's curtain drawn to reveal stacks of her money on stage, night after despairing night. Her money, however, would be the procurer between her need and her object: someone of talent, someone like Yeats, had to do the job of artistic expression for her. Certainly, in many ways, he would not and could not. Horniman once remarked to Yeats, in the midst of other temperamental exasperations, "When I'm dead, your elegy on me should be great literature."[130] It is a fact that, though the list of Yeats's poems to friends is a long, distinguished list, no such elegy was written, no poem at all for his patron, not even an allusion to her during her life or after her death. If he did not speak of her, for her, or to her in his poems or plays, he could and did nonetheless write plays and stage plays answerable to her taste within the theatre she provided, plays that were for the few, that were artistic, in vogue, and not too strenuously Irish.

Yeats liked to brag that his theatre, because of its subsidy, was a place where the authors put on plays they thought good and kept them on stage whether the audience liked them or not; at the Abbey, contrary to the adage, he argued, the piper called the tune.[131] It should be obvious by now that in fact Horniman, who paid the piper, called the tune. But

130. Horniman to WBY, 13 May 1907.
131. WBY, "Notes," *Samhain: 1906*, in Frayne and Johnson, 2:347–48.

her ability to bring forth a music to delight her ears was hampered all around. She lacked not only any capacity for self-expression but also the ability to have a stimulating and encouraging effect upon the people around her. Who composed, who played, to whose ears, at what place, and under whose control: all these she tried to order to her liking, and sometimes did, but she somehow lacked the ability to name the right tune: the Abbey did not play her song. When Holloway told the old folklorist George Sigerson that Horniman paid the piper and had a right to call the tune, Sigerson looked around the empty seats at the Abbey and muttered, "But they don't dance." For although Horniman might howl that the Abbey must articulate her wishes, the actors, playwrights, and audiences of the Abbey would not and could not fully meet the request.

In an interpretation of a passage from *Timon of Athens*, Marx explores the distorting power of money. In the psychology of capitalism, what you can buy is what you are:

> Thus what I am and am capable of is by no means determined by my individuality. I am ugly, but I can buy for myself the most beautiful of women [or most appealing of men]. Therefore I am not ugly, for the effect of ugliness—its deterrent power—is nullified by money. . . . I am brainless, but money is the real brain of all things and how then should its possessor be brainless? Besides, he can buy clever people for himself, and is he who has power over the clever not more clever than the clever? . . . Does not my money, therefore, transform all my incapacities into their contrary?[132]

No, if Horniman is the example, money does not quite transform all incapacities into their contrary. True, its chemically transformative power gave authority to otherwise negligible features of her personality: it converted quirks to shrewdness, piques to official prohibitions, and class prejudice to artistic policy. Her money brought about what Marx calls "the frater-

132. Karl Marx, "Money," *Early Writings,* trans. and ed. T. B. Bottomore (New York: McGraw-Hill, 1963), 190–94.

nisation of impossibilities": it made contradictions embrace, as a rich vulgarian joined forces with the twentieth century's greatest poet. But if Annie Horniman was little without her money, she was not all that she sought to be with it: she could not buy love or self-expression. For Marx is partly wrong to say that "money is the external, universal medium and faculty (not springing from man as man or from human society as human society) for turning an image into reality," because while it is the medium, it is not a sufficient faculty. One must have not only money, but a "real, essential power" within, and that internal, individual power Horniman did not possess; as a result, her image of herself as a woman of the theatre never became real at the Abbey. Marx concludes his discussion of the distorting power of money with a vision of the world with unhappiness and frustration, but without the confusions and transpositions of natural human qualities caused by capital:

> Let us assume *man* to be *man*, and his relation to the world to be a human one. Then love can only be exchanged for love, trust for trust, etc. If you wish to enjoy art you must be an artistically cultivated person; if you wish to influence other people you must be a person who really has a stimulating and encouraging effect upon others. Every one of your relations to man and to nature must be a *specific expression,* corresponding to an object of your will, of your *real individual* life. If you love without evoking love in return, i.e. if you are not able, by the *manifestation* of yourself as a loving person, to make yourself a *beloved person,* then your love is impotent and a misfortune.[133]

Annie Horniman's desire was, for all her capital, to herself *impotent, a misfortune*—she suffered that finely unmediated acquaintance with the inadequacy of her "real individual life." She could by means of her money distort (expand, constrict, thwart) the expression of Irish drama, but, though she screamed and screamed, she could not make it ring true as her self-expression. What she took for a mirror was a cave

133. Ibid., 193–94.

mouth of mysteries, the forbidden entrance to the dark, alien workshop of art. [134]

11

The lasting effect of Horniman's schemes at the Abbey shows itself in one of Lady Gregory's best plays, *Dervorgilla,* first produced on 31 October 1907, but composed (she recollects) "at a time when circumstances had forced us to accept an English stage-manager" and when she sought to move Yeats "from the path of expediency." [135] The secret politics of the business displays itself in the legendary drama, but only as closely knotted needlework appears, *verso,* in the rich illusion of a tapestry.

In Irish folk history, Dervorgilla bears the responsibility of bringing the curse of English rule upon Ireland. The wife of O'Rourke, king of Breffny, she ran away with her lover Diarmuid, king of Leinster, who consequently made a bargain with Norman warriors to defend him against the wrath of O'Rourke in exchange for property in Ireland, the foothold of their future ascendancy. Lady Gregory sets her play at a date in the old age of Dervorgilla, who has retired in remorse to a monastic life behind walls. Only two loyal family retainers— Mona and her husband Flann—know the secret of her identity. Dervorgilla emerges from her solitude at the beginning of the play to dispense money to the poor and prizes to young people for their sports, in the hope of one day being remembered for good deeds. While she is holding court, a songmaker wanders on the scene seeking to impose on her hospi-

---

134. To draw back from the essential sadness of this story and put the situation in larger terms, we can say that the relation of base to superstructure is complex, both enabling and disabling. The economic base of the Abbey does not throw a perfect echo in its superstructure. It does, however, *determine* the activities of the theatre in two restricted senses of the term: *to place limits upon* and *to attempt to force by will.* Mainly, it simply *lies under,* but not quietly or motionlessly, first to raise up and later to subvert the cultural processes of the superstructure.

135. Lady Gregory, *Our Irish Theatre,* 92–93.

tality. Upon payment by Dervorgilla, he offers her a song: it is, horribly, the tale of the coming of the Gall into Ireland through the wickedness of Dervorgilla. The songmaker, getting no praise for his craft, leaves to play his old tricks for a new crowd: the English soldiers. Dervorgilla worries that he will spread the report of her perfidy across the country, and she permits old Flann to go after him and pay the songmaker to leave Ireland altogether. Only moments later, a young man returns with the news that Flann has been killed by the English for trying to stop the songmaker from telling a story. Dervorgilla is tormented that another has died for her sake. When Mona says that she will not blame Dervorgilla for the death of Flann, any more than for O'Rourke's death or Diarmuid's lechery, she unintentionally gives away the secret of Dervorgilla's identity to the young people gathered around. One by one, during a final long sad speech by Dervorgilla, the boys and girls of Ireland lay down their presents—cups and necklaces, hurley stick and silver ball—at the feet of the queen, and walk away, delivering "the swift, unflinching, terrible judgement of the young." [136]

Even though the play is connected to aspects of Abbey "theatre business"—poets who sing for pay, the evil of English invasion, the resentment of young Irish nationalists—it is not an allegory: the audience was in no way invited behind the scenes to gain a perspective on that level of reference. Abbey politics are its motive, not its meaning: the play springs from an inchoate feeling of class guilt, the well of Lady Gregory's creativity, as she sought to make reparations through her privilege, wealth, and talent to the Irish nation. Is there a warrant for seeing Lady Gregory dividing her feelings about Yeats into Diarmuid and the Songmaker, the first a young man not her husband, love of whom brought trouble from the English; the second a poet who imposes on the hospitality of a woman, who is always in need of money, who

---

136. Lady Gregory, *The Collected Plays*, ed. Ann Saddlemyer (New York: Oxford University Press, 1970), 2:110.

sings for anyone that pays (Irish or English), but who always, nonetheless, sings the truth in songs his country will remember? The answer is on the other side of the curtain; what lies on this side, and can be seen, is that the power of the play's conclusion is its dramatization of the fact that the very privilege that makes it possible to make gifts compromises those gifts and leads to further domination. This bitter awakening to her own guilt, and certainly to the venality of songmaker Yeats, was the fruit of Lady Gregory's association with Horniman. She knew only too intimately that Horniman's "generosity" meant foreign domination at the Abbey. In going along with Horniman, Lady Gregory admitted, she "felt as if [she] should be spoken of some day as one who had betrayed her country's trust." Nothing I say can, however, cheat her of the reward of courage in "seeing and knowing that a deed once done has no undoing": the subornation of the Board of Authors of the Abbey Theatre in the ongoing policy that the National Theatre Society not be national.[137]

137. Once Horniman had decisively shifted her capital to the Manchester theatre, Yeats wrote Synge: "There is a remote chance of money coming to us from some other quarter at the end of the patent period and that chance would be much better if we made ourselves a representative Irish institution" (WBY to Synge, 15 August 1907; Saddlemyer, 235). This letter clearly implies that the NTS had not been, had not tried to be, and had not been free to become "a representative Irish institution" while Horniman was involved with it.

6

The Death of the King
and the Lazy Telegraph Boy

The Politics of Culture

In the summer of 1907 Miss Horniman called it quits on her efforts to achieve self-expression through the Abbey Theatre: the £25,000 legacy from her father, once the bait for her reforms in the NTS, would go instead to the establishment of a repertory company in Manchester. She informed the Board of Authors that she would, nonetheless, keep to the bargain of paying the actors' subsidies and part of the overhead at the Abbey until 1910, the end of the patent period, at which point she would close up shop and sell the building. The Board of Authors was generally pleased that even if Annie Horniman was going away angry, at least she was going away. Lady Gregory was "in good spirits on the whole, being . . . really free from Miss H & from further foreign invasions."[1] It was natural for Lady Gregory to feature the event in terms of an invader being driven from the field, especially after Yeats showed her his letter spurning Horniman's request for his plays, with the lofty profession (in Lady Gregory's report of it to Synge) "that he was too old to change his nationality . . . , that he must continue to write for an audience of his own people—& that he could not assign her his plays."[2] Having earlier been impressed with the side of the Horniman coin that declared *freedom through finance*, the Board of Authors had lately come to see the other side: *no freedom from inter-*

1. Lady Gregory to Synge [29 June 1907]; Saddlemyer, 229.
2. Lady Gregory to Synge [20 June 1907]; Saddlemyer, 223.

ference. Synge was positively "overjoyed that we are to be free from [Horniman] in the future—Our *self-respect* I think will gain by the freedom."[3] Of the three authors on the board, Yeats was the least pleased, still worrying that on a pinched budget he could not get performances that would show his plays to their best effect, but he solaced himself by casting a horoscope for Annie Horniman, and, his head "reeling with the queer mathematical terms," put the date of "some great disturbance concerning her to April, May, or June."[4] It would not be long, he prophesied, before Manchester added names to Horniman's "list of truly wicked people."[5] Those in Manchester would learn that to get Horniman's money, they would have to plunge their hands daily to the bottom of a tub of electrified water. Meanwhile, he settled down to the task of turning the National Theatre Society back into "a representative Irish institution" with widespread support in Ireland, so that he could appeal for local government funding at the end of the patent period.

But Annie Horniman did not part company with the little committee of Irish playwrights without a final ominous statement, one that did not bode well for Yeats's plans to reactivate the national character of the theatre. Her 28 June 1907 formal statement of the arrangements for the remainder of the patent period warns the directors, "It must never be forgotten that if the theatre be used politically I am free to close it at once and stop the subsidy."[6] What did Miss Horniman mean by *political?* It was difficult to be sure, but it was comparatively easy to see that she would like to be relieved of paying the subsidy of £800 a year. This made the threat both vague and terribly real. The high spirits of Lady Gregory and Synge were consequently laced with a fear of what Miss Horniman might yet

3. Synge to Lady Gregory, 1 July 1907; Saddlemyer, 229–30.
4. WBY to Florence Farr, 7 October 1907; Wade, 498. In a perfect symmetry that some might find significant, Horniman began her involvement with the Abbey in April 1903 by casting a horoscope; Yeats reviewed her prospects at the Manchester theatre by casting another in October 1907.
5. WBY to Florence Farr [? July 1907]; Wade, 490–91.
6. Saddlemyer, 230.

do. "She is a terror!" Lady Gregory wrote Synge. "I wonder
how soon we shall commit some political crime!"[7] Synge
asked by return of mail if she could not get some information out of Yeats about "whether Miss H. has any particular
phase of political ill-doing in mind."[8] Although Horniman
had moved off a distance, it was only to cast a longer shadow
over the Abbey. If she could not make it into an international
art threatre, she could at least still prevent it from becoming a
full-fledged Irish national theatre, either by planting self-
censorship in the minds of the directors, censoring the NTS
activities herself, or seizing upon a pretext to close the Abbey.

The urgent and practical question for the Board of Authors
was to find out what counted as a political use of the theatre;
otherwise, they might unintentionally forfeit use of it altogether. Although Synge had had little hesitation in calling attacks upon his plays politically motivated, and therefore of no
account, on this occasion Synge's talk of *phases* "of political ill-
doing" suggests that to his present way of thinking, political
life was polymorphous, a spectral affair of changing lights,
darks, and half-lights, and no matter of easy discriminations.
Lady Gregory's indignant, ironical question, How soon shall
we commit some political crime? also reveals a sudden sense
of the difficulty of determining where the political begins and
ends. She knows that nothing she does could really be a
crime, except to the eye of Horniman, but it is less easy to say
what in the perpetual activities of her public role does not
have a dimension bearing to some degree on the great national questions of the day: is there a month, a week, a day, or
a minute that is not stressed with the conflicts of the age?
Under the pressure of Horniman's threat, Lady Gregory and
Synge both began to consider that the definition of politics
could be made very broad indeed, so broad as to be totalizing.
If it were a total category, then it could not be a useful instrument for determining good behavior from "political crime" or
"any particular phase of political ill-doing."

7. Lady Gregory to Synge [29 June 1907]; Saddlemyer, 229.
8. Synge to Lady Gregory, 1 July 1907; Saddlemyer, 230.

This broad, value-free definition of politics was not the basis on which Yeats and Horniman had established their condominium in 1903. The "*Samhain* Principles," constituted as the contract between the INTS and the Abbey owner, defined politics in a narrow and pejorative fashion: politics, mother of propaganda, was illusory and transitory, mere opinion, a frenzy of newspapers and the mob. The other *Samhain* principles—those about decorative staging, elocution, and statuesque acting—had ceased to interest Horniman ("You may do what you like about the *Samhain* principles," she wrote dismissively; "I always thought decorative staging undramatic"),[9] but Yeats's distinction between art and propaganda was her guarantee that she would not bankroll a revolution, just as Horniman's money was Yeats security that he would not be dragooned into service of that revolution. Yeats had never contemplated that this principle of "no politics" might be applied to his own work or that of his friends. They were surely known to be artists, free spirits above the throne of power and the shout of the crowd. Whatever an artist made, quite simply, was art and not propaganda, even if the play in question exhorted to revolution, made heroes of rebels, and stirred Irish audiences to collective action, as *Cathleen ni Houlihan* and *The Rising of the Moon* in fact did. *Cathleen ni Houlihan*, Yeats said, was not propaganda because, inspired by a dream, he had given "thoughts men had felt" "sincere dramatic form," and "did not advocate any kind of opinion"; in short, it was not propaganda because the artist did not intend that it be propaganda.[10] This explanation is good enough only when backed by force and finance, that is, only when it makes no material difference if others disagree. What if Horniman did not care whether a play was by intent art, if in effect it was propaganda? One could hardly then take a cavalier attitude to criticism. Now that Horniman had ap-

9. Horniman to WBY, 31 December 1906.

10. WBY to Horace Plunkett, "Plays Produced by the Irish Literary Theatre and by the Irish National Theatre Society" [1904]; Patent Application (NLI).

parently turned against the NTS directorate itself, she might, as Synge feared, choose to see a revival of such plays in the Abbey stock as "political use of the theatre."[11]

This suspicion, however, was just a shot in the dark. There was more to be feared than the prospect that a few plays, once defined as "non-political," would drop into the class of the "political." What was at issue between the original definition of *politics* in *Samhain* and the new broader sense of the term threatened in Horniman's June 1907 letter was the difference between a simple system of classification applied only to plays and a complex system applied to all uses of the theatre. In a simple system, one divides items according to a significant characteristic into two classes at any one stage: plays are either political or not political; non-political plays are either artistic or not artistic; artistic, non-political plays are either national or non-national, and so on. This dichotomous system of classification inherently retains a conceptual space throughout its divisions for a non-political sphere of activity. A complex, exhaustive classification of all political activities of the theatre, however, distinguishes each possible sub-group at each stage, by degrees dispersing the political element throughout the system. I shall not carry out every step of an exhaustive classification, but for purposes of illustration I list some of the early points of interest by which groups could be divided:

POLITICAL ACTIVITIES OF THE ABBEY

I. By persons
   A. The NTS
      1. Actors   2. Authors   3. Directors
   B. The audience of the NTS
      1. Pit   2. Stalls   3. Balcony
   C. Religion, class, wealth, etc.

II. By place
   A. In the theatre
      1. Onstage

11. Synge to Lady Gregory, 1 July 1907; Saddlemyer, 231.

2. Offstage
   a. Lobby   b. Greenroom   c. Backstage
B. Outside the theatre

III. By time
  A. While at work
    1. During tours
    2. During Dublin residence
      a. During run
        i. During performance
        ii. Before/after performance
      b. During rehearsal
  B. While off work

IV. By acts
  A. Officially political actions (relating to matters of state or party)
    1. Actors, directors, or authors, not at work
      a. participate in marches, demonstrations, or solidarity meetings
      b. donate to candidate, vote for one, or run as candidate for office
      c. sign petitions, write letters to editor, draft protests to government
      d. take posts on committees of political organizations
      e. make public speeches concerning matters of government, etc.
    2. Authors, actors, at work
      a. write political propaganda
        i. against British recruiting
        ii. against emigration
        iii. for militant republicanism
        iv. for Gaelic revival
        v. for land redistribution
        vi. for socialism, etc.
      b. perform in propaganda plays of various kinds
  B. Unofficially political actions
    1. Author/directors, while at work, before performance
      a. write tendentious, though "literary," plays

b. select a program of the most (or least) national works
c. readmit dissident nationalist actors (or not)
d. invite return of nationalist playwrights
e. bill the company as a national organization
f. retitle the company in an unpolitical way
g. schedule plays that offend Dublin Castle
h. cancel plays that offend Dublin Castle
i. hire, or dismiss, foreign employees
2. Actors, while at work, before performance
a. agree or refuse to perform at a certain site
b. agree or refuse to repeat performance of a play the audience likes, or does not like
3. Actors, while at work, during performance
a. characterize roles, by speech, gesture, costume, etc., in a political fashion
4. Authors or actors, while at work, after performance
a. applaud or hiss a partisan audience
b. take or refuse a curtain call
5. Authors or actors, off work, offstage
a. speak (or not) Gaelic
b. buy goods made in Ireland (or England)
c. wear tweed, Connemara cap, or bowler, etc.
d. show sympathy for rights of inherited property, or for universal right to land ownership, etc.

This still somewhat random inventory lists several of the main categories of political life actually practiced by the theatre society during its first five years at the Abbey. When the whole idea of the *res publica* is actively contested, and masses of people are mobilized in social and political revolution, obviously every area of social life is implacably forced to one or the other side of an issue. And not only the social life of the *res publica:* an exhaustive classification would not be complete until it covered private matters as well, reaching some conclusion such as the following: "any act in concert or in conflict with others, any word to others, even to oneself, all thoughts, every moment of being." In the last analysis, one who temporizes, indifferent to claims by any party, one in pursuit of a private project of salvation, is by definition a *politique*, on the side of those who do not take a side. Admittedly, Miss Horniman was no believer in the omnipresence of politics or (in Fredric Jameson's rhetoric) "the grip of Necessity over all such blind zones in which the individual seeks refuge."[12] There would be no point in forbidding political use of the theatre if *every* use were political. But there was no telling which aspects of the totality of activities of the National Theatre Society Horniman might choose to see as tendentious, factious, or clearly rebellious.

There could be little doubt, however, that the Abbey owner would know politics when she saw it, and that the Board of Authors would hear about it when she did. The perception of political interest, Horniman's or another's, depends upon a certain ideological point of view. Other people's politics are "politics"; yours are simply the truth. That is the simple, dichotomous classification by which Horniman, like all people to some degree, unconsciously functioned.[13] It would be obvious to Horniman that Colum's *The Saxon Shillin'*, which depicts a British recruiting sergeant as a villain, was "political"; it would be obvious to an Irish nationalist that the depiction was "natural and self-evident."[14] Politics in a work of literature may be, as Stendhal has it, like a pistol shot in the middle

12. Fredric Jameson, *The Political Unconscious: Narrative as a Socially Symbolic Act* (Ithaca, N.Y.: Cornell University Press, 1981), 20.

13. In the language of Gayatri Spivak, one's own ideology in action is what members of one's group "take to be natural and self-evident, that of which the group, as a group, must deny any historical sedimentation." Contrariwise, what seems unnatural, questionable, and purely partisan is the ideology of an opposed group. See Spivak, "The Politics of Interpretation," in *The Politics of Interpretation*, ed. W. J. T. Mitchell (Chicago: University of Chicago Press, 1982, 1983), 347.

14. After the split in the INTS during the formation of the joint stock company, Horniman demanded "to see a list of all plays proposed to be played [by the dissident Theatre of Ireland] in the Theatre"; she vowed "to refuse its use if she disapprove[d] of the plays, that is, if they are propagandist ones." She would, Yeats said, object to *The Saxon Shillin'*. Lady Gregory to Synge, 20 February 1906; Hogan and Kilroy, 3:61.

of a concert, vulgar but impossible to ignore, but notes that are heard as music by some listeners are pistol shots to others, in a tonal composition of generally aestheticized violence.[15] The immediate problem for the NTS Board of Authors was that nearly every aspect of the Abbey's theatrical activity, to the sensibilities of Annie Horniman, sounded the note of riot against what was decent and English; there was a whiff of gunpowder about the whole affair. What then, of everything, would she choose to single out as a violation of her "No Politics" clause? The Board of Authors could do more to protect their interests than watch what was reported of Abbey performances and await Horniman's letters from London, but, not sharing her Low Church, royalist, capitalist ideology, they could not fully anticipate what particular phase of political ill-doing Miss Horniman had in mind.

2

In addition to their long acquaintance with the temperament of the owner, the directors had, of course, recently experienced Horniman's responses to the riots over *The Playboy of the Western World*. The reception of this play has been exhaustively studied, but a brief review of the salient events will prepare for an examination of Horniman's part in the affair.[16] Although Lady Gregory and Yeats found the play somewhat offensive in rehearsal, and asked him to reduce the frequency with which the characters took the Lord's name in vain, Synge

15. Stendhal, *The Red and the Black*, trans. C. K. Scott-Moncrieff (New York: Liverwright, 1954), 2:189.
16. See James Kilroy, *The 'Playboy' Riots* (Dublin: Dolmen Press, 1971), and Hogan and Kilroy, 3:123–62, for the documentary history of the play's reception. Richard M. Kain gives a colorful and detailed account in "The *Playboy* Riots," in *Sunshine and Moon's Delight: A Centenary Tribute to J. M. Synge 1871–1909*, ed. Suheil Bushrui (New York: Barnes & Noble, 1972), 173–88. For fruitful literary appreciations of the play's bewildering effects, see Nicholas Grene, *Synge: A Critical Study of the Plays* (London: Macmillan 1975), 132–46, and Weldon Thornton, *J. M. Synge and the Western Mind* (Gerrards Cross, Bucks.: Colin Smythe, 1979), 134–43.

made few changes, and with some trepidation on the part of the cast, the play was staged before a full house on Saturday, 26 January 1907.[17] The audience, after respectful attention to *Riders to the Sea*, the curtain-raiser, seemed at first uncertain how to respond to the introduction of the young tramp Christy Mahon into a pub, swearing that with the help of God and a blow of the loy, he had killed his own father. When Pegeen Mike, clearly the heroine, promptly fell in love with the murderer, apparently because he was a murderer, and her father, marching off to the festivities of a distant wake, left his daughter to the protection of a man reddened with the blood of a father, not many in the audience were willing to laugh, though there was polite applause at the curtain. During the second act, while the audience watched the girls of the village bring gifts to Christy, as if to the Messiah himself, or at least to some heathen hero, Lady Gregory saw nothing in the house to keep her from telegraphing Yeats (who was in Scotland) that the play was a success. But smoldering indignation was growing in the audience, needing only the breath of an excuse to break into flame. There was the eroticism of Christy's wild, poetic love-talk to Pegeen, and then the violence of his bloody-headed father coming back to be killed a second time, and then a third time, but what really ignited the rage of the audience was a small violation of the category of the unmentionable: Christy declares that he will take no woman other than Pegeen: "what'd I care if you brought me a drift of chosen females, standing in their shifts itself, maybe, from this place to the Eastern World?"[18]

Shift, a word for a woman's slip, should not have been spoken, it was thought, by a man on a public stage. The concentration on this verbal impropriety (removed after the first performance) was clearly a displacement of anxieties raised by other elements in the play: the satirical treatment of Irish Catholicism, drunkenness, greed, and lawlessness, and the

17. Lady Gregory, *Our Irish Theatre* (1913; rpt., New York: Capricorn Books, 1965), 133.
18. Synge, 4:167.

poetic celebration of passion.[19] By the end of the play, Lady Gregory had wired Yeats a second time, informing him the audience broke up in disorder at the word *shifts*.

Some reviews measured out praise for the actors' skill and the author's wit,[20] but most papers covered the play as an intolerable "unmitigated, protracted libel upon Irish peasant men and women."[21] Nonetheless, Yeats issued a statement declaring that *The Playboy* would be kept on stage for its entire run of a week; meanwhile, he notified the police to be on hand in case of disturbances. On Monday night, though the crowd was small, those who disapproved of the play made so much noise, with groans, shouts, and hisses, that even people at the front of the theatre could not hear much of the dialogue. Police were called into the aisles, but their presence had little effect, and they walked out again. Before the Tuesday performance, Lady Gregory asked a nephew at Trinity College to come with some able-bodied fellow athletes in order to quell a disturbance.[22] These young men arrived drunk and jeered the nationalists in the pit from their seats in the stalls even before the play began.[23] Before the play ended, the conflict between the stalls and the pit moved from applause against hisses, to choruses of "God Save the King" against "A Nation Once Again," to a final outbreak of fisticuffs. The police again were called into the melee, but this time Hugh Lane (a nephew of Lady Gregory) and Yeats insisted that certain protesters against the play be apprehended, with the promise that the theatre would bring charges. The protests and police arrests continued thereafter through the week, amid growing indignation by the public against all concerned. As Sheehy

19. There is also some evidence for believing that the real shock was the entrance of Christy after apparently having murdered his father offstage, just before the "shifts" speech; for a review of this evidence, see Grene, *Synge: A Critical Study*, 144–45.

20. "The Abbey Theatre," *Daily Express*, 28 January 1907, quoted in Hogan and Kilroy, 3:125.

21. Review from the *Freeman's Journal* quoted in Hogan and Kilroy, 3:125.

22. Lady Gregory, *Our Irish Theatre*, 113.

23. "The Abbey Theatre," *Daily Express*, 30 January 1905, quoted in Hogan and Kilroy, 3:128–30.

Skeffington put it, "The play was bad, the organized disturbance worse, and the methods employed to quell the disturbance worst of all." [24]

The trials provided an interesting spectacle. One of the
first men charged by Yeats was the father of Padraic Colum. [25]
Yeats gave evidence against Colum, saying that he was part of
an organized disturbance to prevent Synge's play from being
heard; the play itself was "no more a caricature of the people
of Ireland than Macbeth is a caricature of the people of Scotland." [26] Piaras Beaslai was accused of speaking offensively to
Yeats, but, as the words were addressed in Irish, Yeats was
unable to say what they were, and the defendant claimed
they were entirely edifying. The magistrate in these cases,
Mr. Mahony, agreed with Yeats, and fined the defendants the
maximum penalty for disorderly behavior, forty shillings
(several weeks' wages). However, the magistrate for later
cases, Mr. Wall, took an entirely different view of the matter.
He aimed to discover whether each incident was a case of riot,
disorderly conduct, or rightful expression of an audience's
privilege of censure. If the defendant was simply charged
with hissing and booing, in a theatre that was no crime, even
if the audience was noisy. It seemed to him "an extraordinary
way of administering the law" to arrest a man for hissing such
a play; why not arrest those who applauded indecency? If the
accused man were part of a general disturbance, in which
Trinity boys applauding the play conflicted with nationalists
opposing it, then the proper charge was riotous behavior, not
disorderly conduct. In that event, the whole group—both
those who praised, and those who censured—should be
rounded up and brought to court, and not just a few selected
nationalists. Finally, coming straight to the issue, Magistrate
Wall questioned whether the Abbey directorate should not be
in the dock:

24. "Abbey Theatre Disturbances," *Daily Express*, 5 February 1907,
quoted in Hogan and Kilroy, 3:149.
25. Hogan and Kilroy, 3:132.
26. "Last Night's Row at the Abbey," *Dublin Evening Mail*, 30 January
1907, quoted in Hogan and Kilroy, 3:133.

It might be well to consider on the part of the Crown whether
those who persisted in bringing forward theatrical procedure
of such a character as to excite popular odium and opposition,
and which could not be tolerated, at all events, in Ireland,
where, practically, there were two worlds, one wishing to be at
the throat of the other, and one wishing to avoid what the
other wished to intrude—whether those who were responsible for that should not themselves be brought forward.[27]

In effect, Magistrate Wall charged Yeats, Lady Gregory, and
Synge with a voluntary instigation to political riot, and with
use of the Crown's forces to attack only one party to the dispute. Clearly unhappy with his judicial duty, Wall nonetheless found the accused men guilty of organized disturbance of
the peace, and fined them ten shillings.

Miss Horniman was frankly ecstatic at the first reports
from Dublin of the "Playboy riots." She repeatedly sent the
directors "offers to come and join the fray," but they took no
notice.[28] This was a terrible disappointment, as she told Yeats:
"How I should have loved to be with you, my gems would
have infuriated [the patriots]!" Although she had never liked
Synge before, she was delighted with him now, and compli-
mented him on his "splendid" play.[29] How little she expected
that from such a quarter her "hopes to annoy the Gaelic
League into action would be so violently fulfilled!"[30] William
Boyle had dinner with Horniman during the week of the
Abbey disturbances; she admitted that she "could never have
concealed from him her intense pleasure" at the hostilities between her theatre and the Irish nationalists.[31] Boyle was so
shocked by her "cockcrows" of hatred for the Irish people,
and the antinationalist policy of riding roughshod over pa-

27. "The Scenes at the Abbey Theatre," *Daily Express,* 1 February 1907,
quoted in Hogan and Kilroy, 3:138–39.
28. Horniman to WBY, n.d., quoted in Hugh Hunt, *The Abbey: Ireland's
National Theatre, 1904–1978* (New York: Columbia University Press, 1979), 76.
29. Synge to Molly Allgood [12 Feburary 1907], in *Letters to Molly: John
Millington Synge to Maire O'Neill,* ed. Ann Saddlemyer (Cambridge, Mass.:
Harvard University Press, Belknap Press, 1971), 96.
30. Horniman to WBY, 11 February 1907.
31. Horniman to WBY, 11 February 1907.

triotic sentiment, that he withdrew his plays from the Abbey repertoire.[32] The Board of Authors sent Fay to London to bring Boyle back into the fold, but Fay upon arrival wired back: "Tabby [Miss Horniman] completely upset Boyle. No use waiting here."[33] It had not been Horniman's idea to bring in the police, but in a letter to the Dublin press she "heartily applaud[ed] the strong measures";[34] privately, she remarked to Yeats that the constabulary came cheap as a way of making a point of policy; a few more riots would be a good investment.[35]

It may be difficult to understand how a declared desire to annoy a single political group, to drive them to riot, and then to have them arrested and criminally prosecuted is not a political action even in a narrow sense of the term (it is elective, partisan, and institutionally coercive), but that is just how Horniman saw it. The fight, in her opinion, was not between two political groups, but between one group that was political and another that was not. This was the brunt of a letter she sent to the directors with instructions that it be read out to the cast of *The Playboy*. Hugh Lane had informed her that during performance some actors had hissed the behavior of the drunken students from Trinity College who had come to defend King, Empire, and the Rights of Artists. Horniman scolded those involved:

> This hissing was political . . . it must clearly be understood that I will not allow my theatre to be used for political purposes and the actors must be informed that hissing the drunken vulgarity of the stalls is just as bad as the patriotic vulgarity of the pit. I am fighting for us to stand above all low political spite on either side. I make this protest at once, it is a matter of honour that the directors should do their best to prevent conduct in the actors that would justify my closing of the theatre . . . *I will have no politics.*[36]

32. Boyle to D. J. O'Donoghue, 13 February 1907; quoted in Holloway, 88.
33. Lady Gregory to Synge [5 Feburary 1907]; Saddlemyer, 213.
34. Horniman, letter to the *Evening Telegraph*, 12 February 1907, quoted in Hogan and Kilroy, 3:162.
35. Horniman to WBY, 11 February 1907.
36. Horniman to directors of the INTS, Ltd., 1 February 1907, quoted in Hogan and Kilroy, 3:161.

Horniman's claim of evenhandedness would be more convincing if her wording had been more cautiously considered: the two things she cites as equally bad are hissing West Britons and expressing Irish patriotism, both instances of nationalism. Furthermore, the sentence structure equates "drunken" with "patriotic." Horniman anticipated that the actors would think she sided with the British; she offered in evidence that she did not [bow] low to the Castle" (that is, submit to the British executive housed in Dublin Castle) her proposal that the Abbey revive *Cathleen ni Houlihan* the following week. Does this imply that she regarded *Cathleen* as nationalist propaganda, a challenge to the British authority in Ireland? It appears so. But in that case the Abbey would be used for a political purpose. Horniman's policy was definitively stated— "no politics"—but it was not clear whether in practical terms this meant no nationalist politics, no politics of any kind, or an even balance of antinationalist and nationalist politics.

3

In the May–June 1907 tour of England, Miss Horniman added a new category of political misconduct and a new twist to her working understanding of what was and was not political. After the excitement over *The Playboy* at the Abbey, she was eager to take the company, now under the management of Ben Iden Payne, before her own people, so that they could enjoy the spectacle that had enraged the Irish. The Lord Chamberlain in England was reluctant to license *The Playboy* for performance, however, on the suspicion that the play was immoral or incendiary. Horniman took it upon herself to persuade G. A. Bedford, an official in the Lord Chamberlain's office, that it was not the play that was at fault, but the Gaelic League. Her long letter makes a number of points:

1. "Mr. Synge knows Irish peasant life . . . [but the ideas of young townsmen] come from romantic tales, patriotic poems and flattering political speeches."
2. "There is no touch of ordinary sexual immorality in Mr. Synge's work."

3. "The Gaelic League does not approve of anything written in English."
4. "I glory in being a Londoner; [the Irish] have not economic sense to see their country gains by my spending a quarter of my income in Dublin."
5. "This is a case of jealousy. The Abbey Theatre . . . [has] a standard far above the League's very crude amateur ways."
6. "These various Societies and Leagues are great bullies, they want to destroy everything except the Gaelic language and political agitation and the miserable state of affairs caused by everyone hating everyone else. We have defied [them] for we hold that Art has nothing to do with them." [37]

In brief, the Irish rioted because *The Playboy* was a true, moral, English, London-financed, and well-acted play. The Lord Chancellor did not observe that by this logic, the Irish should have demonstrated against all Abbey shows, for every one was subsidized by Horniman, written in English, and prefaced by declarations of "No Politics." Instead, Bedford wrote back that Horniman's letter confirmed his impression from published accounts that a cabal was behind the Dublin outcry.

Armed with a license for performance, Yeats and Lady Gregory persuaded the reluctant troupe of actors (by means of Easter bonuses, extra pay for *Playboy* performances, and six weeks' vacation salary)[38] to bring the play to the "intellectual centers" of Oxford and Cambridge.[39] They were, however, nonplussed when Synge put his play on the bill for the Birmingham shows: "There are enough slum Irish in Birmingham," Yeats warned, "to stir up a row," and he cancelled the play. Horniman then insisted that *The Playboy* be scheduled for London, slum Irish or not; to refrain from presenting it, she warned, would constitute a political use of the theatre. The actors, who had little love for the play, no desire for obloquy from their countrymen, and a real fear for their safety on stage, nonetheless fulfilled the terms of their contract and

37. Horniman to G. A. Bedford, 17 May 1907.
38. Joseph Holloway, "Impressions of a Dublin Playgoer," 15 July 1907, quoted in Hogan and Kilroy, 3:167.
39. WBY to Synge [27 May 1907]; Saddlemyer, 222.

acted the play in London. At the end of the scheduled run, Horniman asked them to extend the tour with further London performances of *The Playboy.* When they refused, she was irate: *"I consider the refusal . . . as a political* action."[40] She accepted for the moment Yeats's excuse that the actors were motivated by "cowardice," not "politics," but she reaffirmed that such behavior in the future would lead her to stop everything and close the theatre.

It was at this turn of events, in June 1907, that Horniman withdrew her philanthropic attention from Dublin to Manchester, formally warning the authors that she would close the theatre if it were used for any political purpose. The Abbey Board of Authors could reflect on these signal facts: hissing the royalists was political, arresting the nationalists was not; Dublin censure of *The Playboy* was political, London applause for it was not; cancellation of London performances was political, cancellation of Birmingham ones was not; taking bonuses for doing a politically objectionable thing was not political, and not extending such performances was political. The lesson to be learned was that to Horniman's mind practically anything that pleased the Irish, and nothing that annoyed them, was "political."

4

Although Horniman had threatened to close the Abbey for political offenses three times in five months (from February to June 1907), after her final admonition she was relatively quiet for a long time. She had not softened her position or sweetened her attitude to the Abbey; she was simply not directly involved in its affairs. Manchester took up most of her attention; she never visited Dublin. As a result, her contact with the affairs of the Irish theatre came through requests by other groups to lease the theatre, newspaper articles from her cutting agency, or word-of-mouth reports by friends. Yeats, Synge, Lady Gregory, and their actors were thus freed from careful supervision, so that Horniman's formal injunction was

40. Horniman to WBY, 21 June 1907; Saddlemyer, 226.

virtually ineffective. In fact, it can be argued that the injunction, because of its inconsistent, sporadic application, served the advantage of the National Theatre Society in its competition with other Irish theatre groups.

In January 1908 the National Players Society wrote Horniman in Manchester asking to lease the Abbey Theatre on the usual terms granted to other organizations—from a Yiddish opera company to the Salvation Army—when the NTS, Ltd. was not in residence. The National Players Society was a group formed by the Dublin branch of the Gaelic League, with Maud Gonne, Arthur Griffith, and Edward Martyn as officers, performing plays by Douglas Hyde, Seamus Mac-Manus, and Edward Martyn—and Miss Horniman, for a hundred reasons, abominated officers, playwrights, and parent organization. However, the reason that she turned down their request was that "their letter paper makes it clear that they are a political society." [41] What was political about the stationery? The affiliation with the Gaelic League, declared on the letterhead, could not legitimately be called political (at least in Dublin idiom), because President Douglas Hyde notoriously held to the line that the Gaelic League would be conducted as a cultural and educational organization, not involved with either Unionist or Nationalist parties. The more or less honorary officers of the National Players Society— Gonne, Griffith, and Martyn—also held leading positions in the National Council/Sinn Fein, a semi-political but antiparliamentary organization, yet even if an officer of the Player's Society were political (and Griffith and Gonne would have denied they were), one could hardly charge that the whole society was as well. It seems that Horniman's chief article of evidence against the National Players Society was simply its name, clearly for Horniman a banner under which "patriots" would rally. In a postscript to Yeats, attached to a copy of her letter of rejection, she said she would be "flattered by the dislike of 'patriots,' for popularity amongst them would be humiliating to me." [42] For the next few weeks, the question of the

41. Horniman to WBY, 29 January 1908.
42. Horniman to WBY, 29 January 1908.

proper documentation of what she knew in her heart to be the thoroughly seditious character of certain organizations rankled the owner of the Abbey. On 4 February 1908 she warned Yeats that the Abbey notepaper "had better be non-political." Well, as a matter of fact, it bore the insignia of an Irish wolfhound, and the name of an officer—Yeats himself—who was a founding member of the National Council, along with Maud Gonne and Arthur Griffith. In addition, the name of the company—the National Theatre Society—bore the dreaded sign of patriotism. What would she have them do, change their trademark after the business was well established? On 15 February 1908 Horniman realized that, while "the name 'National' should have been abandoned at the start of the enterprise," it was too late to undo the damage. In the matter of notepaper, the policy of Horniman was not even-handed in its application, but it hurt the rivals of the Abbey more than the Abbey itself.

The exclusion of other nationalist theatre organizations from the Abbey stage could have caused the NTS to lose credit with its natural audience,[43] but Yeats shrewdly managed to lay most of the blame upon Horniman, apparently with her consent. For instance, a year after she banned the National Players, the Theatre of Ireland, made up of the dissident INTS actors from the January 1906 split, was successfully competing with Yeats's company on the stage of the Abbey. According to the separation agreement between the dissident players and the INTS, Ltd., they were allowed "to let the theatre on the usual conditions."[44] During 1908 they had Ireland's most popular new playwright, Seamus O'Kelly, and its best tragic actress, Maire nic Shiublaigh. The Abbey Board of Authors had been trying to hire away members of the Theatre of Ireland cast, but many of its leading figures were committed to the democratic, nationalist principles of

43. James W. Flannery, *Miss Annie F. Horniman and the Abbey Theatre*, Irish Theatre Series, no. 3 (Dublin: Dolmen Press, 1970), 28.

44. Language from contract quoted by Seamus O'Connolly, "The Abbey Theatre and the Theatre of Ireland," *Freeman's Journal*, 2 December 1908; Hogan and Kilroy, 3:254.

the amateur society. In November the Theatre of Ireland's productions at the Abbey attracted the notice of a promoter, who invited them to repeat the performances at the vast commercial Gaiety Theatre in Dublin, the first time a small amateur society had made the big time.[45] The Gaiety manager, however, advertised the players as "members of the Abbey theatre company." Horniman received a cutting of this advertisement, and struck. Without further discussion, she published a letter in the *Freeman's Journal* banning the Theatre of Ireland from future use of her theatre, because of their "discourtesy" in appropriating the name of her building. Exclusion from the Abbey stage was a great blow to the viability of the little society. They wrote letters of dismay, they explained that the advertisement was none of their doing, they made reference to their separation agreement with Horniman guaranteeing access to the Abbey stage, they appealed to the honor of Yeats, they declared that they were being unfairly punished because of the superior quality of their work. After they begged Yeats to intercede on their behalf, he privately wrote to D. O'Connell that he had done all that he could to persuade Miss Horniman to relent, but she had given her final word on the matter: nothing he could say could wipe away what she considered discourtesy on the part of the Theatre of Ireland.[46] While unhappy about the outcome, Yeats felt that the letters to the press by the Theatre of Ireland had been "exaggerated" and "unwise." In his own dealings with Horniman, he boldly fibbed, she had been immensely generous and had "never attempted to interfere with our policy in the slightest things." Meanwhile, Horniman wrote to Yeats that she assumed he did not want her to cave in on the Theatre of Ireland issue; otherwise, he would have remonstrated with her more strongly.[47] Annie Horniman may have been a pe-

45. Maire nic Shiublaigh, *The Splendid Years* (Dublin: James Duffy, 1955), 95–96.
46. WBY to D. O'Connell, n.d.; taped into a copy of *Ideas of Good and Evil,* a volume of essays by WBY; ms. 1742, NLI.
47. Horniman to WBY, 9 February 1909.

remptory and arbitrary master, but a shrewd diplomat like Yeats (on occasion, and with her connivance) could make even her worst qualities serve his best interest.

5

Not six months later, however, Horniman took even Yeats by surprise. On 2 July 1908 he opened a letter from the new NTS Ltd. manager, and promising playwright, Norreys Connell:

My dear Yeats,

. . . This morning I had an incomprehensible letter from Miss Horniman from which I gather that she commands me to apologize to her because you did not restrain Sara Allgood from abetting Mrs. Lyttleton in a political demonstration.

I cannot imagine what politics Sally has in common with Mrs. Lyttleton, but I am quite certain that this is the last straw upon the camel's back and that I have finally done with the Abbey Theatre. Please delete my name from the list of directors and believe that I shall always be proud to have been associated with you in this work.

If you will suffer me to give you a piece of advice, it is this— Take in Hone as co-director and bring back the Fays. . . . If Miss Horniman is going to withdraw the subsidy, her aversion from them does not matter.

I am, with all good wishes,

As ever,
Norreys Connell [48]

Connell, because he would not be unreasonably reprimanded, thus followed Moore, Colum, and Boyle as talented playwrights discouraged by the English owner from writing for the Abbey. Yeats was nonetheless not yet willing to take his advice or follow his example in standing up to Annie. He quickly tried to sort out the facts of the matter and talk Horniman out of stopping the subsidy for violation of the taboo on politics.

It turned out that Mrs. Patrick Campbell had asked Sally

48. Norreys Connell to WBY, 2 July 1909; Hogan and Kilroy, 3:273–74.

Allgood to take her place in reciting poetry at a meeting of a ladies' club in the home of Mrs. Edith Lyttleton, where there was to be some discussion of the question of woman's suffrage.[49] Mrs. Lyttleton was a niece of the former Conservative prime minister (1902–5) and chief secretary for Ireland (1887–91) Arthur Balfour; her husband, Alfred Lyttleton, a nephew of Mrs. W. E. Gladstone, had joined the Liberal Unionist party because of his grave doubts about Home Rule. Lyttleton had been head of the Colonial Office under the Conservative government in 1903 when he earned a reputation for attempting to introduce Chinese coolie labor into South Africa. Thus one can understand Connell's surprise at Sally Allgood abetting a Lyttleton scheme. What neither Connell nor possibly even Allgood realized, however, is that the "politics" involved was women's rights, not national independence. Even so, it was difficult to comprehend what was heinous about an actress reciting a poem upon request, or, indeed, how what she did on her own time was any concern of Annie Horniman's. Nonetheless, Horniman demanded that Allgood, Mrs. Patrick Campbell, Mrs. Edith Lyttleton, and each NTS director all write letters begging her forgiveness; if a letter was missing, she would stop the subsidy.[50]

Yeats did not attempt to reason with Horniman about the meaning of the term *politics* and the phrase "use of the theatre"; he rounded up the required apologies, and begged for leniency.[51] The discussion went on for a long time in Horniman's apartment, and Mrs. Helen Rand—a friend of Annie's who happened to be present—testified later that Yeats, with much hand-wringing, accepted her right to require compliance with her political sensitivities; in all their talk, he never

49. Sara Allgood to WBY, 11 July 1909; Finneran, Harper, and Murphy, 1:219.
50. Horniman to Norreys Connell, 1 July 1909.
51. Yeats dictated the letter Sara Allgood was to send; Allgood obliged, but remarked, "Personally I find it most humiliating that I should be compelled to do so" (Allgood to WBY, 11 July 1909; Finneran, Harper, and Murphy, 1:218).

mentioned that he thought she was exceeding her powers.[52] One may doubt Yeats ever believed she had such "rights," but he was certainly kept on his toes by her temperamental application of the carrot and stick: long after Horniman left the room, he spoke to Miss Rand "with much anxiety of the possibility of the theatre being closed."

There is no evidence whether Yeats discovered why Horniman acted in this "incomprehensible" way; he presumably had his hands full keeping her from carrying out her long-standing threat. He must have known that Horniman was jealous of his friendship with Mrs. Pat, especially since the actress and poet had begun to collaborate on his *The Player Queen*, written for Mrs. Pat and to some extent about her. It was also common knowledge that one kink in Horniman's character was that while she was a feminist, she was opposed to women's suffrage. There may have been some further factional dispute among London ladies of high culture that triggered her wrath, so that instead of Horniman stumbling over Irish sensitivities, on this occasion the Irish blundered into the maze of English personality politics. And finally, Connell's hunch was shrewd: Horniman was out to end her association with the Abbey once and for all.

6

In the "Lyttleton affair," Yeats and the Board of Authors were faced quite frankly with an ugly choice: as Arthur Griffith phrased the dilemma in a later crisis, *"Lick my boots or lose my money"* was Horniman's offer. In the relative privacy of Horniman's parlor, Yeats did what he was called upon to do to save the subsidy. However, he got up off his knees looking for a new battleground in which he could fight out the issue of the "No Politics" rule in an honorable public way. It was clear that all the arguments he had made about Horniman's subsidy making the Abbey a sanctuary of artistic freedom, a

52. Helen Rand to Horniman, 18 January 1911.

place of wide tolerance, were basically hollow if she practiced what amounted to arbitrary censorship. Toleration does not mean toleration of doctrines one considers reasonable but of those one considers damnable; and any freedom is insignificant that permits one only to do what is right; it must allow one to do wrong. At present, the NTS was wholly at the mercy of a censor's personal caprice, temper, resentment, bigotry, jealousy, or private conviction.

Fortuitously, just these issues of censorship had become very much a matter of public discussion in England months before the "Lyttleton affair." A parliamentary Select Committee on Stage Plays had been formed and was due to begin meetings in August concerning the role of the Lord Chamberlain in licensing plays for performance. Bernard Shaw, a self-proclaimed "specialist in immoral and heretical plays," rattled the Select Committee with a brilliantly provocative argument against any censorship—of blasphemous libel, seditious libel, or obscene libel.[53] Furthermore, in May the Lord Chamberlain banned Shaw's *The Shewing-Up of Blanco Posnet*, a bizarrely capricious judgment for which he was required to give no proper account. Shaw's work, with its weird combination of Bret Harte language and Shavian forensics, is not a good play, but it is certainly a moral play; in fact, it is a sermon on the working of the spirit of God in a cowboy of the Wild West. During the summer, Shaw offered it to the Abbey Board of Authors, Ireland not being under the Lord Chamberlain's jurisdiction. As Dublin Castle officials soon pointed out to Lady Gregory, *Blanco Posnet* did not deal with an Irish subject, foster an Irish school of drama, or constitute an international literary masterpiece; in short, it was not the sort of play the Abbey was patented to stage.[54] However, for Yeats the play filled the bill to perfection. It enabled him at a single stroke to attack in principle Horniman's capricious censorship

53. George Bernard Shaw, *The Doctor's Dilemma, Getting Married, and The Shewing-Up of Blanco Posnet* (New York: Brentano's, 1911), 346.
54. J. B. Dougherty to Lady Gregory, 20 August 1909; "More about Blanco Posnet," *Evening Telegraph*, 24 August 1909; Hogan and Kilroy, 3:287.

and to earn kudos with Irish nationalists by a direct challenge to British authority over Irish affairs.

The announcement that the Abbey would open its season on 24 August 1909 with Synge's *Playboy* and Shaw's *Blanco Posnet* caused an immediate flurry of diplomatic activity by Dublin Castle, which Yeats promptly aired in daily interviews with the press, stories copied by papers around the world. Throughout the negotiations with the government, Yeats neglected to consult Horniman. This was her time not to speak but to listen. Castle officials shrewdly tried to draw Horniman's interests into the discussion with the Board of Authors. The secretary to the lord lieutenant informed Lady Gregory that his lordship "would deeply regret should it become necessary to take any action which might inflict loss upon the public-spirited lady who founded a home for the Irish National Theatre," [55] but this allusion to the fact that the Irish were imperiling the financial interests of their English philanthropist had no effect upon Yeats or Lady Gregory; they simply turned over the entire correspondence to the Dublin *Evening Telegraph* and went ahead with rehearsals. In effect, they dared the lord lieutenant to censor the play, rescind the patent, sue the owner, and close the theatre. When Horniman requested the statements of Abbey policy be issued by them jointly, Yeats supremely returned that she, as a private person, had no right to object, and they, as artists and public figures, had their obligations.[56] *Blanco Posnet* went on as planned, a tremendous sell-out night after night, with commendatory reviews and triumphant ridicule of the folly of the British censor.

The celebrated conflict of the little Irish theatre with the British Crown cast Yeats in a new role: Celtic David against Saxon Goliath. He built upon his new reputation with nationalists by assuming an entirely new attitude to the Abbey audience. Whereas before he had railed against the mob and its

55. J. B. Dougherty to Lady Gregory, 20 August 1909; "More about Blanco Posnet," *Evening Telegraph,* 24 August 1909, 3; Hogan and Kilroy, 3:287.
56. Horniman to WBY, 16 February 1910.

three sorts of Irish ignorance—of priest, politician, and jour-
nalist—he now used his newspaper interviews to sing the
praises of the Irish theatregoers. The Irish, he said, although
they lied to one another, were true to themselves; the English
"have learned from commerce to be truthful to one another,
but they are great liars when alone." The morally complacent
English audience resents a claim upon the intellect; an Irish
audience, however, "resents not understanding": it allows an
author all means to make his argument with power and passion. Yeats even showed a new conciliatory understanding of
those who hated *The Playboy.* On one hand, a playwright like
Shaw, he said, went over easily with an Irish audience because his argument was clear; on the other hand, a playwright like Synge was precisely the sort that was dangerous
with an Irish audience, because, being "capricious and temperamental," his argument was difficult to follow.[57] This distinction between the English and the Irish national tempera-
ments may be poor social psychology, but it was excellent
public relations. With its coffers full of ticket proceeds, and a
new harmony with the public, the National Theatre Society
was making sudden progress toward becoming "a representative Irish institution."

7

In that case, Horniman wanted out immediately. On 9 September 1909, she made a formal offer to sell the Abbey to the
directors for a £428 down payment, and a £1,000 quittance.
After closing the deal on 1 December 1909, Horniman noted,
Yeats and Lady Gregory would be able to go ahead and sell
sixpenny seats, make up to the Theatre of Ireland, rent the
stage to the Gaelic League, and seek to become a popular na-

57. WBY, "Fighting the Censor," *Irish Independent,* 25 August 1909,
quoted in Hogan and Kilroy, 3:298–99. Compare Yeats's condescending attitude to the audience at the time of the *Playboy* disturbances, when he told
reporters the objectors "had no books in their houses" and parroted the dic-
tates of "societies, clubs and league"; they were "commonplace and ignorant
people" (*Freeman's Journal,* 30 January 1907).

tional theatre.[58] But Yeats was in no hurry: since Horniman was bound by written promise to pay another £800 of subsidy through 1910, the most profitable course for him was delay. He requested that Horniman renew her lease through 1910, so that he could get a formal appraisal of the property, and make a public appeal for a subscription fund enabling the new owners to meet the asking price.[59] Furthermore, Yeats wanted time to bargain Horniman down. Already, she was giving the directors buildings and furniture valued at £9,700, furniture at £750, scenery and properties at £600, and pictures at £250 (total: £11,300) for only £1,438,[60] while throwing in the lease free.[61] Yeats, however, with what he admitted to be "greed, and greed of a singularly monstrous kind," wanted her to lower the price in view of the facts that the building needed painting and that the electric lamps were nearly worn out.[62] These are not ordinary business relations. Yeats's next proposal was positively illegal: he wanted to use the Abbey as collateral in borrowing money to buy it, a "scandalous" suggestion to float the company on Horniman's credit; she threatened to blow the whistle and alert nationalists if he even tried it.[63]

As Yeats strung along the negotiations over the Abbey sale, while promoting the status of the NTS with "patriots," the basically exploitative character of the relationship between poet and patron became glaringly manifest to Horniman. Now that he was openly fighting for his own interest against her, rather than for their common interest against others, Yeats appeared more than ever the tyrant. She admitted she had felt the change in his attitude toward her, felt it acutely, ever since his return from America in 1904, after she had finally bought the Abbey, but it grew and grew, gradually and ever more painfully,[64] until now Lady Gregory and Yeats

58. Horniman to WBY, 9 September 1909.
59. Horniman to WBY, 23 December 1909.
60. Holloway, "Abbey Threatre Valuation," ms. 13267 (10), NLI.
61. Horniman to WBY, 20 December 1909.
62. WBY to Horniman, 15 January 1910.
63. Horniman to WBY, 27 January 1909.
64. Horniman to WBY, 26 December 1909.

openly "associat[ed themselves] with the Sinn Fein and Gaelic League (after the Blanco Posnet fuss)," even though they *knew* she was "very much annoyed."[65] Horniman finally exploded at the "self-indulgence & greed & philistinism" with which the "Superman" treated his "Nitschien [*sic*] 'slave.'"[66] But Horniman served notice that "the time has not yet come that the Supermen are completely paramount, or that revolt [of the slaves] is impossible."[67] And when the time came, as come it would, "even Super People," she glowered, "cannot be expected to enjoy a revolt of slaves."[68]

8

On the occasion of the death of Edward VII, Annie Horniman seized a final opportunity to assert the rights of property, apply her sense of what constituted "political action," and blindside the Irish "Superman." Edward VII died late on Friday, 6 May 1910. The Abbey was scheduled to open on Saturday with Padraic Colum's *Thomas Muskerry*, marking the welcome return to its stage of one of the 1905 INTS dissidents. The young Cork playwright Lennox Robinson, then in charge of the Abbey, rose at 11:30 on Saturday morning to answer the door. The business manager, Henderson, had come with the news of the king's death. Several Dublin theatres were closing out of respect; would the Abbey follow suit? Lennox Robinson was in a quandary: "I knew that the Abbey Theatre had been carried on from the beginning as a purely artistic venture. I knew that its policy was to ignore politics, and I thought if we closed we would be throwing ourselves definitely on one side and that we should remain open taking no notice of a circumstance that had no significance to the arts."[69] Furthermore, Robinson knew for a fact that both Unionists

65. Horniman to WBY, 16 February 1910.
66. Horniman to WBY, 23 December 1909. The spelling is Horniman's.
67. Horniman to WBY, 23 December 1909.
68. Horniman to WBY, 26 December 1909.
69. Lennox Robinson to WBY, n.d.; Lennox Robinson, *Ireland's Abbey Theatre: A History, 1899–1951* (London: Sidgwick & Jackson, 1951), 86.

and nationalists had booked tickets both for the matinee and evening shows, so that the Abbey would not be playing to a crowd of those rejoicing that England's difficulty was Ireland's opportunity. Nonetheless, he was sufficiently acquainted with Annie Horniman to know that doom waited upon such decisions, so, not wanting to act on his own responsibility, at 12:15 Robinson walked around to the Nassau Street post office and wired Lady Gregory for her opinion.[70] The telegram was taken down in Gort at 12:38; by 12:50, a telegraph boy was dispatched by bicycle to Coole, a distance of two miles. Lady Gregory was not long in penciling out her message— "SHOULD CLOSE THROUGH COURTESY"—but the Gort messenger dawdled down the roads and did not show up at the post office until 2:30 (a roundtrip of one hour and forty minutes). Even then, the message was not punched out by the Gort key operator until 3:53, and it was 4:52 by the time Lady Gregory's telegram was delivered at the door of the Abbey.

Meanwhile, Lennox Robinson, with no sign from Lady Gregory, had been forced to decide on his own whether to open the theatre or not for the 3:00 matinee. It was his judgment that making no departure from usual procedure had the least chance of being a political action, so he went ahead with plans as if nothing had happened at Buckingham Palace. *Thomas Muskerry* was proving a big success, when, just before the last act, Lady Gregory's telegram arrived. Robinson then figured that what harm there was in the matter was already done, and not wanting to cause further trouble by disappointing those with evening tickets, he went on with the show on Saturday night.

Horniman of course took a different view of what constituted a political action: keeping the Abbey open the day after the death of the English king was disgusting, infuriating political surliness. The following Thursday, 11 May 1910, she issued a statement to the *Freeman's Journal* briefly stating this

70. The minute-by-minute chronology in this paragraph is taken from a document in the NLI Abbey Theatre Collection (ms. 13068), presumably prepared for legal purposes.

view of the matter, adding, "Unless proper regret is shown in the Press by the directors, my subsidy to the National Theatre Society will cease immediately."[71] Robinson got wind of Horniman's demand and telegraphed Lady Gregory suggesting that they prepare a response to be printed simultaneously with Horniman's statement to the press. Lady Gregory, however, wanted to get Yeats's assent, and she ordered Robinson to "KEEP BACK APOLOGY."[72] He managed in the event to get the editor of the paper to hold up publication of Horniman's demand until the 13th of May, by which time Lady Gregory and Yeats had cannily adjusted the degree of their compliance: two articles were inserted in the same column of the *Freeman's Journal* with Horniman's letter, one a paragraph declaring that Lady Gregory and W. B. Yeats had not been in Dublin during the week of 2 May–8 May (so how could they be responsible?), the other a "Statement by Abbey Theatre Management" that gave the coming week's program and, as a total non sequitur, its "regret that, owing to accident, the theatre remained open on Saturday last."

This plainly did not suffice for Horniman as "proper regret." She wanted her authority to be more clearly observed by public self-criticism: Robinson should be fired. Yeats was not willing to let Robinson go the way of Colum, Moore, Fay, Boyle, and Connell. He instead lodged a complaint with the General Post Office for its inefficiency in carrying Abbey Theatre messages back and forth across the country. By 27 May 1910, the secretary of the GPO responded: "With reference to your application of the 12th instat [*sic*], I beg leave to express regret for any inconvenience caused by the delay of the telegram in question and to inform you that the messenger concerned has been suitably dealt with."[73]

Poor kid from Gort! The weakest, most unknowing link in the chain of responsibility, he got the sack, and all for nothing: Horniman's thirst for punishments was not about to

---

71. Horniman to editor of the *Freeman's Journal*, 11 May 1910.
72. Lady Gregory to Lennox Robinson, 12 May 1910; ms. 13068, NLI.
73. Secretary, GPO, to Lennox Robinson, 27 May 1910; ms. 13068, NLI.

be quenched with a summary judgment upon a bicycle messenger boy.

As Horniman continued to let it be known around Dublin that "a small addition to the ordinary paragraph in advance is not sufficient to save the subsidy," and that "it would be a serious matter for so many people to lose their employment,"[74] Irish nationalists watched carefully to see whether Yeats would find it in himself to display sufficient penitence for lack of proper grief at the death of an English king. In the pages of *Sinn Fein*, Arthur Griffith put the moral situation, for years cloaked from public inspection, now thrown open to the judgment of the crowd, with brutal clarity:

> Mr. Yeats is not in Ireland at present, and circumstances may have prevented him reading the insult which his co-directors have accepted in the spirit of whipped curs. Whether he will permit himself to be whipped in public in return for English money, remains to be seen. We hope not. We remember how Mr. Yeats boasted that in his father's house he was never taught to bend the knee. That was when he was fighting Irish opinion. Whether he is ready to take a public whipping from a rich vulgarian for cash, we doubt. "Lick my boots or lose my money" is the Englishwoman's ultimatum. No gentleman could hesitate in making a choice.[75]

Yeats, of course, wished neither to lick Horniman's boots nor to lose her money. Another thing he learned in his father's house is that "sometimes one is not a gentleman because there is something more important than a gentleman"—such as a condottiere of the civic life.[76] Yeats hired a lawyer, and prepared to fight Horniman through the courts for his subsidy.

Yeats and Lady Gregory took over the Abbey Theatre with their £428 down payment, but they refused to pay Horniman £1,000 quittance until she released the last £200 installments of the subsidy. C. P. Scott of the *Manchester Guardian* was appointed to arbitrate between the lawyers of Yeats and the law-

74. Horniman to J. Roseman Burns, 13 May 1910.
75. Arthur Griffith, "Bootlickers," *Sinn Fein*, 21 May 1910.
76. J. B. Yeats to Ch. Fitzgerald, 30 January 1905; Hone, *W. B. Yeats, 1865–1939* (New York: Macmillan, 1943), 81.

yers of Horniman. W. B. Bailey, of Whitney & Moore, represented Yeats: he made the bold opening gambit that there had
never been an agreement between owner and directors forbidding political action at the Abbey. If there had been such
a "ground understanding," Yeats testified, "it would mean
that Miss Horniman and I arranged a compact of a private
kind without informing Synge and Lady Gregory"—an unthinkable possibility![77] This opening strike was followed by
a slightly contradictory defensive countermove: the events of
7 May 1910, it was argued, were no violation of the agreement, even if there had been an agreement. In fact, Yeats insisted, if Lennox Robinson were dismissed, "his dismissal
would be in itself the first insubordination [*sic*] of Art to Politics that had ever taken place." (Presumably Yeats meant *subordination*, though his slip of the tongue comes as close to the
truth.) In a supplement to Yeats's testimony, Bailey said that,
after going into all the facts, one must conclude that the
theatre's remaining open was merely a regrettable accident.
Lennox Robinson was a person of the highest character, "the
last man who would be deliberately guilty of a disloyal or political action." A survey of public opinion in Ireland showed
that no one took the incident to be political; the explanation of
the directors had been accepted, Bailey reported, "in the
highest official quarters," and, furthermore, "some of the
strongest supporters of the Unionist policy in Ireland have
subscribed to the Endowment Fund with full cognizance of
the controversy."[78]

Annie Horniman furnished her counsel, of the Dendy &
Paterson firm, Manchester, with various documents to prove
that she had made the subsidy conditional upon a "No Politics" rule. The testimony of Helen Rand (mentioned above)
was solicited to show that on an afternoon in July 1909, in the
drawing room at H1, Montague Mansions, Mr. Yeats, by his

---

77. Observations on the Statement of the Case of Lady Gregory and W. B.
Yeats, submitted to C. P. Scott; Flannery, *Horniman and the Abbey Theatre*, 31.
Flannery kindly calls Yeats's testimony "casuistic"; another name for it is
perjury.
78. W. B. Bailey to C. P. Scott, n.d.; ms 13068, NLI.

nervous petitions for pardon, had accepted Horniman's right
to stop the subsidy on account of Sara Allgood's political misbehavior at the suffragette meeting. Finally, to counter arguments that no one in Ireland thought the matter "political,"
Horniman had in her possession letters of sympathy from
Rose Duggan, J. Roseman Burns, and others who, "shocked"
at the "not-closing of the Abbey Theatre," took an oath to
"never again enter its portals."[79] Backed up by the natural
enemies of the National Theatre Society and Abbey boycot-
ters, Horniman awaited the judgment of C. P. Scott.

There is no detailed record of Scott's personal deliberations
through the winter and spring of 1911 before he rendered his
judgment in May, a year after the putative offense. The lawyers for the NTS directors could hardly have proved that Miss
Horniman had to pay the subsidy without furnishing documents that also declared an obligation on their part to avoid
political conduct. But certainly it would have been difficult
for the arbitrator to establish in principle what such conduct
was, or, to put it another way, what restrictions lay upon
Horniman's exercise of her right. There was no evidence of
intent to offend on the part of Lennox Robinson, but there
was some evidence that offense was taken by some parts of
the Irish citizenry, though public criticism did not materialize
until a week after the performance. Surely, if the non-closing
of the Abbey had not originally been a political act, Horniman
herself had made it one by her first letter to the *Freeman's Journal*; afterwards, Unionists and nationalists lined up on either
side of the dispute. The performance of *Thomas Muskerry* was
then caught up in the struggle for power, involved in conflicts
far from its own making, and the Abbey was bound over to
the jurisdiction of a litigator. It seemed a hard thing to make
Horniman, who had freely paid so much to the Abbey, pay
more against her will, but it was a harder thing to find that
there was sedition throughout the seamless web of social discourse, that every thread of thought, word, and deed, and
every person, from King Edward VII to the Gort telegraph

boy, was under contest, pulled both one way and the other by forces that were fundamentally political. While noting that Horniman had behaved admirably during the long months of arbitration, Scott ruled that she was not within her rights in stopping the Abbey subsidy, and that she should pay the Abbey directors £400.

Horniman complained through her lawyers to the lawyers of Yeats that she had been badly treated—there was an agreement, the agreement had been broken, and no money was due.[80] Now, having won their victory in principle, Yeats and Lady Gregory chose to play a noble part: since Horniman did not "accept the integrity of their action," they would not, Whitney & Moore informed Dendy & Paterson, accept her money.[81] With a final perverse turn of the screw, Horniman, hearing that the Abbey directors did not want the £400, paid it forthwith. She then wired Yeats, not through his lawyers, but directly, her last communication to the poet:

YOU HAVE SHOWN ME I DO NOT MATTER IN YOUR EYES THE MONEY IS PAID SUPERMEN CANNOT ASSOCIATE WITH SLAVES MAY TIME REAWAKEN YOUR SENSE OF HONOUR THEN YOU MAY FIND YOUR FRIEND AGAIN BUT REPENTANCE MUST COME FIRST.[82]

9

Repentance did not come from Yeats, nor did he ever resume his friendship with his former patron. Nonetheless, Annie Horniman mattered, mattered even to Yeats, both to the degree that she paid the money, and to the degree that she suppressed the Irish national character of the Irish National Theatre Society. As early as 1903, Yeats trimmed the sails of his policy to catch the wind of her finance. In buying the INTS the Abbey, it may also be said she bought the Abbey the INTS, but she nonetheless took the Irish players out of Camden Street slums and rented lecture halls; she gave them a

80. Dendy & Paterson to Whitney & Moore, 4 May 1911.
81. Whitney & Moore to Dendy & Paterson, 8 May 1911.
82. Horniman to WBY, 5 May 1911.

focus in the center of Dublin, a focus, as James Flannery notes, "either from the audience's viewpoint or the viewpoint of the theatre workers."[83] Without a home, the Irish revival might well have been a poor, unknown, short-lived affair, or it might have found different funding and a different future. Her subsidy for actors' salaries purged the democratic, socialist, republican cadre of actors, and turned the rest into professionals measured by a high standard of proficiency. Her regular guarantee of financial support enabled the NTS to flout public taste and keep unpopular plays on stage—like those of Synge—until their odium faded and their quality was recognized.[84] Finally, her administration and her attempted censorship of the theatre strengthened the Abbey against its rivals, while taking a severe toll of its own personnel: Moore, Colum, Boyle, Connell, and the Fays all suffered eviction. Indeed, Annie Elizabeth Fredericka Horniman fundamentally mattered; she was (to commit a pharisaical borrowing) "The stone in the midst of all," the "stone to trouble the living stream." It is useless to blame, with Arthur Griffith, this "rich vulgarian," whose wealth without merit and literally blind partisanship were not so much personal shortcomings as embodiments of the way the world was then, is now, and will continue for some time to be: vastly unequal in its distribution of wealth and caught up in struggles for power. In a moment of rare clarity, William Boyle wrote Joseph Holloway that it was no good to blame Horniman and the directors for the loss of the Fays, because what had Ireland done to keep them? No good either, he went on, to blame "the Abbey lords" for "playing their own hand," because no other Irishmen had the same zeal for drama. If a

---

83. Flannery, *Horniman and the Abbey Theatre*, 33. Flannery's estimate of the importance of Horniman's role in the creation of the Abbey Theatre is excellent; my differences from his summary are matters of emphasis. He stresses the positive, liberating effects of her generosity; I stress its determinative effects.

84. Not all plays, of course, became popular simply because they were regularly revived: several of Yeats's plays failed to improve upon the audience's further acquaintance.

thousand people in Ireland could have been found to sub-
scribe a pound each, "Ireland wouldn't need the money of an
Irish-hating Englishwoman to set up a drama on its own."[85]
Even if local funding had been discovered, the Irish National Theatre Society would not thereby have become necessarily more free and less repressed, a kind of dramatic *vox
populi*, political *saeculum saeculorum*, and artistic *aetas aurea*
rolled into one. The case of Annie Horniman vividly illustrates two principles effectively involved to some degree in all
examples of artistic production. First, money is the condition
of artistic freedom, and artistic freedom is conditioned by
money. Second, a principle obvious in the abstract, and ex-
quisitely apparent in Horniman's experience with the Abbey,
all works of art are involved in the human struggle, which
shapes them as they shape it. To open the doors of the Abbey
was a political act; to close the doors of the Abbey was a political act; and everything that moved within its walls was
flooded with the inspiriting turmoil of the nation in the streets.

Bibliography

I. MANUSCRIPTS

Footnotes in the text to letters not published in books are located in the following National Library of Ireland (NLI) manuscript collections. Letters by A. E. F. Horniman, where not otherwise noted in the text, are drawn from ms. 13068, the Horniman papers.

Abbey Theatre Management. Financial Accounts, business correspondence, patents, 1904–32. National Library of Ireland, ms. 13068.

Denson, Alan. Letters of George Russell [Æ]. National Library of Ireland, ms. 9967.

Fay, Frank J. Lectures and Articles on the Theatre. National Library of Ireland, mss. 10951–52.

———. Nine letters to Maire Garvey (April to November 1904). National Library of Ireland, ms. 8320.

———. Letters to J. M. Synge, 1903–7. National Library of Ireland, P 5381.

Fay, W. G. Articles and Letters, including Horniman's account of expenses. National Library of Ireland, ms. 10952.

Financial Statement, July 1907 to November 1910. Henderson Press Cuttings. National Library of Ireland, ms. 1733.

Holloway Papers. Seventy-eight letters of William Boyle. National Library of Ireland, ms. 13267.

Horniman, A. E. F. Letters to Abbey Theatre directors and to W. B. Yeats, 1903–11. National Library of Ireland, ms. 13068.

———. Letters to Reverend Canon James O. Hannay (George Birmingham). National Library of Ireland, ms. 2259.

Roberts, George, Collection. Minutes of the Irish National Theatre Society and letters to Maire Garvey from Frank Fay and others. National Library of Ireland, mss. 5651–52, 7267, 5320.

II. Irish Journals and Periodicals

The Academy and Literature. A weekly review. London, 1869–1916.
The Arrow. An occasional publication of the National Theatre Society. Edited by W. B. Yeats. Dublin & London, 1906–9.
Beltaine. An occasional publication. Organ of the Irish Literary Theatre. Edited by W. B. Yeats. Dublin, 1899–1900.
Dana. A magazine of independent thought. Edited by John Eglinton and Frederick Ryan. Dublin: Hodges, May 1904–April 1905.
The Leader. A review of current affairs, literature, politics, art, and industry, biweekly. Edited by Denis Patrick Moran. Dublin, September 1900–.
Samhain. An occasional publication. Organ of the National Theatre Society. Edited by W. B. Yeats. Dublin: Sealy & Byers, London: Fisher Unwin, 1901–5, 1908.
The United Irishman. A national weekly review. Edited by Arthur Griffith. Vols. 1–16, nos. 1–372 (4 March 1899–14 April 1906). Dublin: Bernard Doyle, 1899–1906.

III. Published Primary Sources

Blunt, Wilfrid Scawen. *My Diaries: Being a Personal Narrative of Events, 1888–1914.* London: Wecker, 1921.
Colum, Mary. *Life and the Dream.* 1958; rev. ed., Dublin: Dolmen Press, 1966.
Colum, Padraic. *Three Plays.* Edited by John Eglinton [William Kirkpatrick Magee]. Dublin: Figgis, 1963.
———. *The Road round Ireland.* New York: Macmillan, 1926.
Cousins, James H., and Margaret E. Cousins. *We Two Together.* Madras: Ganesh, 1950.
Eglinton, John [William Kirkpatrick Magee]. *Irish Literary Portraits.* London: Macmillan, 1935.
Eglinton, John [William Kirkpatrick Magee], W. B. Yeats, Æ, and W. Larminie. *Literary Ideals in Ireland.* London: Fisher Unwin, 1899. Reprint. New York: Lemma Press, 1973.
Fay, Frank J. *Towards a National Theatre: The Dramatic Criticism of Frank J. Fay.* Edited by Robert Hogan. Irish Theatre Series, no. 1. London: Oxford University Press; Dublin: Dolmen Press, 1970.
Fay, William George, and Catherine Carswell. *The Fays of the Abbey Theatre: An Autobiographical Record.* London: Rich & Lowan; New York: Harcourt, Brace, 1935.
Finneran, Richard, George Mills Harper, and William M. Murphy, eds. *Letters to W. B. Yeats.* 2 vols. New York: Columbia University Press, 1977.

Gonne, Maud. *A Servant of the Queen*. 1938. Reprint. Suffolk: Boydell Press, 1983.

Gregory, Isabella Augusta, Lady. *Our Irish Theatre*. 1913. Reprint. New York: Capricorn Books, 1965.

———. *The Collected Plays*. 4 vols. Edited by Ann Saddlemyer. Vol. 1, *The Comedies*. Vol. 2, *The Tragedies and Tragic-comedies*. Vol. 3, *Wonder and the Supernatural*. Vol. 4, *Translations, Adaptations, and Collaborations*. New York: Oxford University Press, 1970.

———. *Seventy Years: Being the Autobiography of Lady Gregory*. Edited by Colin Smythe. Gerrards Cross, Bucks.: Colin Smythe, 1973; New York: Macmillan, 1974.

———. *Lady Gregory's Journals, Volume One, Books One to Twenty-nine, 10 October 1916–24 February 1925*. Edited by Daniel J. Murphy. 1947. Reprint. New York: Oxford Universty Press, 1978.

———. ed., *Ideals in Ireland*. London: At the Unicorn, 1901.

Hogan, Robert, and James Kilroy, eds. *Lost Plays of the Irish Renaissance*. Gerrards Cross, Bucks.: Colin Smythe, Newark, Del.: Proscenium Press, 1970.

Hogan, Robert, general ed. *Modern Irish Drama: A Documentary History*. Vols. 1–4. Dublin: Dolmen Press; Atlantic Highlands, N.J.: 1975–79. Vol. 1, *The Irish Literary Theatre 1899–1901*, edited by Robert Hogan and James Kilroy. Vol. 2, *Laying the Foundations 1902–1904*, edited by Robert Hogan and James Kilroy. Vol. 3, *The Abbey Theatre, the Years of Synge 1905–1909*, edited by Robert Hogan and James Kilroy. Vol. 4, *The Rise of the Realists 1910–1915*, edited by Robert Hogan, Richard Burnham, and Daniel P. Poteet.

Holloway, Joseph. *Joseph Holloway's Abbey Theatre: A Selection from His Unpublished Journal "Impressions of a Dublin Play-Goer."* Edited by Robert Hogan and Michael J. O'Neill. Carbondale: Southern Illinois University Press; London: Feffer & Simmons, 1967.

Mitchell, Susan. *Aids to the Immortality of Certain Persons in Ireland, Charitably Administered by Susan L. Mitchell*. 1908. Dublin: Maunsel, 1913.

Moore, George. *Hail and Farewell! Ave, Salve*, and *Vale*. 3 vols. 1911–14. Reprint. London: Heinemann, 1937.

Nic Shiublaigh, Maire. *The Splendid Years*. Dublin: James Duffy, 1955.

O'Sullivan, Seumas [James Starkey]. *The Rose and Bottle*. Dublin: Talbot Press, 1946.

Payne, Ben Iden. *A Life in a Wooden O: Memoirs of the Theatre*. New Haven: Yale University Press, 1977.

Robinson, Lennox. *I Sometimes Think*. Dublin: Talbot Press, 1956.

Rothenstein, William. *Men and Memories: Recollections of William Rothenstein*. 3 vols. New York: Coward-McCann, 1937.

Russell, George. *Letters from AE*. Edited by Alan Denson. London: Abelard-Schuman, 1962.

Saddlemyer, Ann, ed. *Theatre Business: The Correspondence of the First Abbey Theatre Directors: William Butler Yeats, Lady Gregory, and J. M. Synge.* Gerrards Cross, Bucks.: Colin Smythe; University Park: Pennsylvania State University Press, 1982.

Synge, John Millington. *Collected Works.* General editor: Robin Skelton. London: Oxford University Press; Gerrards Cross, Bucks.: Colin Smythe; Washington, D.C.: Catholic University of America Press, 1962–68. 4 vols. Vol. 1, *Poems*, edited by Robin Skelton. Vol. 2, *Prose*, edited by Alan Price. Vols. 3 and 4, *Plays*, edited by Ann Saddlemyer.

————. *Letters to Molly: John Millington Synge to Maire O'Neill, 1906– 1909.* Edited by Ann Saddlemyer. Cambridge, Mass.: Harvard University Press, Belknap Press, 1971.

————. *Some Letters of John M. Synge to Lady Gregory and W. B. Yeats.* Edited by Ann Saddlemyer. Dublin: Cuala Press, 1971.

Yeats, John Butler. *J. B. Yeats: Letters to His Son W. B. Yeats and Others, 1869–1922.* Edited by Joseph Hone. 1944. Reprint. London: Secker & Warburg, 1983.

Yeats, William Butler. *Poems.* London: T. Fisher Unwin, 1899.

————. *Poems.* London: T. Fisher Unwin, 1901.

————. *The Letters of W. B. Yeats.* Edited by Allan Wade. London: R. Hart-Davis, 1954. Reprint. New York: Octagon Books, 1980.

————. *The Autobiography of William Butler Yeats.* 1938. Reprint. New York: Collier, 1961.

————. *Essays and Introductions.* New York: Macmillan, 1961.

————. *Explorations.* New York: Macmillan, 1962.

————. *The Variorum Edition of the Plays of W. B. Yeats.* Edited by Russell K. and Catherine C. Alspach. New York: Macmillan, 1966.

————. *Memoirs: Autobiography—First Draft, Journal.* Edited by Denis Donoghue. New York: Macmillan, 1972.

————. *Uncollected Prose by W. B. Yeats.* Edited by John P. Frayne and Colton Johnson. 2 vols. New York: Columbia University Press, 1976.

————. *The Collected Letters of W. B. Yeats.* Edited by John Kelly and Eric Domville. Vol. 1. Oxford: Clarendon Press, 1986.

————, ed. *Fairy and Folk Tales of Ireland.* Edited by Mary Helen Thuente. Foreword by Kathleen Raine. Reprint of *Fairy and Folk Tales of the Irish Peasantry,* ed. W. B. Yeats (London, 1888), and *Irish Fairy Tales,* ed. W. B. Yeats (London, 1892). Gerrards Cross, Bucks.: Colin Smythe, 1977.

IV. Secondary Sources

Archibald, Douglas. *John Butler Yeats.* Lewisburg, Pa.: Bucknell University Press, 1974.

————. *Yeats.* Syracuse, N.Y.: Syracuse University Press, 1983.

Bax, Clifford, ed. *Florence Farr, Bernard Shaw and W. B. Yeats; Letters.* New York: Dodd, Mead, 1942.

Bloom, Harold. *Yeats.* New York: Oxford University Press, 1970.

Bohlmann, Otto. *Yeats and Nietzsche: An Exploration of Major Nietzschean Echoes in the Writings of William Butler Yeats.* Totowa, N.J.: Barnes & Noble, 1982.

Bowen, Zack. *Padraic Colum.* Carbondale: Southern Illinois University Press, 1970.

Boyce, D. George. *Nationalism in Ireland.* Baltimore: Johns Hopkins University Press, 1982.

Boyd, Ernest. *Ireland's Literary Renaissance.* New York: Knopf, 1922.

Brown, Malcolm. *The Politics of Irish Literature: From Thomas Davis to W. B. Yeats.* Seattle: University of Washington Press, 1972.

Bushrui, Suheil. *Yeats's Verse Plays: The Revisions 1900–10.* London: Oxford University Press, 1965.

————, ed. *Sunshine and the Moon's Delight: A Centenary Tribute to J. M. Synge 1871–1909.* New York: Barnes & Noble, 1972.

Cardozo, Nancy. *Lucky Eyes and a High Heart: The Life of Maud Gonne.* New York: Bobbs-Merrill, 1978.

Carpenter, Andrew, ed. *Place, Personality, and the Irish Writer.* Irish Literary Studies, 1. New York: Barnes & Noble, 1977.

————. *The Dramatic Imagination of W. B. Yeats.* Dublin: Gill & Macmillan, 1978.

Colum, Padraic. *The Road round Ireland.* London: Macmillan, 1927.

————. *Ourselves Alone! The Story of Arthur Griffith and the Origin of the Irish Free State.* New York: Crown, 1959.

————. "Vagrant Voices: A Self-Portrait." *Journal of Irish Literature* 2, no. 1 (January 1973): 63–75.

————. "Ninety Years in Retrospect." Interview with Zack Bowen. *Journal of Irish Literature* 2, no. 1 (January 1973): 14–34.

Connell, K. H. *The Population of Ireland, 1750–1845.* 1950. Reprint. Westport, Conn.: Greenwood Press, 1975.

Connolly, James. *Selected Political Writings.* Edited by Owen Dudley Edwards and Bernard Ransome. London: Jonathan Cape, 1973.

Corkery, Daniel. *Synge and Anglo-Irish Literature.* London, New York: Longmans, 1931.

Cosgrave, Patrick. "Yeats, Fascism, and Conor O'Brien." *London Magazine* 7, no. 4 (July 1967): 22–41.

Coxhead, Elizabeth. *Daughters of Erin: Five Women of the Irish Renaissance.* London: Secker & Warburg, 1965.

————. *Lady Gregory: A Literary Portrait.* New York: Harcourt, Brace, 1961.

Cross, K. G. W., and A. Norman Jeffares, eds. *In Excited Reverie.* London: Macmillan; New York: St. Martin's Press, 1965.

Cullingford, Elizabeth. *Yeats, Ireland and Fascism.* New York: New York University Press, 1981.

Denson, Alan, ed. *Letters from AE.* London: Abelard-Schuman, 1961.

Dulac, Edmund. "Yeats, as I Knew Him." *Irish Writing* 8 (July 1949): 77–87.

Edwards, Hilton, and Micheál MacLiammóir. Interviewed by Gordon Henderson, *Journal of Irish Literature* 2, no. 3 (May 1973): 79–97.

Edwards, Ruth Dudley. *James Connolly.* Dublin: Gill & Macmillan, 1981.

Ellmann, Richard. *Yeats: The Man and the Masks.* New York: Dutton, 1948.

———. *The Identity of Yeats.* New York: Oxford University Press, 1964.

Fay, Gerard. *The Abbey Theatre: Cradle of Genius.* New York: Macmillan, 1958.

Fingall, Elizabeth, countess of, and Pamela Hinkson. *Seventy Years Young.* London: Collins, 1937.

Flannery, James W. *Miss Annie F. Horniman and the Abbey Theatre.* Irish Theatre Series, no. 3. Dublin: Dolmen Press; London: Oxford University Press, 1970.

———. *W. B. Yeats and the Idea of a Theatre: The Early Abbey Theatre in Theory and Practice.* New Haven: Yale University Press, 1976.

Freyer, Grattan. *W. B. Yeats and the Anti-Democratic Tradition.* Totowa, N.J.: Barnes & Noble, 1981.

Friedman, Barton. *Adventures in the Deeps of the Mind: The Cuchulain Cycle of W. B. Yeats.* Princeton: Princeton University Press, 1977.

Greene, David H., and Edward M. Stephens. *J. M. Synge, 1871–1909.* New York: Macmillan, 1959.

Grene, Nicholas. *Synge: A Critical Study of the Plays.* London: Macmillan, 1975.

———. "Stephen McKenna on Synge." *Irish University Review* 12, no. 2 (Autumn 1982): 141–51.

Gwynn, Denis. *Edward Martyn and the Irish Literary Theatre.* 1930. Reprint. New York: Lemma Press, 1974.

Harper, George Mills. "Intellectual Hatred and Intellectual Nationalism." In *Theatre and Nationalism in Twentieth-Century Ireland,* edited by Robert O'Driscoll. Toronto: University of Toronto Press, 1971.

———. *Yeats's Golden Dawn.* New York: Barnes & Noble, 1974.

Hone, Joseph. *The Life of George Moore.* New York: Macmillan, 1936.

———. *The Life of W. B. Yeats, 1865–1939.* New York: Macmillan, 1943.

Hunt, Hugh. *The Abbey: Ireland's National Theatre, 1904–1978.* New York: Columbia University Press, 1979.

Jeffares, A. Norman. *W. B. Yeats: The Critical Heritage.* London: Routledge & Kegan Paul, 1977.

Jochum, K. P. S. *WBY: A Classified Bibliography of Criticism.* Urbana: University of Illinois Press, 1978.

Kavanagh, Peter. *The Story of the Abbey Theatre, from Its Origins in 1899 to the Present.* New York: Devin-Adair, 1950.

Kelly, John S. *The Fall of Parnell and the Rise of Irish Literature: An Investigation.* Anglo-Irish Studies, 2. Bucks, England: Alpha Academic, 1976.

Kilroy, James. *The 'Playboy' Riots.* Dublin: Dolmen Press, 1971.

King, Mary C. *The Drama of J. M. Synge.* Syracuse: Syracuse University Press, 1985.

Kohfeldt, Mary Lou. *Lady Gregory: The Woman behind the Irish Renaissance.* London: André Deutsch; New York: Atheneum, 1985.

Knowland, A. S. *W. B. Yeats, Dramatist of Vision.* Irish Literary Studies, 17. Gerrards Cross, Bucks.: Colin Smythe; Totowa, N.J.: Barnes & Noble, 1983.

Kuch, Peter. *Yeats and A.E.: The Antagonism that Unites Dear Friends.* Gerrards Cross, Bucks.: Colin Smythe; Totowa, N.J.: Barnes & Noble, 1986.

Lyons, F. S. L. *Ireland since the Famine.* 1971. rev. ed., London: Fontana/Collins, 1973.

———. *Charles Stuart Parnell.* New York: Oxford University Press, 1977.

———. *Culture and Anarchy in Ireland, 1890–1939.* New York: Oxford University Press, 1979.

McCormack, W. J. *Ascendancy and Tradition.* Oxford: Clarendon Press, 1985.

MacDonagh, Oliver. *States of Mind: A Study of Anglo-Irish Conflict, 1790–1980.* London: George Allen & Unwin, 1983.

———. *Ireland: The Union and Its Aftermath.* London: George Allen & Unwin, 1977.

Malins, Edward. "Annie Horniman, Practical Idealist." *Canadian Journal of Irish Studies* 3, no. 2 (November 1977): 18–26.

Marcus, Phillip L. *Yeats and the Beginning of the Irish Renaissance.* Ithaca, N.Y.: Cornell University Press, 1970.

Mikhail, E. H., ed. *Lady Gregory: Interviews and Recollections.* London: Macmillan; Totowa, N.J.: Rowman & Littlefield, 1977.

———, ed. *W. B. Yeats: Interviews and Recollections.* London: Macmillan; New York: Barnes & Noble, 1977.

Miller, Liam. *Noble Drama of W. B. Yeats.* Dublin: Dolmen Press; Atlantic Highlands, N.J.: Humanities Press, 1977.

Moody, T. W. *Davitt and Irish Revolution, 1846–82.* Oxford: Clarendon Press, 1982.

Moore, John Rees. *Masks of Love and Death: Yeats as Dramatist.* Ithaca, N.Y.: Cornell University Press, 1971.

Munch-Pedersen, Ole. "Yeats's Synge-Song." *Irish University Review* 6, no. 2 (Autumn 1976): 204–13.

Murphy, William M. *Prodigal Father: The Life of John Butler Yeats (1839–1922)*. Ithaca, N.Y.: Cornell University Press, 1978.

O'Brien, Conor Cruise. *Writers and Politics*. London: Chaffo & Windus, 1965.

———. "Passion and Cunning: An Essay on the Politics of W. B. Yeats." In *In Excited Reverie: A Centenary Tribute to William Butler Yeats, 1865–1939*, edited by A. Norman Jeffares and K. G. W. Cross. New York: St. Martin's Press, 1965.

O'Brien, Joseph V. *"Dear, Dirty Dublin": A City in Distress, 1899–1916*. Berkeley and Los Angeles: University of California Press, 1982.

O'Neill, William. "Yeats on Poetry and Politics." *Midwest Quarterly* 25, no. 1 (Autumn 1983): 64–73.

Oppel, Frances Nesbitt. *Mask and Tragedy: Yeats and Nietzsche, 1902–1910*. Charlottesville: University Press of Virginia, 1987.

O Suillebhain, Sean. "Synge's Use of Irish Folklore." In *J. M. Synge, Centenary Papers, 1971*, edited by Maurice Harmon. Dublin: Dolmen Press; New York: Humanities Press, 1972.

Parkin, Andrew. *The Dramatic Imagination of W. B. Yeats*. Dublin: Gill & Macmillan; New York: Barnes & Noble, 1978.

Pogson, Rex. *Miss Horniman and the Gaiety Theatre, Manchester*. Foreword by St. John Ervine. London: Rockcliff, 1952.

Price, Alan. *Synge & Anglo-Irish Drama*. London: Methuen, 1961.

Robinson, Lennox. *Ireland's Abbey Theatre: A History, 1899–1951*. London: Sedgwick & Jackson, 1951.

———. *The Noble Drama of William Butler Yeats*. Dublin: Dolmen, 1977.

Robinson, Paul N. "Peasant Play as Allegory: J. M. Synge's *Shadow of the Glen*." *CEA Critic* 36, no. 4 (May 1974): 36–38.

Rogers, William Garland. *Ladies Bountiful*. London: Gollancz, 1968.

Ronsley, Joseph, ed. *Myth and Reality in Irish Literature*. Waterloo, Ontario: Wilfrid Laurier University Press, 1977.

Saddlemyer, Ann, and George Gmelch. *J. M. Synge in Wicklow, West Kerry, and Connemara*. Totowa, N.J.: Rowman & Littlefield, 1980.

Sekine, Masaru, ed. *Irish Writers and the Theatre*. Irish Literary Studies, 23. Gerrards Cross, Bucks.: Colin Smythe, 1987.

Skelton, Robin, and Ann Saddlemyer, eds. *The World of W. B. Yeats: Essays in Perspective*. 1965. rev. ed. Seattle: University of Washington Press, 1967.

Skene, Reg. *The Cuchulain Plays of W. B. Yeats: A Study*. New York: Columbia University Press, 1974.

Summerfield, Henry. *That Myriad-Minded Man: A Biography of George William Russell "A.E." 1867–1935*. Gerrards Cross, Bucks.: Colin Smythe, 1975.

Taylor, Richard. *A Reader's Guide to the Plays of W. B. Yeats.* London: Macmillan; New York: St. Martin's Press, 1984.
Thornton, Weldon. *J. M. Synge and the Western Mind.* Gerrards Cross, Bucks.: Colin Smythe, 1979.
Torchiana, Donald T. *W. B. Yeats and Georgian Ireland.* Evanston: Northwestern University Press, 1966.
Tuohy, Frank. *Yeats.* New York: Macmillan, 1976.
Ure, Peter. *Yeats the Playwright: A Commentary on Character and Design in the Major Plays.* London: Routledge & Kegan Paul, 1963.
Watson, G. J. *Irish Identity and the Literary Revival.* New York: Barnes & Noble, 1979.
West, Trevor. *Horace Plunkett, Co-operation and Politics.* Gerrards Cross, Bucks.: Colin Smythe, 1986.
Weygandt, Cornelius. *Irish Plays and Playwrights.* London: Constable; Boston: Houghton Mifflin, 1913. Reprint. Port Washington, N.Y.: Kennikat Press, 1966.
Worth, Katharine. "O'Casey, Synge and Yeats." *Irish University Review* 10, no. 1: 103–17.
———. *The Irish Drama of Europe from Yeats to Beckett.* Atlantic Highlands, N.J.: Humanities Press, 1978.
Zwerdling, Alex. *Yeats and the Heroic Ideal.* New York: New York University Press, 1965.

V. OTHER SOURCES

Adorno, Theodor W., and Max Horkheimer. Translated by John Cumming. *Dialectic of Enlightenment.* 1944. Reprint. New York: Herder & Herder, 1972.
Benjamin, Walter. "The Artist as Producer." In *The Essential Frankfurt School Reader.* Edited by Andrew Arato and Eike Gerhardt. 1937. Reprint. New York: Urizen, 1978.
Bettelheim, Bruno. *The Uses of Enchantment: The Meaning and Importance of Fairy Tales.* New York: Knopf, 1976.
Cantor, Jay. *The Space Between: Literature and Politics.* Baltimore: Johns Hopkins University Press, 1981.
Darnton, Robert. *Mesmerism and the End of the Enlightenment in France.* Cambridge, Mass.: Harvard University Press, 1968.
Ellul, Jacques. *Propaganda: The Formation of Men's Attitudes.* Translated by Konrad Kellen and Jean Lerner. New York: Knopf, 1966. Reprint. New York: Vintage Books, 1973.
Engels, Friedrich, and Karl Marx. *The German Ideology.* Edited by C. J. Arthur. New York: International Publishers, 1972.
Foucault, Michel. *Discipline and Punish: The Birth of the Prison.* Translated by Alan Sheridan. New York: Pantheon Books, 1977.
———. *Power/Knowledge: Selected Interviews and Other Writings, 1972–*

77. Edited by Colin Gordon. New York: Pantheon Books, 1972; rev. ed., 1980.

Foulkes, A. P. *Literature and Propaganda*. New York: Methuen, 1983.

Horkheimer, Max. *Critical Theory: Selected Essays*. Translated by Matthew J. O'Connell et al. New York: Herder & Herder, 1972.

———. *The Eclipse of Reason*. New York: Continuum, 1974.

Jameson, Frederic. *The Prison-House of Language*. Princeton: Princeton University Press, 1972.

———. *The Political Unconscious: Narrative as a Socially Symbolic Act*. Ithaca, N.Y.: Cornell University Press, 1981.

Lentricchia, Frank. *Criticism and Social Change*. Chicago: University of Chicago Press, 1983.

Marcuse, Herbert. *Counterrevolution and Revolt*. Boston: Beacon Press, 1972.

Marx, Karl. *Early Writings*. Translated and edited by T. B. Bottomore. New York: McGraw-Hill, 1963.

Mitchell, W. J. T., ed. *The Politics of Interpretation*. Chicago: University of Chicago Press, 1982, 1983.

Morris, Charles. *Writings on the General Theory of Signs*. The Hague: Mouton, 1971.

Pocock, J. G. A. "Verbalizing a Political Act: Towards a Politics of Speech." In *Language and Politics*. Edited by Michael Shapiro. New York: New York University Press, 1984.

Propp, Vladimir. *The Morphology of the Folktale*. Translated by Laurence Scott. Austin: University of Texas Press, 1968.

Shapiro, Michael J., ed. *Language and Politics*. New York: New York University Press, 1984.

Smart, Barry. *Foucault, Marxism, and Critique*. London: Routledge & Kegan Paul, 1983.

Stendhal [Marie-Henri Beyle]. *The Red and the Black*. Translated by C. K. Scott-Moncrieff. Two volumes in one. New York: Liveright, 1954.

Taylor, Richard. *Film Propaganda: Soviet Russia and Nazi Germany*. London: Croom Helm; New York: Barnes & Noble, 1979.

Williams, Raymond. *Keywords: A Vocabulary of Culture and Society*. New York: Oxford University Press, 1976.

Index

Abbey Theatre (building): history of, xv, 108, 108n; description of, 171–72; opening of, 108–13, 171–72; ownership of, xiii; ticket prices for, 171n, 173–74, 174n; use of, by other groups, 221–25; value of, 231, 235. *See also* Irish National Theatre Society; National Players Society; National Theatre Society; Theatre of Ireland

Abbey Theatre (theatre company): name of, 187n. *See also* Irish National Theatre Society; National Theatre Society

Actors: creators of the theatre movement, xiii, 50–59, 50n, 110–13, 111n, 112n, 113n; democrats, 120–23; dissidents in the INTS, Ltd., 116, 120, 122–25; interpreters of plays, 74–75, 188, 188n; professionalization of, 122–35; and star system, 189, 191–92. *See also* Allgood, Sara; Campbell, Mrs. Patrick; Colum, Padraic; Darragh, Florence; Fay, Frank; Fay, W. G.; nic Shiublaigh, Maire; Roberts, George; Theatre of Ireland; Walker, Frank

Adorno, Theodor, 33–36, 34n, 35n

Æ. *See* Russell, George

Allgood, Molly, 111, 157–58, 186n. *See also* Actors

Allgood, Sara (Sally): acting of, 111, 188, 188n, 191n; wages of, 124–25, 126, 127; offense to Horniman by, 225–27; quoted 226n.

See also Actors; Irish National Theatre Society

Archer, William, 1

Archibald, Douglas, 149, 149n

Ascendancy, Protestant, 11–20, 28, 36–41, 69–70. *See also* Class, classes

Ashbourne Act (1885), 37

Atkinson, Robert, 27. *See also* Ascendancy, Protestant; Folklore

Audience, Irish: Catholic Nationalist members of, 7–9, 11–12, 19, 24–25, 59, 69–70, 81, 85; compared to English audiences, 67, 169, 230; considered as "mob," 2, 2n, 24–25, 67–68, 80–82, 81n, 214–17; genteel elements in, 9–10, 44, 170–71, 174, 174–75n, 233, 237; reaction to *The Countess Cathleen*, 1–23; reaction to *In the Shadow of the Glen*, 73–74, 79–93; reaction to *The King's Threshold*, 64–73; reaction to *The Playboy of the Western World*, 213–21; sophistication of, xiii, xv, xvi–xx, 67–68, 67n, 230

Authoritarian personality, 31–36, 33n, 142–44

Bailey, W. B., 236–38

Balfour, Arthur, and Lady Elizabeth, 10

Balzac, Honoré, 85

Bedford, G. A., 219–20

Beerbohm, Max, 1

Benjamin, Walter, 136–37. *See also* Adorno, Theodor; Horkheimer, Max; Marcuse, Herbert

Compositor: G & S Typesetters, Inc.
Text: 10/12 Palatino
Display: Palatino
Printer: Edwards Brothers, Inc.
Binder: Edwards Brothers, Inc.